INTRODUCTION TO BIBLE DOCTRINE

Ten Foundational Truths behind Christianity

By Reid A. Ashbaucher

Reid Ashbaucher Publications | Toledo, Ohio U. S. A.

Reid Ashbaucher Publications
Toledo, Ohio U.S.A.
https://ra-publications.us

Introduction to Bible Doctrine:
Ten Foundational Truths behind Christianity

Copyright © 2020 by Reid A. Ashbaucher
All rights reserved.

No part of this publication may be reproduced, stored in a retrieval system, or transmitted in any form or by any means electronic, mechanical, photocopying, recording, or otherwise, without the prior written permission of the author.

Any resources used in this work should not be seen as an endorsement of any kind towards the content of this book.

Due to the changing nature of the Internet, any website address or links contained in this book may have been modified or deleted since publication and may no longer be functional.

All Scripture quotations are taken from the New American Standard Bible® (NASB), Copyright © 1960, 1962, 1963, 1968, 1971, 1972, 1973, 1975, 1977, 1995 by the Lockman Foundation, unless otherwise noted. Used by permission. www.Lockman.org

Scripture quotations marked HCSB are been taken from the Holman Christian Standard Bible®, Copyright © 1999, 2000, 2002, 2003 by Holman Bible Publishers. Used by permission. Holman Christian Standard Bible®, Holman CSB®, and HCSB® are federally registered trademarks of Holman Bible Publishers.

Scriptures are taken from The Darby Bible. (1890 Edition)

Scriptures are taken from the King James Version of the Bible.

Library of Congress Control Number: 2020950105
ISBN: 978-1-7350948-2-3 pbk.
ISBN: 978-1-7350948-3-0 hbk.

Printed in the United States of America
U.S. Printing History
First Edition: December 2020

CONTENTS

Preface 7
Introduction 9

1. The Doctrine of God 11
2. The Doctrine of Christ 35
3. The Doctrine of the Holy Spirit 69
4. The Doctrine of the Scriptures 89
5. The Doctrine of Humanity 105
6. The Doctrine of Angels 119
7. The Doctrine of Salvation 135
8. The Doctrine of the Church 159
9. The Doctrine of Heaven and Hell 189
10. The Doctrine of Eschatology 211

Works Cited 235
Scripture Index 241
Subject Index 251

PREFACE

Introduction to Bible Doctrine is not just the title of this book, it was once the course title used in many Bible colleges and Universities in the United States as an entry-level Bible course. Today these courses may be 100, 200, or even 300 level courses, such as Introduction to Biblical Theology, New Testament Survey, Old Testament Survey, The Gospels or the Life of Christ, and so on.

This volume was written as a recommended prerequisite study to the author's textbook, *Dispensational Theology: A Textbook on Eschatology in the Twenty-First Century*. The purpose behind Introduction to *Bible Doctrine: Ten Foundational Truths behind Christianity* is to provide the student of the Word with the necessary tools to build a biblical and understandable foundation to one's theology to facilitate further growth in one's spiritual life in today's world.

When the reader completes their study of this volume, the reader will have gain knowledge of the foundational truths of the Christian faith from a non-denominational Biblicists perspective, which is systematic in its approach and attempts to stay true to the belief that there are no contradictions in Scripture, for biblical truth to be true, it must agree with all other biblical truths.

It is the author's view that this book would be equivalent to a 100 or 200 level course on Introduction to Bible Doctrine or a Biblical Theology course in any 21st century Bible college or University, making it a good textbook or supplemental reading material to any Biblical Theology course today.

The author fully supports the historical view of God existing as a triune being that represents God as three individual persons sharing a single nature. Within this traditional view, the author interjects his independent biblical study of 27-years to explain a nontraditional view of how the trinity exists, communicates, and functions within the world they created, thereby bringing clarity to the truth of the historical teaching of a triune God from a biblical perspective. Consequently, this volume relies on the support of one additional work of the author. *Made in the Image of God: Understanding the Nature of God and Mankind in a Changing World* (Third Revised Edition).

The end of each chapter contains a section called Chapter Discussion Notes, a place where the author expresses his personal views and expands on the chapter topics, while providing the reader space to make notes and express their thoughts on the subject matter presented.

INTRODUCTION

We may define *Bible doctrine* as spiritual truths and concepts expressed within the Word of God; while defining *concepts* as biblical constructs of truths rather than abstract thoughts of the mind.

In Titus 1:9 and 2:1, the Scriptures tell us to teach sound doctrine to the church. God gives the church leaders who are to promote sound doctrine through the following process.

> And He gave some as apostles, and some as prophets, and some as evangelists, and some as pastors and teachers, for the equipping of the saints for the work of service, to the building up of the body of Christ; until we all attain to the unity of the faith, and of the knowledge of the Son of God, to a mature man, to the measure of the stature which belongs to the fulness of Christ. As a result, we are no longer to be children, tossed here and there by waves, and carried about by every wind of doctrine, by the trickery of men, by craftiness in deceitful scheming; but speaking the truth in love, we are to grow up in all aspects into Him, who is the head, even Christ, from whom the whole body, being fitted and held together by that which every joint supplies, according to the proper working of each individual part, causes the growth of the body for the building up of itself in love. (Ephesians 4:11-16)

The result of good teaching (doctrine) is stability in one's life, providing a shield to protect oneself from the enemy of God, Satan, who sows thoughts of doubt and confusion to the *body of Christ*. When doubts come, any individual can overcome them by going to the Scriptures for clarity and truthfulness as to what God states to be right or wrong on any issue. Satan's strategy from the beginning was to get people to doubt God's words, as illustrated in Genesis 3:1-6 where his first words to Eve were, "Indeed, has God Said...?"

In First Timothy 4:6-8, the Apostle Paul tells Timothy to ignore storytelling (fables), but instead rely on God's instructions as found in his Word. Later Paul explains why this is important as he writes, "For the time will come when they will not endure sound doctrine; but wanting to have their ears tickled, they will accumulate for themselves teachers in accordance to their own desires; and will turn away their ears from the truth, and will turn aside to myths" (2 Timothy 4:3-4).

The purpose of this volume is to help the *body of Christ* know and understand the foundational truths of God's Word—the Scriptures.

This volume has not been written for pastoral instruction, but to aid every member of the *body of Christ* in knowing and understanding the foundational truths of the Scriptures, thereby bringing lifelong stability to one's spiritual life for the well-being of their soul and body. This sound doctrine also provides a scriptural foundation to build on, aiding in the continuation of one's spiritual growth.

The approach of this volume's hermeneutical interpretations comes through a Grammatical-Historical Method, defined by Paul Lee Tan (Th.D.) as a literal method, focused on the normal usage of words through their normal Grammatico-historical context.[1]

It should be remembered that the Holy Spirit of God is our ultimate teacher, and we should bathe all teaching in clear thought and prayer (John 14:26; 1 Corinthians 2:10-16). A second thought to remember is, the power behind the Christian faith is the Holy Spirit working through the Word of God as we are obedient to it. Second Corinthians 10:5-6 states, "We are destroying speculations and every lofty thing raised up against the knowledge of God, and we are taking every thought captive to the obedience of Christ, and we are ready to punish all disobedience, whenever your obedience is complete."

---

[1] Paul Lee Tan, *The Interpretation of Prophecy* (Winona Lake, Indiana: Assurance Publishing, 1974), 29.

One

THE DOCTRINE OF GOD

GOD'S NATURE AS TRIUNE

The Scriptures present God as a triune being. This is revealed from the very first chapter in the Old Testament in Genesis 1:26 which reads, "Then God said, 'Let Us make man in Our image, according to Our likeness; and let them rule over the fish of the sea and over the birds of the sky and over the cattle and over all the earth, and over every creeping thing that creeps on the earth.'" Then in Genesis 11:7 we see, "And the Lord said, 'Behold, they are one people, and they all have the same language. And this is what they began to do, and now nothing which they purpose to do will be impossible for them. Come, let Us go down and there confuse their language, that they may not understand one another's speech.'"

Later, through the progressive revelation provided through the New Testament, the terms *Us* and *Our* as spoken through Old Testament passages are presented in the form of three individual persons—God the Father, God the Son, and God the Holy Spirit.

We read in Romans 1:7, "... to all who are beloved of God in Rome, called as saints: Grace to you and peace from God our Father and the Lord Jesus Christ." Here we see God represented as our heavenly Father.

Hebrews 1:8 reads, "But of the Son He says, 'Thy throne, O God, is forever and ever, And the righteous scepter is the scepter of His kingdom.'" The context of this passage is God declaring his Son to be equal in nature with himself, as the writer quotes Psalm 45:6.

Acts 5:3-4 records the Apostle Peter's words, "But Peter said, 'Ananias, why has Satan filled your heart to lie to the Holy Spirit, and to keep back some of the price of the land? While it remained unsold, did it not remain your own? And after I sold it, was it not under your control? Why is it that you have conceived this deed in your heart? You have not lied to men, but to God.'"

Here we see Peter declaring the Holy Spirit to be God, warning that by lying to the Holy Spirit you have lied to God. The only way for this to be legitimate would be if both entities are the same in nature. To lie to one person does not mean you have lied to someone else unless both persons share something metaphysically in common. Here, both persons share the same singular nature as God.

To grasp the concept of a triune God, one needs to understand the distinction between God's nature and God's personhood. Within the Scriptures, God is revealed as having a singular nature consisting of three separate persons. Because of this seeming paradox, we need to understand what represents God's nature and what represents His personhood—the three persons within God's singular nature. These concepts are fully vented and introduced to us through the book, *Made in the Image of God: Understanding the Nature of God and Mankind in a Changing World* (Third Revised Edition).

Within this present work, we will touch on this subject for purposes of better understanding.

To understand the difference between God's nature and personhood, one needs to understand the difference between the concepts of *soul* and *spirit*. When the Scriptures use the term *soul*, 99% of the time it refers to personhood, that part of a person that contains intellect, emotion, and will. This is true in both the Old and the New Testament. When the Scriptures use the term spirit, its meaning involves quite a bit more study.

We can arrange the term spirit under nine separate categories, with nine different definitions for each category. With a relationship to God's nature, spirit represents the part of God that reflects power, communication between entities, generates attitudes, and represents life itself. The soul and spirit work collectively as an entity, not independently as separate parts. Just as our bodies cannot function without a heart, personhood cannot function without the functionality of a spirit. Soul and spirit work together to create a complete individual.

When we put these two concepts together, we conclude that God consists of a single spirit representing His nature, with three souls functioning within that singular spirit. Thus, God is three persons unified by their singular spirit nature. Because of these factors, we can say that the Godhead comprises God the Father, God the Son, and God the Holy Spirit. The term God represents its nature and the terms Father, Son, and Holy Spirit represent their individual personhood as three persons.

To gain a better visual understanding of this concept, draw a large circle on a piece of paper. Now place three smaller circles of equal size inside the big circle and label all four according to the following description. The big circle represents God's nature as spirit while the three smaller circles represent God's personhood, reflected as three souls. (Leviticus 26:11; Psalm 11:5; Hebrews 10:38; Matthew 26:38; John 12:27). [1] Each soul represents intellect, emotion, and will; while the spirit nature represents the part of God that manifests power, attitudes, communications, and life itself. The souls (personhood) and spirit (nature) together represent God as three persons sharing a singular spirit nature.

John 4:24 states, "God is spirit, and those who worship Him must worship in spirit and truth." God is spirit, singular. Through a study of the Scriptures, we can see that each person of the trinity has their own intellect, emotion, and willpower. This idea is so vast and complex it requires another book on the topic, which has already been mentioned.

THE ATTRIBUTES OF GOD'S NATURE

The nature of God is best explained through the categories of what we consider natural and moral. These natural attributes deal with non-moral issues such as God's presence and power. His moral attributes deal with issues of attitude, which translates into morality, as God defines it, and as shown to us in the form of love, justice, kindness, and so on. Like soul and spirit, we do not mean these natural and moral

---

[1] Reid A. Ashbaucher, *Made in the Image of God: Understanding the Nature of God and Mankind in a Changing World*, 3 rev ed. (Toledo: Reid Ashbaucher Publications, 2020), 68-69.

attributes function independently from each other, instead, they work together to portray God's metaphysical nature.

When we speak about the metaphysical nature of God, we are speaking about the reality of God's existence and what that looks like in terms of human understanding. God's metaphysical make-up represents all the properties that explain God's existence. Such as, God is spirit in nature and possesses unique attributes, and within this spirit exists three persons with their unique attributes. God's metaphysical existence consists of all these attributes collectively, representing God as three individual persons sharing a single nature, to which the church has held to historically since its formation.

These attributes display God's essence and character. We will discuss the attributes of God within the category they represent as follows.

NATURAL ATTRIBUTES

Omnipresent—The word omnipresent means to be present everywhere at the same time. The Scriptures express it this way,

> *Where can I go from Thy Spirit?*
> *Or where can I flee from Thy presence?*
> *If I ascend to heaven, Thou art there;*
> *If I make my bed in Sheol, behold, Thou art there.*
> *If I take the wings of the dawn,*
> *If I dwell in the remotest part of the sea,*
> *Even there Thy hand will lead me,*
> *And Thy right hand will lay hold of me.*[2]

God's spirit, represented in Scripture as being omnipresent, is not the same as an angelic being which can only be in one place at a time. God's spirit is like the air of our world, it is present everywhere we are as a single element. Jesus explained this concept to a religious ruler of his day named Nicodemus, who came to Jesus seeking a better understanding of who He was. When the question concerning the spirit came

---

[2] Ps. 139:7-10.

up, Jesus explained it this way, "That which is born of the flesh is flesh, and that which is born of the Spirit is spirit. Do not marvel that I said to you, 'You must be born again.' The wind blows where it wishes and you hear the sound of it, but do not know where it comes from and where it is going; so is everyone who is born of the Spirit." [3] Jesus equated the spirit world to the wind or air around us; a conceptual concept God revealed to us because he wanted us to understand.

When we understand the concept of spirit and air as similar in nature, it helps us grasp how God exists all around us, how he can be everywhere at the same time. When looked at in this light, it brings a whole new meaning to the omnipresence of God.

Omnipotent—The omnipotence of God means God is all-powerful. This means God can do anything he chooses with no one able to oppose him. The Scriptures express God's limitations this way: God cannot lie (Titus 1:2). God cannot be tempted by evil (James 1:13). God cannot deny himself (2 Timothy 2:13). And, God cannot change his nature (Malachi 3:6).

Sometimes the question is asked by a skeptic; Can God make a rock he cannot lift? Based on the limitations God has provided us, the answer is no, because to do so would violate his nature, which states God cannot deny himself. If God made a rock he could not lift, he would have to deny his power or his very nature.

Back to the seriousness of the concept of God's power. Remember, God is in control of all things; there is no being on any level who can oppose his will. This truth is forever unchangeable.

Eternal— God is eternal. The Merriam-Webster Dictionary defines the term in several ways, using words like everlasting, perpetual, and timeless.

We can interpret the eternalness of God through the evidence proving the first law of thermodynamics, otherwise known as the law of conservation of energy. Simply put, energy can change forms, but it

---

[3] John 3:6-8.

cannot be created or destroyed. If you cannot create or destroy energy, which consists of atoms, then by extension atoms have a property of eternalness. The second law of thermodynamics tells us there is no such thing as perpetual motion, or that there are no sources of energy that are 100% efficient.

So what holds the atom together and controls its eternal property? The only source that has such properties outside natural energy is GOD, who is eternal by nature. The Scriptures express it this way, "And He built His sanctuary like the heights, Like the earth which He has founded forever." [4] A concept that the earth is forever is express to us in Colossians 1:15-17, as it reads, "And He is the image of the invisible God, the first-born of all creation. For by Him all things were created, both in the heavens and on earth, visible and invisible, whether thrones or dominions or rulers or authorities—all things have been created by Him and for Him. And He is before all things, and in Him all things hold together." These statements tell us the source or power behind what holds everything together. It is God! This is further illustrated to us in Second Corinthians 4:17-18, as we read: "For momentary, light affliction is producing for us an eternal weight of glory far beyond all comparison, while we look not at the things which are seen, but at the things which are not seen; for the things which are seen are temporal, but the things which are not seen are eternal."

Like water that can change its state but always exists, matter is the same way. A piece of steel may rust and deteriorate, but all the atoms that make it up still exist. The matter that formed the original steel piece only changed from one form to another through the rusting process; from what we see, to something we can no longer see. But all the atoms that made up that steel are still present because it consists of energy (atoms) that cannot be destroyed. Thus, the earth is forever, just as the Scriptures proclaim. The atom is eternal because God's nature that holds all things together is eternal. This is true, even if we split the atom because the energy just changes to another form of energy.

---

[4] Ps. 78:69.

God affirms his eternalness in Deuteronomy 33:27, Isaiah 9:6, Romans 16:26, and First Peter 5:10-11, which reads, "And after you have suffered for a little while, the God of all grace, who called you to His eternal glory in Christ, will Himself perfect, confirm, strengthen and establish you. To Him be dominion forever and ever. Amen." God reinforces this, as he declares for himself, "I am the Alpha and the Omega," says the Lord God, "who is and who was and who is to come, the Almighty." [5]

Omniscience—The omniscience of God means a God who has all knowledge and knows everything. We do not have a great deal of revelation about this topic, but what we do know is conveyed through three passages within the Scriptures.

Psalm 147:5 states, "Great is our Lord, and abundant in strength; His understanding is infinite." This shows infinite understanding is tied to God's eternalness. If God is eternal, then everything about God's metaphysical makeup would be infinite. The Scriptures call us to reason together with the teachings of God in Isaiah 1:18. It would stand to reason if God created everything we can know and experience, then God would need to have a complete understanding of everything he designed and made. Therefore, based on God being the creator of all things and being eternal in nature, God is omniscient or all-knowing.

The Scriptures continue this line of thinking by pointing out that God not only understands everything external to himself, He also understands everything internal about himself. This stands in stark contrast to human understanding, as expressed by the prophet Jeremiah, "The heart is deceitful above all things, and desperately wicked: who can know it?" [6]

First Corinthians 2:10-12 provides us this revelation about God. "For to us God revealed them through the Spirit; for the Spirit searches all things, even the depths of God. For who among men knows the thoughts of a man except the spirit of the man, which is in him? Even so the thoughts of God no one knows except the Spirit of God."

---

[5] Rev. 1:8.
[6] Jer. 17:9 KJV (King James Bible).

The Apostle John confirms that God knows man's heart as well as everything else pertaining to his creation, as he writes, "We shall know by this that we are of the truth, and shall assure our heart before Him, in whatever our heart condemns us; for God is greater than our heart, and knows all things." [7]

To summarize what the Scriptures reveal to us, we can say that God understands everything about himself and his creation. And because God's nature is eternal, God's knowledge and understanding are infinite.

Immutable— The immutability of God means God cannot change or is incapable of change. God declares this himself in Malachi 3:6. "For I, the Lord, do not change; therefore you, O sons of Jacob, are not consumed."

When we plug this concept into Bible doctrine through a closer study, we learn the immutability of God refers to God's nature, not his personhood. We derive this assessment from several passages that speak of changes in God's emotions as found in Numbers 32:14 where God becomes angry at Israel, and in Matthew's account of God being well-pleased with his Son when John the Baptist baptized Jesus, showing that God's emotions can change (Matthew 3:16-17). We also see through the Scriptures that God sometimes changes his mind toward judgment after repentance takes place on an individual's part (Exodus 32:11-14; Psalm 106:44-46). Or God's resolute mind that he will not change his mind that Christ will be a High Priest on the order of Melchizedek forever (Psalm 110:4; Hebrews 7:21).

So we see that although God can change within the relationship of his emotions and will, His natural or moral attributes never change. God's omnipotence, omnipresence, or eternalness never change.

MORAL ATTRIBUTES

We tie all of God's moral attributes to His holiness. Therefore, the holiness of God is the foundational attribute tied to all other moral

---

[7] 1 John 3:19-20.

attributes represented in the Godhead. We should also note that these moral attributes reflect God's attitudes toward His creation and is thus seen as the unifying and controlling attributes of the Godhead. These concepts are better understood through the following expositions.

Holiness— God declares his holiness this way, "For I am the Lord your God. Consecrate yourselves therefore, and be holy; for I am holy. And you shall not make yourselves unclean with any of the swarming things that swarm on the earth." [8] When we evaluate this statement, we see God's command to consecrate ourselves, meaning to devote, to commit, and to separate ourselves from unclean things. As we search the Scriptures, we see this concept expanded to include moral issues, not just the contextual things relating to Jewish dietary laws. God is holy, and all things related to God such as the Holy Scriptures, a holy priesthood, and those that are part of the body of Christ—the church—all referenced in Scripture as to be holy, meaning, separated from that which is unclean or unrighteous (Ephesians 5:27; 1 Peter 1:15-16; Romans 1:2).

Righteous—The righteousness of God means God is in right standing with himself and his holiness. The scriptures express it like this, "But the Lord of hosts will be exalted in judgment, And the holy God will show Himself holy in righteousness." [9] The Scriptures go on to say, "The Rock! His work is perfect, For all His ways are just; A God of faithfulness and without injustice, Righteous and upright is He." [10] Within this context God's works, reasoning, character, and morals are right or righteous concerning himself. This means God is the standard for all life represents. It is God who determines what is right or wrong in life since he is the creator of all things and sovereign over it. "The Lord is righteous in all His ways, And kind in all His deeds." [11] The prophet Isaiah writes, "Declare and set forth your case; Indeed, let them

---

[8] Lev. 11:44.
[9] Isa. 5:16.
[10] Deut. 32:4.
[11] Ps. 145:17.

consult together. Who has announced this from of old? Who has long since declared it? Is it not I, the Lord? And there is no other God besides Me, A righteous God and a Savior; There is none except Me." [12]

The Scriptures are full of references supporting these concepts that God is holy and righteous, and is the only one who sets the standard for living with any proper authority. We can validate these truths; one only needs to seek them out to find them (see Romans 3:10-18; 2 Thessalonians 1:5; 1 John 2:29; Revelation 15:4; 16:5; 19:2).

Goodness—The psalmist writes, "Good and upright is the Lord; Therefore He instructs sinners in the way." [13] Because of this, the psalmist also writes, "Thou art good and doest good; Teach me Thy statutes." [14]

The concept of *good* relates directly to God's actions. We first see this in Genesis Chapter 1 regarding God's creative acts—which are all referenced as good. Because of this, everything God does is good according to his holiness. The psalmist writes, "How blessed is the one whom Thou dost choose, and bring near to Thee, to dwell in Thy courts. We will be satisfied with the goodness of Thy house, Thy holy temple."[15] We cannot separate the holiness and goodness of God, they are inherently connected to God's nature. There is no such thing as one without the other. This is true about all of God's moral attributes.

Love—The love of God is portrayed in Scripture as an attitude, not an emotion; just as all of God's moral attributes are. The Apostle John writes, "For God loved the world in this way: He gave His One and Only Son so that everyone who believes in Him will not perish but have eternal life." [16] God's love resulted in his willingness to take action to give and save his creation. We are later told that God's people cannot be separated from this loving attitude.

---

[12] Isa. 45:21.
[13] Ps. 25:8.
[14] Ps. 119:68.
[15] Ps. 65:4.
[16] John 3:16 HCSB (Holman Christian Standard Bible).

Who shall separate us from the love of Christ? Shall tribulation, or distress, or persecution, or famine, or nakedness, or peril, or sword? Just as it is written,

> '*For Thy sake we are being put to death all day long;*
> *We were considered as sheep to be slaughtered.*'

But in all these things we overwhelmingly conquer through Him who loved us. For I am convinced that neither death, nor life, nor angels, nor principalities, nor things present, nor things to come, nor powers, nor height, nor depth, nor any other created thing, shall be able to separate us from the love of God, which is in Christ Jesus our Lord. [17]

As further evidence God's love is part of his nature, scripture provides a list of attributes stemming from that nature. "But the fruit of the Spirit is love, joy, peace, patience, kindness, goodness, faithfulness, gentleness, self-control; against such things there is no law." [18] We can classify all these attributes as being generated from God's nature—a single spirit. Because everyone born again through the Holy Spirit of God can possess God's nature, all these attitudes become available to them with faith in Christ. The result of faith in Christ is becoming new individuals in Christ, getting new attitudes to live by. The Scriptures express it this way, "Therefore if any man is in Christ, he is a new creature; the old things passed away; behold, new things have come." [19]

As a side note, we should also understand that emotions are a product of attitudes. Therefore, all of God's emotions are a by-product of attitudes that stem from his nature. [20] John 11:35 states that Jesus wept, an emotion that stems from Jesus' attitude of love and mercy.

---

[17] Rom. 8:35-39.
[18] Gal. 5:22-23.
[19] 2 Cor. 5:17.
[20] Ashbaucher, *Made in the Image of God*, 84-86.

Mercy—The mercy of God is shown to us in Exodus 25:17-22, with God's instructions for Moses to build a mercy seat, which visually symbolized God's temporary provision of forgiveness of sins—a propitiatory, through his attitude of mercy toward the sinfulness of humanity. This action foreshadowed God's mercy through the grace of Jesus Christ, as Christ permanently replaced the symbolism and application of the mercy seat—a propitiatory act—for believers in Christ as reflected in Hebrews 9:1-28 and Romans 3:25.

Jesus parable recorded in Matthew 18:33 illustrates what the mercy of God looks like when applied toward others. "Should you not also have had mercy on your fellow slave, even as I had mercy on you?" Mercy is an attitude of forgiveness toward someone not deserving of such forbearance or kindness. This is further reflected in Scripture in Ephesians 2:4-7 and Titus 3:4-8.

Wisdom—The wisdom of God is illustrated in James 3:13-18:

> Who among you is wise and understanding? Let him show by his good behavior his deeds in the gentleness of wisdom. But if you have bitter jealousy and selfish ambition in your heart, do not be arrogant and so lie against the truth. This wisdom is not that which comes down from above, but is earthly, natural, demonic. For where jealousy and selfish ambition exist, there is disorder and every evil thing. But the wisdom from above is first pure, then peaceable, gentle, reasonable, full of mercy and good fruits, unwavering, without hypocrisy. And the seed whose fruit is righteousness is sown in peace by those who make peace.

The wisdom of God is an attribute with characteristics expressed to be pure (holy), peaceable, gentle, and reasonable, reflecting mercy and good fruits (acts of good deeds). This is the opposite of human wisdom, which is portrayed as having an attitude of arrogance, selfishness, jealousy, and opposes the real truth—God's Word (John 17:17).

The psalmist writes, "O Lord, how many are Thy works! In wisdom Thou hast made them all; The earth is full of Thy possessions." [21] Here we see a declaration that everything in the known here and now is established on God's wisdom, a foundational attribute tied to God's holiness and love.

King David express the result of this concept as he writes,

> O Lord, our Lord, How majestic is Thy name in all the earth, Who hast displayed Thy splendor above the heavens! From the mouth of infants and nursing babes Thou hast established strength, Because of Thine adversaries, To make the enemy and the revengeful cease.
>
> When I consider Thy heavens, the work of Thy fingers, The moon and the stars, which Thou hast ordained; What is man, that Thou dost take thought of him? And the son of man, that Thou dost care for him? Yet Thou hast made him a little lower than God, And dost crown him with glory and majesty! Thou dost make him to rule over the works of Thy hands; Thou hast put all things under his feet, All sheep and oxen, And also the beasts of the field, The birds of the heavens, and the fish of the sea, Whatever passes through the paths of the seas.
>
> O Lord, our Lord, How majestic is Thy name in all the earth! [22]

The thoughts expressed here are that of worship and recognition of God's works through the preordination of the *son of man* to the world, who came in the form of Jesus Christ to save the world from its sins, just as the Gospel of Luke proclaims it, all because of God's wisdom.

---

[21] Ps. 104:24.
[22] Ps. 8:1-9.

DIVINE SIMPLICITY

The doctrine of Divine Simplicity is developed mostly within the discipline of philosophical theology or scholastic philosophy, having its definitions expressed several ways.

John Frame (D.D.), the author of *The Doctrine of God*, seems to conclude from his study that God is not part of a godhood species or part of a class of gods, nor is God accidental. He did not come into being by causation or accident, but God is essential to his being and is his essence without metaphysical parts. [23]

Thomas Morris, who wrote *Our Idea of God*, seems to suggest that God contains no spatial parts, temporal parts, or is without metaphysical complexity. [24]

Ronald Nash (Ph.D.), who authored *The Concept of God*, defines this doctrine in the following manner: "The doctrine of simplicity is the belief that God is identical with His nature or His properties. Another aspect of the theory teaches that God's essence is indivisible in the sense that God's properties are not parts of God's nature. Simplicity is therefore said to be unique to God; it marks off one of the fundamental differences between God's nature and human nature." [25]

From *Stanford Encyclopedia of Philosophy* on the subject of "Divine Simplicity," we read,

> According to the classical theism of Augustine, Anselm, Aquinas and their adherents, God is radically unlike creatures and cannot be adequately understood in ways appropriate to them. God is simple in that God transcends every form of complexity and composition familiar to the discursive intellect. One consequence is that the simple God lacks parts. This lack is not a deficiency but a positive feature. God is

---

[23] John Frame, *The Doctrine of God* (Phillipsburg: P & R Publishing Co., 2002), 226.

[24] Thomas Morris, *Our Idea of God* (Downers Grove: Intervarsity Press, 1991), 113.

[25] Ronald Nash, *The Concept of God* (Grand Rapids: Zondervan Publishing House, 1983), 85.

ontologically superior to every partite entity, and his partlessness is an index thereof. Broadly construed, 'part' covers not only spatial and temporal parts (if any) but also metaphysical 'parts' or ontological constituents. To say that God lacks metaphysical parts is to say inter alia that God is free of matter-form composition, potency-act composition, and existence-essence composition. There is also no real distinction between God as subject of his attributes and his attributes. God is thus in some sense identical to each of his attributes, which implies that each attribute is identical to every other one. God is omniscient, then, not in virtue of instantiating or exemplifying omniscience—which would imply a real distinction between God and the property of omniscience—but by being omniscience. And the same holds for each of the divine omni-attributes: God is what he has as Augustine puts it in The City of God, XI, 10. As identical to each of his attributes, God is identical to his nature. And since his nature or essence is identical to his existence, God is identical to his existence. This is the doctrine of divine simplicity (DDS). [26]

The reality of this doctrine is that God is complete within himself and needs no outside entity or resource to provide completeness. God is self-existent, with no beginning and no ending to themselves. God expressed this to Moses by saying, "And God said to Moses, 'I AM WHO I AM'; and He said, 'Thus you shall say to the sons of Israel, I AM has sent me to you.'" [27]

The doctrine of simplicity also reasons that God is the product of all his attributes, both natural and moral, without exception. Although aspects to this doctrine are debated within the metaphysical makeup of God, it is undeniable that God is a self-existing and eternal being,

---

[26] *The Stanford Encyclopedia of Philosophy* (Spring 2019 Edition), s.v. "Divine Simplicity," by William F. Vallicella, ed. Edward N. Zalta, available from https://plato.stanford.edu/archives/spr2019/entries/divine-simplicity/; Internet; accessed 25 June 2020.

[27] Ex. 3:14.

having no dependencies on anything or anyone outside of his metaphysical makeup as a single nature triune being.

THE NAMES FOR GOD

The meaning behind names for God in the Scriptures is important, as they command respect and provide descriptive meanings for the various attributes of God. While numerous books and articles have been written on this subject, we will only focus on that which is essential for the best understanding of God's identity through the use of names presented to us within the Scriptures.

We begin with God introducing himself by providing us his name. "I am the Lord, that is My name; I will not give My glory to another, Nor My praise to graven images." [28] The term *Lord* is an English translation for the Hebrew term *YHWH*, Yahweh, or *Jehovah*. Most English translations use the name *Lord* for God, as reflected over 4,100 times in most translations. A few earlier translations such as the American Standard Version (ASV) and The Darby Bible transliterate *Jehovah* in place of *Lord*. Within the King James Version, the name *Jehovah* appears four times, two of which use the phrase *Lord Jehovah*. The New King James Bible never references the name *Jehovah,* but instead uses the name *Lord* in its place.

The name for God in Hebrew, the original language of the Old Testament, is *YHWH*, the Hebrew translation for what most English Bibles translate as *Lord*. The Septuagint, a Greek translation of the Hebrew Old Testament scriptures into the Greek language of Jesus' day, translates YHWH (Yahweh) as θεος (Theos), meaning God, Lord, or sometimes Creator.

Throughout the Scriptures, many other names and titles are used regarding God for a contextual emphasis of His natural and moral attributes. When other words follow the term *Jehovah*, it expands the meaning to mean something more. We see this in terms like:

---

[28] Isa. 43:8.

Jehovah-Shalom—Lord of peace (Judges 6:24)
Jehovah-Rapha—The Lord who heals (Exodus 15:26)
Jehovah-Nissi—The Lord our banner (Exodus 17:15)
Jehovah-Jireh—The Lord will provide (Genesis 22:14)
Jehovah-Elohim—Lord God (Genesis 2:4)
Jehovah-Tsidqenuw—The Lord our righteousness (Jeremiah 33:16)
Jehovah-M'Kaddesh—The Lord that sanctifies or makes holy (Leviticus 20:8)

Each of these Scriptures references the translation of the Hebrew word represented here. As expected, in the "Complete Jewish Bible" the word for *Jehovah* is translated as *Adonai*.

OTHER NAMES AND TITLES FOR GOD

Elohim—*Elohim* is the English translation for the Hebrew name for God in some scriptural passages, and is translated as such in The Darby Bible forty times. The word is a plural term translated in most English versions as God. John Nelson Darby, an English scholar of the 1800s, translated the Old Testament term with the term *Jehovah*, translated in other versions as *Lord*. We find an example from The Darby Bible in Genesis 2:4-5, which is translated to read, "These are the histories of the heavens and the earth, when they were created, in the day that Jehovah Elohim made earth and heavens, and every shrub of the field before it was in the earth, and every herb of the field before it grew; for Jehovah Elohim had not caused it to rain on the earth, and there was no man to till the ground." [29]

Other translations would translate *Jehovah Elohim* as *Lord God* while translating the Hebrew words into the English term *YHWH Elohim*. When examining the use of the term *Elohim*, the context seems to reflect a unifying action by God toward his creation; demonstrating a triune God acting with power and authority; thus the purpose of the term being plural in nature.

---

[29] Gen. 2:4-5 (The Darby Bible).

Adonai— *Adonai* is another translation from the Hebrew name for Lord. Although most English Bibles translate *Adonai* as *Lord*, The Darby Bible translates this term only once, in First Kings 2:26 which reads, "And the king said to Abiathar the priest, Go to Anathoth, to thine own fields; for thou art worthy of death; but I will not at this time put thee to death, because thou didst bear the ark of Adonai Jehovah before David my father, and because thou hast been afflicted in all wherein my father was afflicted."

Here the Hebrew word is translated as *Adonai*. The Hebrew term comes from the root word *Adon* meaning rule; sovereign; or controller. Other translations use the term *Lord* in the place of *Adonai*.

The term used here makes sense when understood within the context usage. A priest is being judged, but because of his relationship to the only sovereign God, or Adonai Jehovah, the judgment will be suspended.

The Complete Jewish Bible published by Jewish New Testament Publications uses the term *Adonai* in place of the Hebrew word *YHWH* and is referenced 5,000 times in its translation.

Because of Leviticus 24:16, the Jewish community at large believes that to even speak the name of God is forbidden, therefore they shorten the name *Yahweh* to *YHWH* in the Hebrew text to prevent God's name from being spoken aloud. The Complete Jewish Bible has taken this one step further by replacing *YHWH* with *Adonai*. Since both terms carry the same connotation, the sovereign one, the creator, the I AM that I AM, this substitution carries with it very little difficulty in understanding its true meaning or purpose.

El Shaddai—The term *El Shaddai* in Genesis 17:1 is self-interpreted for us to mean *God Almighty*. In the context of Exodus 6:1-8, we see the meaning carries the connotation of the Lord of power who delivers his people out of bondage. It is a term used to show a God of compassion with glorious power to act on behalf of his people. God introduces this term to show us that God is not just the God of a covenant promise, but a God who has the power to deliver on that promise.

Summary of Names for God

Throughout the Scriptures, many names or titles are used to emphasize the many attributes of a triune God. Within the doctrine of Christ, there will be additional discussions on this topic that are directly related to Jesus Christ, the second person of the Godhead—of the Trinity.

{ CHAPTER DISCUSSION NOTES }

Doctrine on the Trinity

The doctrine of the trinity has been under attack for centuries. Most religious cults deny the concept of the Trinity, along with some who claim Christianity as their faith in practice.

This is one reason for the need of a new approach in explaining a triune God, to help answer the questions of how God can be one and also three at the same time? And how can Jesus be both fully God and Man at the same time? I find these questions are best answered through my biblical study where I supply answers to these traditional perspectives by presenting a nontraditional concept of a soul and spirit combination as being representative of God's metaphysical make-up, proving both the reality of a triune God and the deity of Jesus Christ as God's Son without contradicting what the Scriptures tell us when we study them using the Grammatical-Historical Method of interpretation. The evidence behind this non-traditional approach in the explanation of these doctrines can be found in my book, *Made in the Image of God: Understanding the Nature of God and Mankind in a Changing World* (Third Revised Edition).

The teaching of the triune God is important and best understood through reasoning through the Scriptures.

The New Covenant found in Jeremiah Chapter 31 states that God will put His laws within the heart of his people, teach them concerning things about himself, and provide forgiveness of sins forever. The question becomes, considering these facts, how will God accomplish all this? The answer comes through understanding New Testament revelation where Christ introduces the Holy Spirit as the one who will become our teacher and indwell believers forever, not just temporarily (John 14:16-17, 25-26; 16:13-14).

We realize that the forgiveness of sins forever comes through the teaching of Christ as the Son of God, the Messiah, the Savior of the world (Titus 2:11-14; Romans 1:1-4; Isaiah 53:12; 1 Peter 2:24-25). This can only be true if Christ is, being God by nature, a perfect substitutionary sacrifice to God as payment for the penalty of personal sin.

The trinity's existence allows for the fulfillment of the New Covenant, providing the world an opportunity to achieve reconciliation with God—its creator. Without the Trinity, it would be impossible to reconcile the world to God, which includes the salvation of humanity from its sins. This is clear throughout the Scriptures from Genesis to Revelation as they speak to God's judgment on sin, and His requirement to satisfy that judgment represented in Christ.

NATURAL ATTRIBUTES OF GOD

Within the relationship of the gods of Greek and other ancient mythologies, we sometimes ask, what kind of god can forgive wrongdoing (sin), or provide peace of mind, or even guarantee eternal life? The God of the Bible can do all these things and more.

Why is it important that God be omnipotent? If he was not, there would be no one able to guarantee anything in life or have the power to carry it out. With power comes the concept of authority. Those in authority generally have the means to back it up. A weak god means another stronger god could overcome him in a coup. If the laws of the evolutionist pertained to the creator God, the universe we live in would be in a perpetual state of chaos. There would always be a struggle over who was in charge for eternity when in reality God states He is in control and there is no one besides himself with any legitimate authority. This means God grants all other authority that exists in the world. This includes angels, family, human government, or even the church. The entire structure of humanity, saved or lost, is granted authority by its creator—God.

It is said that God is immutable, meaning God cannot, and will not ever change. What if God could be tempted by evil, deny himself, lie, or change his nature in any way? The logical conclusion would be that there would be no stability in the universe God created. No one would know where they stood in their relationship with God. Everyone would be second-guessing how to live or what is right or wrong in life, with no ultimate standards. In the end, everyone would do what is right in their own eyes (Judges 17:6).

Satan, who is currently the prince of this world, is the tempter, the liar, the one who changes to whatever you want him to be. Thus, we live in a world already in chaos. If God were the same way, there would be no hope of rescue, no hope for the future, no salvation from sin and death.

So, by understanding the doctrine of God and what it means in actuality, we gain hope and understanding of the true realities in life vs. the lies of Satan—God's enemy.

THE MORAL ATTRIBUTES OF GOD

Morality is a standard God determines, not human beings. We see this first revealed to us in Genesis Chapter 3 when Adam and Eve sinned against God through their disobedience to God's set standards. Later in the New Testament, we read the account of God speaking to Peter in a vision revealing God changed the dietary rules found in the Mosaic Law that God originally dictated to Moses. This was to later carry more meaning than what was originally understood (see Acts 10:9-11:18).

We can define morality as the knowledge of good and evil, as God defines it, where good is the right moral choice. Therefore, anything God declares or defines as good within his written word is morally good and the right choice regarding right living. Morality then becomes an act of doing what is good vs. engaging in what is bad based on God's standards. Without God revealing what is good and evil, humanity would be left without understanding what is right or wrong in their everyday living. We base this understanding of good and evil on divine and human nature as they exist today. The concept of good is represented by, and comes from God's nature, while the concept of evil is represented by, and comes from its originating source of Satan's nature, which affected and corrupted human nature. We see this explained in Romans 3:10-12 where we are told, "There is none righteous, not even one; There is none who understands, There is none who seeks for God; All have turned aside, together they have become useless; There is none who does good, There is not even one."

We can see all these concepts in the first three chapters of Genesis. God is good, and from his good nature, he creates what is good. Satan, who was created and existed from the beginning, became the father of sin and evil, affecting all he came into contact with, beginning with Adam and Eve. As a result, through our fallen human nature, sin was passed down to all of humanity, just as the Scriptures proclaim in Romans 5:12.

THE NAMES FOR GOD

The name of God is important because it brings personalization to God and his creation. How close would you feel to someone if you never knew their name but could only refer to them as "hey, you"? Names sometimes carry meaning behind them, giving another sense of understanding to the individual's existence. Another aspect of God's name is that it commands respect and a sense of honor, just as the titles of a king, ambassador, or president. Lord with a capital "L" instantly commands respect and homage to such a person. It also paints an instant picture of who is in charge and who is subservient to whom. The other names for God are simply titles given to help us understand God's nature and character by using descriptive language we can understand and relate to in our own vocabulary.

It should be noted that God places great emphasis on his name and lets his creation know that there is no one else like him in all of creation.

Personal Notes

Two

THE DOCTRINE OF CHRIST

THE NATURE OF CHRIST

The uniqueness of Jesus Christ is established by his possession of two natures—a divine and a human nature. This understood reality is revealed within the Holy Scriptures and was debated among early church leadership in the third and fourth centuries. As a result of these debates, two church Creeds, among others, were finalized and universally adopted by these Christian leadership councils.

The first was the Nicene Creed of A.D. 325, later amended and universally excepted as the Nicene/Constantinople Creed in A.D. 381. The language of the creed proclaimed that God, in its essence, consists of three persons sharing a single nature, with an emphasis on God the Father and God the Son being equal in nature. They adopted a second creed in A.D. 451 at the council of Chalcedon, known as the Chalcedonian Creed, which proclaimed Jesus Christ to be of the same nature as God the Father, but possessing two sinless natures as a single person, both divine and human. The English translation of the Chalcedonian Creed states the following:

> We, then, following the holy Fathers, all with one consent, teach men to confess one and the same Son, our Lord Jesus Christ, the same perfect in Godhead and also perfect in manhood; truly God and truly man, of a reasonable [rational] soul and body; consubstantial [coessential] with the Father according to the Godhead, and consubstantial with us according to the Manhood; in all things like unto us, without sin; begotten before all ages of the Father according to the Godhead, and

in these latter days, for us and for our salvation, born of the Virgin Mary, the Mother of God, according to the Manhood; one and the same Christ, Son, Lord, Only-begotten, to be acknowledged in two natures, *inconfusedly, unchangeably, indivisibly, inseparably;* the distinction of natures being by no means taken away by the union, but rather the property of each nature being preserved, and concurring in one Person and one Subsistence, not parted or divided into two persons, but one and the same Son, and only begotten, God the Word, the Lord Jesus Christ, as the prophets from the beginning [have declared] concerning him, and the Lord Jesus Christ himself has taught us, and the Creed of the holy Fathers has handed down to us. [1]

SCRIPTURAL EVIDENCE OF CHRIST'S NATURES

Divine Nature—Genesis 1:26, 3:22, 11:7; Isaiah 6:8 speaks to God referencing himself in the plural, speaking in terms of *Us* and *Our*. This *We* factor highlights the fact that God represents himself to the world as a God of pluralism concerning his singular nature as God.

The expansion of God's revelation of the Scriptures continues this theme of *We* through God's prophets in both the Old and New Testaments. The messianic statement of Isaiah 48:16 and 61:1-2 reflects that the Son of God or coming Messiah will be sent with the Holy Spirit to the world. Later in Luke 4:17-21, we see Jesus' statement concerning himself supporting the prophet's words spoken in Isaiah Chapters 48 and 61.

The Apostle John reinforces Jesus' claims by writing, "In the beginning was the Word, and the Word was with God, and the Word was God. He was in the beginning with God. All things came into being by Him, and apart from Him nothing came into being that has come into

---

[1] Philip Schaff, *The Creeds of Christendom, with a History of Critical Notes*, vol 2, (New York: Harper & Brothers, Franklin Square, 1877), 62; available from https://archive.org/details/TheCreedsOfChristendomV2/page/n83/mode/2up; Internet; accessed 8 July 2020.

being. And the Word became flesh, and dwelt among us, and we beheld His glory, glory as of the only begotten from the Father, full of grace and truth." [2] Later the Apostle Paul explains the dual nature of Christ by saying,

> Have this attitude in yourselves which was also in Christ Jesus, who, although He existed in the form of God, did not regard equality with God a thing to be grasped, but emptied Himself, taking the form of a bond-servant, and being made in the likeness of men. And being found in appearance as a man, He humbled Himself by becoming obedient to the point of death, even death on a cross. Therefore also God highly exalted Him, and bestowed on Him the name which is above every name, that at the name of Jesus every knee should bow, of those who are in heaven, and on earth, and under the earth, and that every tongue should confess that Jesus Christ is Lord, to the glory of God the Father. [3]

The writer of Hebrews provides the argument in support of God the Son having the same nature as God the Father with power and authority, stating, "God, after He spoke long ago to the fathers in the prophets in many portions and in many ways, in these last days has spoken to us in His Son, whom He appointed heir of all things, through whom also He made the world. And He is the radiance of His glory and the exact representation of His nature, and upholds all things by the word of His power." [4]

The historical record of the Gospels tells us that Christ accepted the premise that every knee shall bow to Christ and call him Lord with God the Father's blessing, as Jesus is seen accepting the worship of others with the recognition of the title Lord, as recorded for us in Matthew 2:11, 8:2-4, 14:33, 28:9, 17; Luke 5:8, 7:6-10; John 11:27-45, and John 9:35-38, which reads, "Jesus heard that they had put him out; and

---

[2] John 1:1-3, 14.
[3] Phil. 2:5-11.
[4] Heb. 1:1-3.

finding him, He said, 'Do you believe in the Son of Man?' He answered and said, 'And who is He, Lord, that I may believe in Him?' Jesus said to him, 'You have both seen Him, and He is the one who is talking with you.' And he said, 'Lord, I believe.' And he worshiped Him."

Divine Nature Attributes—Because Christ is part of a triune entity, unified by a single nature, there are attributes shared among all three persons of that trinity. Among these are Omnipresent, Omnipotent, Eternal, Immutable, Holy, Loving, Righteous, Goodness, Merciful, and Wisdom. This means, as the Scriptures express it, that Christ cannot lie (Titus 1:2), change his divine nature (Malachi 3:6), be tempted by evil (James 1:13), or deny himself (2 Timothy 2:13).

When evaluating these facts, we come to understand that it was Christ's human nature that was tempted, not his divine nature. And because Christ cannot change his nature or deny himself, He remains the eternal God through His death, burial, and resurrection experiences. At no point in his life, death, or resurrection did Christ give up his deity or become separated from his divine nature; to teach such understandings would be heresy, and require the denial of key parts of Scriptural teaching. Remember, there are no contradictions in Scripture. For biblical truth to be true, it must agree with all other biblical truths. This is why we are instructed to "Study to show thyself approved unto God, a workman that needeth not to be ashamed, rightly dividing the word of truth" (2 Timothy 2:15; KJV).

Human Nature—The coming of God in human flesh was proclaimed by the prophets of God throughout the Old Testament. King David in a messianic Psalm writes,

> Why are the nations in an uproar, And the peoples devising a vain thing? The kings of the earth take their stand, And the rulers take counsel together Against the Lord and against His Anointed: Let us tear their fetters apart, And cast away their cords from us!
>
> He who sits in the heavens laughs, The Lord scoffs at them. Then He will speak to them in His anger And terrify

them in His fury: But as for Me, I have installed My King Upon Zion, My holy mountain.

I will surely tell of the decree of the Lord: He said to Me, 'Thou art My Son, Today I have begotten Thee. Ask of Me, and I will surely give the nations as Thine inheritance, And the very ends of the earth as Thy possession. Thou shalt break them with a rod of iron, Thou shalt shatter them like earthenware.'

Now therefore, O kings, show discernment; Take warning, O judges of the earth. Worship the Lord with reverence, And rejoice with trembling. Do homage to the Son, lest He become angry, and you perish in the way, For His wrath may soon be kindled. How blessed are all who take refuge in Him![5]

Here we see God proclaiming that God the Father will be installing a future King to sit on the throne of David, who is stated to be God's Son. Zion is represented in the Scriptures as a place on earth, a kingdom to be established by God where every knee shall bow and every tongue shall confess Jesus the Son of God, as Lord of Lords and King of Kings. The Apostle Paul writes to Timothy confirming the writings of the prophets, as he writes,

I charge you in the presence of God, who gives life to all things, and of Christ Jesus, who testified the good confession before Pontius Pilate, that you keep the commandment without stain or reproach until the appearing of our Lord Jesus Christ, which He will bring about at the proper time—He who is the blessed and only Sovereign, the King of kings and Lord of lords; who alone possesses immortality and dwells in unapproachable light; whom no man has seen or can see. To Him be honor and eternal dominion! Amen.[6]

---

[5] Ps. 2:1-12.
[6] 1 Tim. 6:13-16.

The fulfillment of the Old Testament prophecies moves forward with the angel Gabriel's announcement to Mary, the mother of Jesus, as he proclaims, "... Do not be afraid, Mary; for you have found favor with God. And behold, you will conceive in your womb, and bear a son, and you shall name Him Jesus. He will be great, and will be called the Son of the Most High; and the Lord God will give Him the throne of His father David; and He will reign over the house of Jacob forever; and His kingdom will have no end." [7]

With this pronouncement, Jesus, God's coming Son to the earth, will take on human nature through the virgin birth of Mary. It is because of the nature of Jesus' birth that his human nature was without sin. This is reflected in the teachings of the Scriptures throughout the New Testament.

The concept of how sin is passed onto others is explained to us by the Apostle Paul as he writes,

> Therefore, just as through one man sin entered into the world, and death through sin, and so death spread to all men, because all sinned—for until the Law sin was in the world; but sin is not imputed when there is no law. Nevertheless death reigned from Adam until Moses, even over those who had not sinned in the likeness of the offense of Adam, who is a type of Him who was to come. But the free gift is not like the transgression. For if by the transgression of the one the many died, much more did the grace of God and the gift by the grace of the one Man, Jesus Christ, abound to the many. And the gift is not like that which came through the one who sinned; for on the one hand the judgment arose from one transgression resulting in condemnation, but on the other hand the free gift arose from many transgressions resulting in justification. For if by the transgression of the one, death reigned through the one, much more those who receive the abundance of grace and of the gift of righteousness will reign in life through the One,

---

[7] Luke 1:30-33.

Jesus Christ. So then as through one transgression there resulted condemnation to all men, even so through one act of righteousness there resulted justification of life to all men. For as through the one man's disobedience the many were made sinners, even so through the obedience of the One the many will be made righteous. [8]

This passage expresses that through one man, Adam, sin was passed down from one human being to the next, which can only happen through the birth process. But because the embryo in the virgin Mary's womb was the final product of the Holy Spirit, Jesus was born without a sin nature, representing a second Adam, just as Paul implies when he wrote, "… Adam, who is a type of Him who was to come." In another later letter, Paul emphasizes this point when he writes, "So also it is written, 'The first man, Adam, became a living soul.' The last Adam became a life-giving spirit." [9] Irenaeus of Lyons (A.D. 130-202), defends this position in his writings called *Against Heresies* where he writes,

If, then, the first Adam had a man for his father, and was born of human seed, it were reasonable to say that the second Adam was begotten of Joseph. But if the former was taken from the dust, and God was his Maker, it was incumbent that the latter also, making a recapitulation in Himself, should be formed as man by God, to have an analogy with the former as respects His origin. Why, then, did not God again take dust, but wrought so that the formation should be made of Mary? It was that there might not be another formation called into being, nor any other which should [require to] be saved, but that the very same formation should be summed up [in Christ as had existed in Adam], the analogy having been preserved. [10]

---

[8] Rom. 5:12-19.
[9] 1 Cor. 15:45.
[10] Irenaeus of Lyons Against Heresies 3, 21.10. *Ante-Nicene Fathers*, vol. 1. ed. Alexander Roberts, James Donaldson, and A. Cleveland Coxe. trans. Alexander

This lack of sin in the life of Christ is testified to by the Apostles through the Holy Spirit's teaching. The Apostle Paul writes, "Therefore, we are ambassadors for Christ, as though God were entreating through us; we beg you on behalf of Christ, be reconciled to God. He made Him who knew no sin to be sin on our behalf, that we might become the righteousness of God in Him." [11] The Apostle John states, "And you know that He appeared in order to take away sins; and in Him there is no sin." [12] These statements are further supported in principle and implied throughout the Scriptures, as represented in Isaiah 53:9, and reads, "His grave was assigned with wicked men, Yet He was with a rich man in His death, Because He had done no violence, Nor was there any deceit in His mouth."

THE LIFE OF CHRIST

Christ's Birth—The importance of the birth of Christ is evaluated in light of Christ's humanity and the fulfillment of Messianic prophecies which speak to Christ's divinity. We find the starting place for this evaluation in the genealogical record of Christ. Lord Arthur Hervey (M.A.) writes,

> The genealogy of our Lord Jesus Christ, as by the evangelists St. Matthew and St. Luke, has been a subject of acknowledged difficulty and perplexity to commentators from the earliest days of Christianity. Nor are the difficulties of one kind only, or confined to one gospel. They are, on the contrary, manifold and multiform. They attach to the principle as well as to the details of the statements. They comprise questions of history, of chronology, of law, of grammar, of criticism, of agreement between inspired writers, of harmony

---

Roberts and William Rambaut (Buffalo, NY: Christian Literature Publishing Co., 1885.) Revised and edited for New Advent by Kevin Knight. http://www.newadvent.org/ fathers/0103321.htm.

[11] 2 Cor. 5:20-21.
[12] 1 John 3:5.

between the Old and New Testament; in short, they are difficulties of every kind which can beset a passage of Scripture. But though the most learned and able of the fathers and doctors of the Church in all ages have labored to the utmost to disentangle these perplexities, and have in some points labored successfully, still the subject continues to be involved in very considerable obscurity, and there is, consequently, still a great diversity of opinion about it. [13]

The approach we will be taking is one of Grammatical-historical hermeneutics, answering the question, what is the purpose of the book being studied.

Current debates have centered on two separate genealogies that represent Christs' family line, with the first recorded in the Gospel of Matthew and the second in the Gospel of Luke. Because of the differences found within these two genealogies, a theological debate has arisen about why these differences exist. The best answer must come from reasoning through the Scriptures and within its historical context. The key to this issue is to find an answer that contains the least amount of contradictions, both in historical facts and in theological and hermeneutical considerations throughout all of Scripture.

The Gospel of Matthew was written to persuade a Jewish audience that Jesus Christ is their prophesied Messiah and the rightful legal King to the throne of David. Matthew starts his evidence by establishing Christ's genealogy as the son of David (Matthew 1:1), stemming from Abraham, to Isaac, to Jacob, to David, to Solomon, to Eliud, to Joseph, the husband of Mary. The entire list within this genealogy represents forty-two generations (Matthew 1:1-17).

Why start the genealogy from Abraham and not David? The answer lies with the fact that the throne of David was established through the Davidic Covenant, as founded on the Abrahamic Covenant for its foundation, both are classified as everlasting covenants. If one nullifies any of these covenants as being replaced or no longer in effect, the

---

[13] Lord Arthur Hervey, M.A., *The Genealogies of Our Lord and Saviour Jesus Christ* (Cambridge: Macmillan and Co., 1853) 1-2.

concept of the throne of David and the coming of any kingdom from God becomes meaningless.

Matthew's genealogy, both in fact and purpose, is straightforward. The debate arises out of the gospel of Luke, who writes his account from a human perspective to reflect the humanity of Christ for both Jews and Gentiles, using the phrase *Son of Man* twenty-six times. This is best evidenced in Luke's writings, which read,

> And he came in the Spirit into the temple; and when the parents brought in the child Jesus, to carry out for Him the custom of the Law, then he took Him into his arms, and blessed God, and said,
>
> Now Lord, Thou dost let Thy bond-servant depart
> In peace, according to Thy word;
> For my eyes have seen Thy salvation,
> Which Thou hast prepared in the presence of all peoples,
> A light of revelation to the Gentiles,
> And the glory of Thy people Israel. [14]

> To what then shall I compare the men of this generation, and what are they like? They are like children who sit in the market place and call to one another; and they say, 'We played the flute for you, and you did not dance; we sang a dirge, and you did not weep.' For John the Baptist has come eating no bread and drinking no wine; and you say, 'He has a demon!' The Son of Man has come eating and drinking; and you say, 'Behold, a gluttonous man, and a drunkard, a friend of tax-gatherers and sinners!' Yet wisdom is vindicated by all her children. [15]

---

[14] Luke 2:27-32.
[15] Luke 7:31-35.

It is within these passages we see the message of the phrase *Son of Man*. A message meant for all of humanity, presenting Christ as a human, mingling with other humans.

The debate within Luke's genealogy is found in the difference between the names listed and that they stem from two different sons of King David to the last name mentioned in both lists, Joseph, Mary's husband, who is not biologically Jesus' earthly father.

One of the key points of Matthew's gospel is that Jesus is legally the rightful heir to the throne of David because the genealogy placed Joseph as a descendent of David through his son Solomon. Even if Jesus had been an adopted son of Joseph, by Jewish custom, this would make him a legal heir as the first son. Concerning Luke's gospel, it is believed the genealogy represents Mary's line, not her husband's. Even though both Mary and Joseph are direct descendants of David, their genealogy differs through brother relationships, leaving open the question as to why the last name listed in Luke's genealogy is Joseph and not Mary?

We find the answer in the historical setting of the day. Per God's instructions, they did not mention Jewish women in the genealogy lines, only the men or husbands. The evidence of this history is best explained in Numbers 27:1-11 and Numbers 36:1-12. Here God establishes through his prophet Moses how family genealogies and the family line's inheritances would be preserved.

The inheritance of daughters of men who have no sons will be preserved through other male relatives within the same tribes. By following the two genealogies of Joseph and Mary, it appears they are both of the same family lines through two different sons of David—Solomon and Nathan. And it is reported that Heli (Eli), the father of Mary only had one daughter.[16] Thus, it named Joseph, by custom, in the genealogy line.

Summarizing genealogy issues, it should be noted that the gospel of Matthew reflects Joseph's bloodline as the rightful legal heir of David's throne, while Luke's genealogy establishes the bloodline of Mary,

---

[16] Palestinian "Talmud", Haggigah, Book 77, # 4.

Jesus' biological mother, representing seventy-seven generations, traced back through Nathan, the son of King David, to King David, going back to the first man Adam (Luke 3:23-38), identifying the humanity of Christ with Adam as the starting point of all of creation. When comparing all the facts and issues in careful research, it is this author's view that this explanation is the one with the least amount of contradictions and best fits the narrative and purpose of the Scriptures as a whole. [17]

History behind Christ's Birth—Jesus was born between 3 and 2 B.C.[18] We derive this date by reasoning, through Roman history, the writings of the early Church fathers, Christ's life history, astronomy, and the narrative of scriptural accounts surrounding Christ's life. A few of these sources would include the writings of Cassiodorus Senator, St. Irenaeus of Lyon, St. Clement of Alexandria, Tertullian of Carthage, Julius Africanus, St. Hippolytus of Rome, Hippolytus of Thebes, Origen of Alexandria, Eusebius of Caesarea, and Epiphanius of Salamis.[19]

It is believed that Jesus was not born in the winter months. Research shows that December 25 was first celebrated as Christ's birthday by the Church of Alexandria between A.D. 427-433. Cyril Charles Martindale summarizes this history as follows:

> Christmas was not among the earliest festivals of the Church. Irenaeus and Tertullian omit it from their lists of feasts; Origen, glancing perhaps at the discreditable imperial Natalitia, asserts (in Lev. Hom. viii in Migne, P.G., XII, 495) that in the Scriptures sinners alone, not saints, celebrate their

---

[17] Complete-bible-genealogy.com, "Genealogy of Jesus," [article online]; available from https://www.complete-bible-genealogy.com/genealogy_of_jesus.htm; Internet; accessed 13 July 2020.

[18] Jack Finegan, *Handbook of Biblical Chronology: Principles of Time Reckoning in the Ancient World and Problems of Chronology in the Bible* (Princeton, New Jersey: Princeton University Press, 1964), 176, 233.

[19] Jimmy Akin, "What Year was Jesus Born? The Answer may Surprise You," Strangenotions.com [article online]; available from https://strangenotions.com/what-year-was-jesus-born-the-answer-may-surprise-you/; Internet; accessed 16 July 2020.

birthday; Arnobius (VII, 32 in P.L., V, 1264) can still ridicule the "birthdays" of the gods.

The first evidence of the feast is from Egypt. About A.D. 200, Clement of Alexandria (Stromata I.21) says that certain Egyptian theologians "over curiously" assign, not the year alone, but the day of Christ's birth, placing it on 25 Pachon (20 May) in the twenty-eighth year of Augustus. [Ideler (Chron., II, 397, n.) thought they did this believing that the ninth month, in which Christ was born, was the ninth of their own calendar.] Others reached the date of 24 or 25 Pharmuthi (19 or 20 April). With Clement's evidence may be mentioned the "De paschæ computes," written in 243 and falsely ascribed to Cyprian (P.L., IV, 963 sqq.), which places Christ's birth on 28 March, because on that day the material sun was created. But Lupi has shown (Zaccaria, Dissertazioni ecc. del p. A.M. Lupi, Faenza, 1785, p. 219) that there is no month in the year to which respectable authorities have not assigned Christ's birth. Clement, however, also tells us that the Basilidians celebrated the Epiphany, and with it, probably, the Nativity, on 15 or 11 Tybi (10 or 6 January). At any rate this double commemoration became popular, partly because the apparition to the shepherds was considered as one manifestation of Christ's glory, and was added to the greater manifestations celebrated on 6 January; ... John Cassian records in his "Collations" (X, 2 in P.L., XLIX, 820), written 418-427, that the Egyptian monasteries still observe the "ancient custom;" but on 29 Choiak (25 December) and 1 January, 433, Paul of Emesa preached before Cyril of Alexandria, and his sermons (see Mansi, IV, 293; appendix to Act. Conc. Eph.) show that the December celebration was then firmly established there, and calendars prove its permanence. The December feast therefore reached Egypt between 427 and 433. [20]

The Childhood of Christ—As the Scriptures explain to us in Matthew Chapter 2, Jesus was born in the "city of David, which is called Bethlehem." The Scriptures tell us this was because Jesus' parents were of the lineage of King David. [21] Later, Mary and Joseph took Jesus to Egypt for a short time as directed by God because of the threat of King Herod. It is believed that Herod the Great died in 1 B.C., [22] allowing for the return of Jesus back into Israel soon after. From the gospel text of Matthew Chapter 2, we know that Jesus had a history in Nazareth because others have testified to such facts (Luke 4:16, John 1:45-46, Acts 10:38).

Not until the gospel account in Luke Chapter 2 do we hear of Christ's interaction with the teachers of Israel in the temple at Jerusalem. At age twelve, we are told of Christ's progress in his human development. Following this event, the Scriptures make no further mention of Christ until his baptism by the prophet John the Baptist, just before the start of his ministry around age thirty. We find this sequence of events recorded in Matthew Chapters 3 and 4, and Luke Chapter 3.

Christ's Ministry— The four New Testament gospels provide historical context to Christ's ministry on earth. Each gospel provides a record of Christ's life from four differing viewpoints as designed through the inspiration of the Holy Spirit. Matthew, Mark, and Luke are called the synoptic gospels because they record Christ's life in similar details, with an overlap in the descriptions of the same events.

Because some details of similar events differ between each gospel account, a controversy has arisen over the validity of the accounts. We

---

[20] *The Catholic Encyclopedia*, vol. 3, s.v. "Christmas," by Cyril Charles Martindale (New York: Robert Appleton Company, 1908.) 26 Apr. 2010 http://www.newadvent.org/cathen/03724b.htm.

[21] Luke 2:4.

[22] Complete-bible-genealogy.com, "Jesus Birth and When Herod the Great Really Died," [article online]; available from https://strangenotions.com/jesus-birth-and-when-herod-the-great-really-died/; Internet; accessed 14 July 2020.

can account for these discrepancies if the reader understands the purpose behind the gospel book being written as reflecting a particular point of view. The other element of this debate that many times gets left out is the working and inspiration of the Holy Spirit, who causes God's word to be without contradiction in its message presented while upholding the validity of its details, even when its interpreters lack understanding (2 Timothy 3:16; 2 Peter 1:20-21).

The gospel of John was the last of the gospel accounts written, for a different readership, and from a different perspective.

Matthew, Mark, and Luke were written with the Jewish reader of the day in mind, proclaiming Christ as the Jewish Messiah, while the gospel of John was written for the Gentile people of the day, proclaiming Jesus Christ as the Son of God, the Savior of the world.

We should also note that eyewitness accounts from different witnesses often reflect differing details of the same event based on that witnesses' perspective. Therefore, to understand Christ's life, the four gospels should be studied collectively to obtain the best information regarding the historical Jesus.

The following subheadings reflect a summarization of the individual gospels referenced as the historical account of Christ's ministry on earth.

The Gospel of Matthew

The gospel according to Matthew presents Christ as the messianic King that has come. Matthew uses the phrase *the kingdom of heaven* twenty-eight times which does not appear anywhere else in the New Testament and reflects an emphasis within the book. The Apostle Matthew presents to the reader Jesus' ministry as the Messiah, the prophesied King of Israel who has come. We see other evidence that reflects the purpose of Matthew's writings in the phrase, *spoken through the prophets might be fulfilled* and appears seven times in the book which does not appear in the other Gospels. Matthew also uses more Old Testament quotes than any other book, reflecting the messianic nature of Christ's life. [23]

The key points within the book, are the virgin birth and genealogy of Christ in Chapters 1 and 2, the Messiah being rejected by the leadership of Israel in Chapter 12, the Apostle Peter's recognition of Jesus as the Christ (Messiah), the Son of God in Chapter 16, and the commissioning of Christ's Apostles to go out and build Christ New Testament Church, the *body of Christ* in Chapter 28.

THE GOSPEL OF MARK

The gospel according to Mark presents Christ as the *servant*. Mark's emphasis on Christ's ministry presents one who is serving the Jewish people of Israel. We notice this in the absence of any genealogy or even a mention of the virgin birth. This is also clear in Mark's descriptive word *immediately*, used forty times in his writings reflecting the nature of Jesus' service as being compassionate and active toward the physical and spiritual needs of the people. [24]

Another aspect of Mark's writings is the showing of Christ's power and authority within his servanthood, reflecting Jesus as the *Son of God*. (Mark 1:1; 3:11; 15:39)

A key verse that reflects the theme of the book reads, "For even the Son of Man did not come to be served, but to serve, and to give His life a ransom for many." [25]

Like Matthew, there is a turning point in the direction of Christ's ministry. This change occurs in Mark 8:29 with Peter's confession of his recognition of Jesus as the *Christ*. Chapter 1 through 8 shows Christ's service to the Jewish people—Israel. Then, in the remaining part of the book until the ending in Chapter 16, Christ's focus becomes

---

[23] New American Standard Bible, The Open Bible Expanded Edition, "The Christ of Matthew" (Nashville: Thomas Nelson Publishers, 1985) 959.

[24] New American Standard Bible, The Open Bible Expanded Edition, "The Christ of Mark" (Nashville: Thomas Nelson Publishers, 1985) 996.

[25] Mark 10:44.

the preparation of his disciples for his death being the final servant sacrifice for the sins of the world.

The Gospel of Luke

The gospel according to Luke presents Christ's life and ministry as the prophesied coming of the *Son of Man*, emphasizing the human nature of Christ as the God/Man who came to save his people from their sins. Luke, a medical doctor who traveled extensively with the Apostle Paul, and possibly a gentile Christian, shows this in his writings by providing a complete account of Jesus' birth, genealogy, and the growing up experience of Jesus the Messiah, who came with compassion and understanding while sharing the human experience through his birth, the temptation of Satan and finally his suffering on a Roman cross where he died.

But, as is the message of all the gospels, the good news is that Christ rose from the dead and presently sits on the right hand of God the Father (Matthew 28:7; Luke 22:69, 24:45-47).

Luke highlights the theme of his writings in Luke 19:10 when he writes, "For the Son of Man has come to seek and to save that which was lost." The key element of Luke's gospel is its emphasis on Christ's compassion through his humanity as the God/Man.

The Gospel of John

The gospel according to John presents Christ as deity and the incarnate Son of God. This is evident throughout John's writings as he quotes Jesus' seven *I am* statements. *I am the bread of life* (6:35, 48); *I am the light of the world* (8:12; 9:5); *I am the door* (10:7, 9); *I am the good shepherd* (10:11, 14); *I am the resurrection and the life* (11:25); *I am the way, the truth, and the life* (14:6); *I am the true vine* (15:1-5).

The Apostle John continues this theme of deity as he cites seven signs as proof of Christ's true identity, along with five eyewitnesses attesting to his divine nature. John also ties the meaning behind the Old

Testament statement "I AM WHO I AM" (Ex. 3:14) to Christ in verses 4:25, 26; 8:24, 28, 58; 13:19; 18:5, 6, 8. [26]

The Apostle John's writings clearly reflect the deity of Jesus Christ, he also provides a clear path to understanding Christ's humanity. We see this in the very first chapter where John tells us that the Word was God, and the Word became flesh and dwelt among us (1:1, 14). John shows the humanity of Christ through Christ's experiences in travel as he became weary and thirsty (4:6, 7), at the death of Lazarus when Jesus wept (11:35), in Jesus' statement to his disciples that he was troubled (12:27), then in the upper room at the last supper of Christ, Jesus is found reflecting on his humanity, his going to prepare a place for his church (14:2-3), and finally, that which comes to all of humanity, his death. [27]

We find key references in this gospel in 1:1; 8:58; 10:30; 14:9, and 20:28; all of which points to Christ deity.

John opens the book with statements of Christ being the living Word of God in Chapter 1, performing his first miracle in Chapter 2 to validate his ministry, then ends the book with the statement, "Many other signs therefore Jesus also performed in the presence of the disciples, which are not written in this book; but these have been written that you may believe that Jesus is the Christ, the Son of God; and that believing you may have life in His name." [28]

THE PERSON OF CHRIST

The Messianic Message—The fall from perfection to a state of sin for humanity is recorded in Genesis Chapter 3 and provides the reason for the need of redemption for God's creation. Within that same chapter, God introduces the first messianic prophecy which states,

---

[26] New American Standard Bible, The Open Bible Expanded Edition, "The Christ of John" (Nashville: Thomas Nelson Publishers, 1985) 1060.
[27] Idid.
[28] John 20:30-31.

> And the Lord God said to the serpent,
> Because you have done this,
> Cursed are you more than all cattle,
> And more than every beast of the field;
> On your belly shall you go,
> And dust shall you eat
> All the days of your life;
> And I will put enmity
> Between you and the woman,
> And between your seed and her seed;
> He shall bruise you on the head,
> And you shall bruise him on the heel. [29]

The enmity expressed here is between two things; the woman representing all of humanity, and Satan, represented by his kingdom rule. The two seeds represent Christ, who is birthed by the woman into humanity, while the other seed represents Satan.

The prophecy is stating that through Christ the coming Messiah, Satan will be destroyed as represented by the bruising or crushing of the head representing a mortal wound, and the attacks of Satan on humanity can be healed through Christ who is to come, represented by the bruising of the heel.

Other interpretive applications show that Christ's birth, then death, burial, and resurrection was the fulfillment of this prophecy; as Christ provided a way of redemption and escape from Satan's control, and God's final judgment on Satan's kingdom and all of sinful humanity. From Genesis 3 forward, God provides messianic prophecies that point his people to the expectation of the coming Messiah, as Christ is expressed in the gospel accounts.

Christ was not only prophesied to be the saving Messiah, but an eternal priest who continually intercedes for his people, and he will be the ruling King of his kingdom to come.

---

[29] Gen. 3:14-15

Christ as Lord (Messiah)—Jesus provides us some insight into who he is, and where his authority comes from through his prayer to God in the presence of his disciples. "These things Jesus spoke; and lifting up His eyes to heaven, He said, 'Father, the hour has come; glorify Thy Son, that the Son may glorify Thee, even as Thou gavest Him authority over all mankind, that to all whom Thou hast given Him, He may give eternal life. And this is eternal life, that they may know Thee, the only true God, and Jesus Christ whom Thou hast sent.'" [30]

The prophet Danial prophesies of the coming Messiah in Danial 9:24-27, which reads in part, "Then after the sixty-two weeks the Messiah will be cut off and have nothing, and the people of the prince who is to come will destroy the city and the sanctuary. And its end will come with a flood; even to the end there will be war; desolations are determined." The Psalmist supports this message as we read: "The Lord is at Thy right hand; He will shatter kings in the day of His wrath." [31] The Apostle John expanse this thought as he writes, "These will wage war against the Lamb, and the Lamb will overcome them, because He is Lord of lords and King of kings, and those who are with Him are the called and chosen and faithful." [32]

Christ as Prophet— God establishes Christ as the prophet who will one day come and bring God's message to Israel, as the prophet Moses stated, "The Lord your God will raise up for you a prophet like me from among you, from your countrymen, you shall listen to him." [33] The prophet Isaiah confirms this prophecy by saying, "The Spirit of the Lord God is upon me, Because the Lord has anointed me To bring good news to the afflicted; He has sent me to bind up the brokenhearted, To proclaim liberty to captives And freedom to prisoners." [34]

---

[30] John 17:1-4.
[31] Ps. 110:5.
[32] Rev. 17:14.
[33] Deut. 18:15.
[34] Isa. 61:1.

Later we are reminded by Luke of who and why this Prophet is unique from all the other prophets.

> Repent therefore and return, that your sins may be wiped away, in order that times of refreshing may come from the presence of the Lord; and that He may send Jesus, the Christ appointed for you, whom heaven must receive until the period of restoration of all things about which God spoke by the mouth of His holy prophets from ancient time. Moses said, 'The Lord God shall raise up for you a prophet like me from your brethren; to Him you shall give heed in everything He says to you. And it shall be that every soul that does not heed that prophet shall be utterly destroyed from among the people.' And likewise, all the prophets who have spoken, from Samuel and his successors onward, also announced these days. It is you who are the sons of the prophets, and of the covenant which God made with your fathers, saying to Abraham, 'And in your seed all the families of the earth shall be blessed.' For you first, God raised up His Servant, and sent Him to bless you by turning every one of you from your wicked ways. [35]

Christ as Priest—Psalm 110:4 states, "The Lord has sworn and will not change His mind, 'Thou art a priest forever According to the order of Melchizedek.'" The writer of Hebrews explains Christ's role as this priest in this way,

> Since then we have a great high priest who has passed through the heavens, Jesus the Son of God, let us hold fast our confession. For we do not have a high priest who cannot sympathize with our weaknesses, but One who has been tempted in all things as we are, yet without sin. Let us therefore draw near with confidence to the throne of grace, that we may receive mercy and may find grace to help in time of need.

---

[35] Acts 3:19-26.

For every high priest taken from among men is appointed on behalf of men in things pertaining to God, in order to offer both gifts and sacrifices for sins; he can deal gently with the ignorant and misguided, since he himself also is beset with weakness; and because of it he is obligated to offer sacrifices for sins, as for the people, so also for himself. And no one takes the honor to himself, but receives it when he is called by God, even as Aaron was. So also Christ did not glorify Himself to become a high priest, but He who said to Him,

'Thou art My Son, Today I have begotten Thee';
just as He says also in another passage,
Thou art a priest forever
According to the order of Melchizedek.' [36]

Christ as King—The kingship of Christ was established through God the Father. King David writes, "But as for Me, I have installed My King Upon Zion, My holy mountain." [37] David continues to support this concept by writing, "The Lord is King forever and ever; Nations have perished from His land." [38] "Who is this King of glory? The Lord of hosts, He is the King of glory." [39]

God sent the angel Gabriel to the Virgin Mary, and "he said to her, 'Hail, favored one! The Lord is with you.' But she was greatly troubled at this statement and kept pondering what kind of salutation this might be. And the angel said to her, 'Do not be afraid, Mary; for you have found favor with God. And behold, you will conceive in your womb, and bear a son, and you shall name Him Jesus. He will be great, and will be called the Son of the Most High; and the Lord God will give Him the throne of His father David; and He will reign over the house of Jacob forever; and His kingdom will have no end.'" [40]

---

[36] Heb. 4:14-5:6.
[37] Ps. 2:6.
[38] Ps. 10:16.
[39] Ps. 24:10.
[40] Luke 1:28-33.

The Scriptures tell us that foreign magi came to King Herod, seeking Christ the King, and asked, "Where is He who has been born King of the Jews? For we saw His star in the east, and have come to worship Him." [41]

The Apostle Paul writes,

> I charge you in the presence of God, who gives life to all things, and of Christ Jesus, who testified the good confession before Pontius Pilate, that you keep the commandment without stain or reproach until the appearing of our Lord Jesus Christ, which He will bring about at the proper time—He who is the blessed and only Sovereign, the King of kings and Lord of lords; who alone possesses immortality and dwells in unapproachable light; whom no man has seen or can see. To Him be honor and eternal dominion! Amen. [42]

The Scriptures as a whole support the kingship of Christ, and thus, Christ's coming kingdom.

NAMES USED OF CHRIST

Like the various names for God the Father, a variety of names are used to describe Jesus Christ, most of which are titles or names reflecting his attributes, position, or ministerial functions. The following are examples of such name usages in the New Testament Scriptures. [43]

Advocate—1 John 2:1
Alpha and Omega—Revelation 1:8; 22:13
The Almighty—Revelation 1:8
Amen—Revelation 3:14

---

[41] Matt. 2:2.
[42] 1 Tim. 6:13-16.
[43] Msgr. Charles Pope, "150 Titles of Christ from the Scriptures," Community in Mission [article online]; available from http://blog.adw.org/2012/05/150-titles-of-christ-from-the-scriptures/; Internet; accessed 22 July 2020.

Apostle and High Priest of our Confession—Hebrews 3:1
Author and Finisher of our Faith—Hebrews 12:2
Beloved—Matthew 12:18
Beloved Son—Colossians 1:13
Bread of God—John 6:33; 50
Bread of Life—John 6:35
Living Bread—John 6:51
Bridegroom—John 3:29
Brother—Matthew 12:50
Captain of our Salvation—Hebrews 2:10
Carpenter—Mark 6:3
Carpenter's Son—Matthew 13:55
Chief Shepherd—1 Peter 5:4
Chosen One—Luke 23:35
Christ—Matthew 16:20
Christ Jesus—1 Timothy 1:15; Colossians 1:1.
Christ of God—Luke 9:20
Christ the Lord—Luke 2:11
Christ who is above all—Romans 9:5
Consolation of Israel—Luke 2:25
Chief Cornerstone—Ephesians 2:20; 1 Peter 2:6
Dayspring—Luke 1:78
Deliverer—Romans 11:26
Deliverer from the wrath to come—1 Thessalonians 1:10
Eldest of many brothers—Romans 8:29
Emmanuel—Matthew 1:23
Faithful and True Witness—Revelation 1:5; 3:14.
First and Last—Revelation 1:17; 2:8
Firstborn among many brothers—Romans 8:29
First born from the dead—Revelation 1:5
Firstborn of all creation—Colossians 1:15
First Fruits—1 Corinthians 15:20
Friend of tax collectors and sinners—Matthew 11:19
Gate of the sheepfold—John 10:7
Glory—Luke 2:32
Good Shepherd—John 10:11; 14

Grain of Wheat—John 12:24
Great Shepherd of the sheep—Hebrews 13:20
Head—Ephesians 4:15
Head of the Church—Colossians 1:18; Ephesians 1:22.
Hidden Manna—Revelation 2:17
High Priest—Hebrews 3:1; 4:14; 7:26
He Who Holds of the Keys of David—Revelation 3:7
He who is coming amid the clouds—Revelation 1:7
Holy One—Acts 2:27
Holy One of God—Mark 1:24
Holy Servant—Acts 4:27
Hope—1 Timothy 1:1
Horn of Salvation—Luke 1:69
I Am—John 8:58
Image of God—2 Corinthians 4:4; Colossians 1:15.
Indescribable Gift—2 Corinthians 9:15
Intercessor—Hebrews 7:25
Jesus—Matthew 1:21
Jesus the Nazarene—John 18:5
Judge of the World—2 Timothy 4:1; Acts 10:42.
Just One—Acts 7:52
Just Judge—2 Timothy 4:8
King—Matthew 21:5
King of Israel—John 1:49
King of Kings—Revelation 17:14; 19:16; 1 Timothy 6:15
King of Nations—Revelation 15:3
King of the Jews—Matthew 2:2
Lamb of God—John 1:29
Last Adam—1 Corinthians 15:45
Leader—Matthew 2:6; Hebrews 2:10.
Leader and Perfecter of Faith—Hebrews 12:2
Leader and Savior—Acts 5:31
Life—John 14:6; Colossians 3:4.
Light—John 1:9; John 12:35.
Light of all—Luke 2:32; John 1:4.
Light of the world—John 8:12

Lion of the tribe of Judah—Revelation 5:5
Lord—Luke 1:25
One Lord—Ephesians 4:5
My Lord my God—John 20:28
Lord both of the dead and the living—Romans 14:9
Lord God Almighty—Revelation 15:3
Lord Jesus—Acts 7:59
Jesus is Lord—1 Corinthians 12:3
Lord Jesus Christ—Acts 15:11
Lord of all—Acts 10:36
Lord of Glory—1 Corinthians 2:8
Lord of lords—1 Timothy 6:15
Lord of Peace—2 Thessalonians 3:16
The Man—John 19:5
Master—Luke 5:5
Mediator—1 Timothy 2:5
Messiah—John 1:41; 4:25
Morning Star—2 Peter 1:19; Revelation 2:28; Revelation 22:16.
Nazarene—Matthew 2:23
Passover—1 Corinthians 5:7
Power and wisdom of God—1 Corinthians 1:24
Power for salvation—Luke 1:69
Priest forever—Hebrews 5:6
Prince of Life—Acts 3:15
Rabboni—John 20:16
Ransom—1 Timothy 2:6
Rescuer from this Present Evil Age—Galatians 1:4
Radiance of God's Glory—Hebrews 1:3
Resurrection and Life—John 11:25
Rising Sun—Luke 1:78
Root of David—Revelation 5:5
Root of David's line—Revelation 22:16
Ruler—Matthew 2:6
Ruler of the kings of the earth—Revelation 1:5
Ruler and Savior—Acts 5:31
Savior—2 Peter 2:20; 3:18

Savior of the world—1 John 4:14; John 4:42.
Second Adam—Romans 5:14
Servant of the Jews—Romans 15:8
Shepherd and Guardian of our souls—1 Peter 2:25
Slave—Philippians 2:7
Son—Galatians 4:4
Beloved Son—Colossians 1:13
Firstborn Son—Luke 2:7
Son of Abraham—Matthew 1:1
Son of David—Matthew 1:1
Son of God—Luke 1:35
Son of Joseph—John 1:45
Son of Man—John 5:27
Son of Mary—Mark 6:3
Son of the Blessed One—Mark 14:61
Son of the Father—2 John 1:3
Son of the Living God—Matthew 16:16
Son of the Most High—Luke 1:32
Son of the Most High God—Mark 5:7
Only Son of the Father—John 1:14
Source of God's creation—Revelation 3:14
Spiritual Rock—1 Corinthians 10:4
Living Stone—1 Peter 2:4
Stone rejected by the builders—Matthew 21:42; 1 Peter 2:8
Stumbling Stone—1 Peter 2:8
Teacher—Matthew 8:19; Matthew 23:10.
Testator of the New Covenant—Hebrews 9:16
True God—1 John 5:20
True Vine—John 15:1
The Way the Truth and the Life—John 14:6
The One who is, is was, and who is to come—Revelation 3:7
Wisdom of God—1 Corinthians 1:24
Wonderful Counselor—Isaiah 9:6
Word—John 1:1; 14
Word of God—Revelation 19:13
Word of Life—1 John 1:1

The Old Testament also makes references to Christ through the following descriptions. [44]

The Glory of the Lord (Isaiah 40:5)
The Lord of Hosts (Psalm 24:7-10)
Offspring of the Woman (Genesis 3:15)
Kinsman Redeemer (Ruth chapters 1-4)
Messenger of the Covenant (Malachi 3:1)
Refiner's Fire and Launderer's Soap (Malachi 3:2-3)
Sun of Righteousness (Malachi 4:2)
The Rose of Sharon and the Lily of the Valleys (Song of Solomon 2:1)
The Desire of All Nations (Haggai 2:7)
The Servant of the Lord (Isaiah 52:13)
The Arm of the Lord (Isaiah 53:1)
The Branch (Zechariah 3:8)
The Lord our Righteousness (Jeremiah 23:6)
One from the Days of Eternity (Micah 5:2)
Prince of Peace—Isaiah 9:6
Redeemer—Isaiah 59:20
Mighty God—Isaiah 9:6
Root of Jesse—Isaiah 11:10
Father Forever—Isaiah 9:6

---

[44] Pope, "150 Titles of Christ from the Scriptures," [article online]; available from http://blog.adw.org/2012/05/150-titles-of-christ-from-the-scriptures/. Note: Scripture's referenced in the list of both New and Old Testament name titles are not part of book's Scripture Index.

THE DOCTRINE OF CHRIST | 63

{ CHAPTER DISCUSSION NOTES }

The Two Natures of Christ

Historically the dual natures of Christ have been debated for centuries. Even the disciples, despite being intimate with Jesus for the better part of his ministry, struggled with his true identity. This is seen in their response to Jesus' actions throughout Christ's 3 ½ years of ministry. This fact becomes evident in Mark 4:39-41 which reads, "And being aroused, He rebuked the wind and said to the sea, 'Hush, be still.' And the wind died down and it became perfectly calm. And He said to them, 'Why are you so timid? How is it that you have no faith?' And they became very much afraid and said to one another, 'Who then is this, that even the wind and the sea obey Him?'" This lack of understanding was also noted in Mark 6:52 and 7:37. We read in Mark 8:14-21:

> And they had forgotten to take bread; and did not have more than one loaf in the boat with them. And He was giving orders to them, saying, 'Watch out! Beware of the leaven of the Pharisees and the leaven of Herod.' And they began to discuss with one another the fact that they had no bread. And Jesus, aware of this, said to them, 'Why do you discuss the fact that you have no bread? Do you not yet see or understand? Do you have a hardened heart? Having eyes, do you not see? And having ears, do you not hear? And do you not remember, when I broke the five loaves for the five thousand, how many baskets full of broken pieces you picked up?' They said to Him, 'Twelve.' 'And when I broke the seven for the four thousand, how many large baskets full of broken pieces did you pick up?' And they said to Him, 'Seven.' And He was saying to them, 'Do you not yet understand?'

It is clear from these passages that even at the mid-point of Jesus' ministry, the disciples were still without understanding as to who Christ truly was. Even John the Baptist had doubts, as we see demonstrated by his sending two disciples to Jesus to verify who he was (Matthew

11:2). Why did those earnestly looking for the Messiah to come not understand who the Messiah truly was? — God incarnate.

The answer to this question is best explained within the context of the Old Testament. Those looking for the prophesied Messiah did not see this Messiah as God coming to save their souls, but as a great warrior king sent by God to deliver them from their oppressors and usher in the promised millennial kingdom under another mortal king along the lines of King David. They originally saw this coming kingdom as a continuous extension of the existing Old Testament system.

The second component of their lack of understanding was their belief that God was one, not three in one. The Jewish people of that day, and even today, lack an understanding of the concept of a triune God; this is evident as we read the following passage, "And one of the scribes came and heard them arguing, and recognizing that He had answered them well, asked Him, 'What commandment is the foremost of all?' Jesus answered, 'The foremost is, Hear, O Israel! The Lord our God is one Lord; and you shall love the Lord your God with all your heart, and with all your soul, and with all your mind, and with all your strength.'"[45]

The hardness of the disciple's hearts was not because of the sin of denial (Mark 16:14; Luke 22:24), but a sin of national pride apart from God's actual plan. They were not looking for a Savior, but a deliverer from oppression by the Roman empire and the promised kingdom on earth (2 Samuel 7:14-18). Christ provides us an explanation of how the disciples finally came to understand the truth, as recorded in Luke 24:44-49:

> Now He said to them, 'These are My words which I spoke to you while I was still with you, that all things which are written about Me in the Law of Moses and the Prophets and the Psalms must be fulfilled.' Then He opened their minds to understand the Scriptures, and He said to them, 'Thus it is written, that the Christ should suffer and rise again from the dead

---

[45] Mark 12:28-30.

the third day; and that repentance for forgiveness of sins should be proclaimed in His name to all the nations, beginning from Jerusalem. You are witnesses of these things. And behold, I am sending forth the promise of My Father upon you; but you are to stay in the city until you are clothed with power from on high.'

Luke's gospel tells us that Christ opened the eyes of his disciples to fully understanding the Old Testament Scriptures concerning the coming Messiah, that would not just bring them their inheritance of an earthly kingdom, but also provide them a way of eternal life through the New Covenant, also promised, that was not to replace, but to come alongside the Davidic Covenant. The New Covenant reads,

'But this is the covenant which I will make with the house of Israel after those days,' declares the Lord, 'I will put My law within them, and on their heart I will write it; and I will be their God, and they shall be My people. And they shall not teach again, each man his neighbor and each man his brother, saying, Know the Lord, for they shall all know Me, from the least of them to the greatest of them,' declares the Lord, 'for I will forgive their iniquity, and their sin I will remember no more.' [46]

The two natures of Christ can then be seen in the dual purpose of his ministry, providing redemption to the world from sin and providing the inheritance promised to Israel through the Davidic Covenant. These goals could only be accomplished through one person in the form of the God/Man—Jesus Christ. (Romans 5:12-15)

THE LIFE OF CHRIST

It is interesting to note that every aspect of Christ's life can be found in the prophetic utterances of the Old Testament, hundreds, and even over

---

[46] Jer. 31:33-34.

a thousand years before their fulfillment; these are what we understand to be the messianic prophecies. We see this in the details of Christ's birth, flight to Egypt, ministry, death, and resurrection. The following passages reflect this observation (Jeremiah 31:15; Matthew 2:18; Matthew 2:23; Isaiah 7:14; Matthew 1:23; Isaiah 53:9-12; Matthew 27:57-60; Psalm 22:18; Luke 23:34; Psalm 69:21; Matthew 27:34; Psalm 22:1; Matthew 27:46; Psalm 34:20; John 19:36; Zechariah 12:10; John 19:34; Psalm 16:10; Mark 16:6-7).

THE PERSON OF CHRIST

Christ, who came as Prophet, Priest, and King, is significant because of what that represents within God's revelation to the world.

The Prophet—Christ was to be the final prophet sent by Jehovah God who would come with all authority and speak to the final matters concerning humanity to the world. Deuteronomy 18:18-19 reads, "I will raise up a prophet from among their countrymen like you, and I will put My words in his mouth, and he shall speak to them all that I command him. And it shall come about that whoever will not listen to My words which he shall speak in My name, I Myself will require it of him." Jesus said, "When you lift up the Son of Man, then you will know that I am He, and I do nothing on My own initiative, but I speak these things as the Father taught Me." [47] As the prophecy states, Jesus the prophet only spoke those things the Father said to him.

The Priest—The tabernacle of God and the functionality of the priesthood within that temple was established before the foundations of the world, and introduced to humanity through the prophet Moses (Exodus 25:8-9).

The purpose of the biblical priesthood and Christ's role as our High Priest is explained in Hebrews Chapters 7 through 9. As the writer of Hebrews expresses it, Christ is of an eternal priestly line after the order of Melchizedek, making Christ eternally available to be our intercessor

---

[47] John 8:28.

before God. The eternalness of the tabernacle of God is seen in Revelation 21:3: "Behold, the tabernacle of God is among men."

The King—The concept of kings came about in Scripture when the Nation of Israel asked God for a king to rule over them like all the other nations; this king would stand in the place of God, who was too Holy and unapproachable in their current sinful condition. God granted them this request, but in his eternal purposes, God provided a way for this to be an everlasting concept before the whole world. Thus, God over time established the Abrahamic and Davidic Covenants, allowing for a future God/Man King who would become an everlasting King who will physically sit on an earthly throne, not just over a Jewish Israel, but over all nations, representing both Jews and gentiles (Daniel 7:14).

> Personal Notes

Three

THE DOCTRINE OF THE HOLY SPIRIT

THE PERSON OF THE HOLY SPIRIT

The Holy Spirit's existence and nature are progressively revealed in Scripture in incremental stages. To understand the trinity and how each person relates to one another, it is important to understand what personhood means regarding a relationship to a triune God.

The Scriptures tell us that God is spirit (John 4:24), meaning the metaphysical makeup of God is in a spirit form, similar to the air we breathe. Jesus provides a metaphor for this concept in John 3:6-8. "That which is born of the flesh is flesh, and that which is born of the Spirit is spirit. Do not marvel that I said to you, 'You must be born again.' The wind blows where it wishes and you hear the sound of it, but do not know where it comes from and where it is going; so is everyone who is born of the Spirit."

The word for spirit is *ruwach* in the Old Testament and *pneuma* in the New Testament. It can be categorized into nine separate categories,[1] bringing some confusion as to how we should interpret its meaning and usage. Because of this complexity, we will only point out that the metaphysical makeup of God as spirit differs from when we speak about the person of the Holy Spirit. This difference then requires us to define the term spirit when referencing God and the Holy Spirit's personhood.

---

[1] Reid A. Ashbaucher, *Made in the Image of God: Understanding the Nature of God and Mankind in a Changing World*, 3 rev ed (Toledo, Ohio: Reid Ashbaucher Publications, 2020), 41.

We read in Genesis 1:2, "the Spirit of God was moving over the surface of the waters." For centuries, this passage has been presumed to be a reference to the Holy Spirit. But if we look at this from another perspective, another interpretation is very plausible. If God is spirit, representing the single nature of a triune God, then the spirit of God or the very nature of God's single essence as a triune being could move over the surface of the waters, not just the person of the Holy Spirit. When seen in this light, we come to a better understanding that it was not just the Holy Spirit who has power or creative ability, but a triune God collectively has this power that works in the world. This interpretation is the result of my 27-year study on the nature of God and Man, resulting in my first book, *Made in the Image of God: Understanding the Nature of God and Mankind in a Changing World* and would provide additional support on the topic.

Following this line of reasoning, we need to define what makes a person a person. Or concerning God, what is personhood? The answer to that question comes to us from a thorough study of the Scriptures. The short answer is, the spirit of God or the single nature of God carries the attributes of power, communication, presence, and most importantly, attitudes, all of which represent God's morality such as, holiness, righteousness, wisdom, and love. God's personhood represents the attributes of emotion, intellect, and will. Through the Scriptures, it can be proven that each person of the trinity has their own individual ability to show intellect, emotion, and will. [2]

Regarding the person of the Holy Spirit, we see this in Acts 16:16 where He forbids something from taking place, representing an act of the will. In Acts 15:28 we see the Holy Spirit reasoning with believers as to the best action to take under the circumstances. This shows independent reasoning ability, or intellect. Then in Ephesians 4:30, we see that we can grieve the Holy Spirit, showing that, as an individual, the Holy Spirit has emotions. We can also show this concerning God the Father and God the Son. [3]

---

[2] Ashbaucher, *Made in the Image of God*, 63-93.
[3] Ibid., 65-72.

Keeping this study simple, the unifying factor to all three persons is their single nature which produces not only their power, communications, and presence but also unifying attitudes, reflecting that all three persons of the Trinity share the exact same attitudes, which further study will prove to be the controlling factor of their personhoods.

The person of the Holy Spirit is just that, an individual person who is God in nature, who acts in the world according to the will of God the Father and God the Son's direction (John Chapters 14 and 15). We see this in Jesus' introduction of the Holy Spirit to the world in John 14:16, where we are told that a *helper* will come and abide in us as believers forever. This helper and the Holy Spirit are later defined in the same text (John 14:26).

SUMMARY OF PERSONHOOD

Summarizing these points; the Holy Spirit is a person who is spirit in nature. When the Scriptures use the term *Holy Spirit* it is referencing a person, not specifically referring to the very nature of God, for God is spirit, is he not? Many questions arise within this discussion of a triune God, which is why it requires another book to deal with such issues.

The main point of this discussion is that the Holy Spirit is a person who shares the unifying nature of God that is also spirit in nature. So when we see the word "spirit" used in Scripture, we should not assume that it always automatically refers to the person of the Holy Spirit, instead, it could be a reference to God's nature as spirit or some other defined use of spirit, such as the spirit of attitude found in Numbers 14:24 and Proverbs 16:32, or evil spirits spoken of in Acts 19:15 and First Samuel 16:23, showing there are other usages of this term *spirit* reflected in the Scriptures.

We should also note that when the Scriptures use the phrase *Spirit of the Lord* (2 Corinthians 3:17-18), it is always in reference to the person of the Holy Spirit. But when we see the phrase *Spirit of God* (Genesis 41:38 KJV), this is much more difficult to interpret in context, but in all cases, it is a reference to God's natural attributes as his spirit nature, not God's intellect, emotion or will attributes, or associated with personal pronouns reflecting a person. We see this in the New

American Standard Bible translating this phrase as a *divine spirit*. Remember, everywhere the person of the Holy Spirit goes, he takes his God nature with him, which is also spirit in nature, for God is spirit, is he not? (John 4:24)

Think of it this way. Your personhood lies inside your body. So everywhere your body goes, your personhood goes with you. So it is with the Holy Spirit. Everywhere the person of the Holy Spirit goes, so goes his nature, known as the spirit of God.

THE NATURE OF THE HOLY SPIRIT

HOLY SPIRIT'S NATURE REFLECTED IN THE O.T.

The person of the Holy Spirit shares in the same nature as God the Father and God the Son. We find the first mention of the person of the Holy Spirit in Numbers 11:17 where God states, "and I will take of the Spirit who is upon you and will put Him upon them...." Here we see the Spirit personalized as *who* and *Him*. This is repeated in verse 25 which expresses the same concept. Not until the writings of the prophets do we see four additional references to the person of the Holy Spirit; as we read, "Do not cast me away from Thy presence, And do not take Thy Holy Spirit from me." [4] Isaiah writes, "But they rebelled And grieved His Holy Spirit; Therefore, He turned Himself to become their enemy, He fought against them. Then His people remembered the days of old, of Moses. Where is He who brought them up out of the sea with the shepherds of His flock? Where is He who put His Holy Spirit in the midst of them...?" [5] We find the fourth reference in Isaiah 59:21.

Because the Old Testament speaks little directly about the person of the Holy Spirit, the concept of a triune God was not understood or known among the Jewish nation—Israel. The teaching God commanded Moses concerning his being, reflected in the instructions Moses provided to God's people, as recorded in Deuteronomy 6:4-9:

---

[4] Ps. 51:11.
[5] Isa. 63:10-11.

> Hear, O Israel! The Lord is our God, the Lord is one! And you shall love the Lord your God with all your heart and with all your soul and with all your might. And these words, which I am commanding you today, shall be on your heart; and you shall teach them diligently to your sons and shall talk of them when you sit in your house and when you walk by the way and when you lie down and when you rise up. And you shall bind them as a sign on your hand and they shall be as frontals on your forehead. And you shall write them on the doorposts of your house and on your gates.

HOLY SPIRIT'S NATURE REFLECTED IN THE N.T.

Not until Jesus introduces the person of the Holy Spirit do we see a triune God presented to the world through God's ongoing revelation, demonstrating the progressive nature of God's revelation up to John's writing of his last book, the Apocalypse, or what the Scriptures reference as, *The Revelation of Jesus Christ* (Revelation 1:1).

The concept of the term Holy Spirit comes early in the gospel writings, as we are told by the angel Gabriel that the birth of Jesus Christ will come about through the work of the Holy Spirit (Matthew 1:18-20).

Then comes John the Baptist's pronouncement: "As for me, I baptize you with water for repentance, but He who is coming after me is mightier than I, and I am not fit to remove His sandals; He will baptize you with the Holy Spirit and fire." [6] This pronouncement brings no real meaning to the term since the people of that day did not understand what or who the Holy Spirit was, or how the Holy Spirit would baptize anyone. Later, Luke tells us that Jesus was filled with the Holy Spirit and led him through the wilderness during his forty-days of fasting and his temptation confrontation with Satan. [7] Not until the final rejection of Christ by the leaders of the Nation of Israel, through their denial of not only Christ but the power of the Holy Spirit in Christ's ministry

---

[6] Matt. 3:11.
[7] Luke 4:1-13.

(Matthew 12), do we find Christ introducing the Holy Spirit to the world.

Christ introduces the person of the Holy Spirit to his disciples following his rejection by the Nation of Israel. Jesus opens this introduction by saying, "And I will ask the Father, and He will give you another Helper, that He may be with you forever; that is the Spirit of truth, whom the world cannot receive, because it does not behold Him or know Him, but you know Him because He abides with you, and will be in you." [8] Jesus clarifies this statement by saying, "These things I have spoken to you, while abiding with you. But the Helper, the Holy Spirit, whom the Father will send in My name, He will teach you all things, and bring to your remembrance all that I said to you." [9]

It is through the gospel accounts that we learn the Holy Spirit is not just associated with power, but a person who comes from God carrying similar attributes as God himself.

Within Christ's introduction, we learn that the Holy Spirit will permanently reside in all believers in Christ. Later, more was revealed about the work and ministry of the person of the Holy Spirit through the continuing revelation of the Scriptures as they were being written and unfolding before us.

THE DEITY OF THE HOLY SPIRIT

We come to understand the Holy Spirit's deity through several Scripture passages. The prophet Isaiah tells us of the origins of the Holy Spirit, referring to, *His Holy Spirit* (Isaiah 63:10); where the pronoun *His*, is a reference to God. Through the gospel accounts, we know that all believers or *the body of Christ* (the church) are indwelt by the person of the Holy Spirit, who is God.

Then in Acts 16:6, it gives this newly formed body direction regarding what to do in their gospel ministry by the Holy Spirit, providing us understanding that the Holy Spirit carries authority as deity. This understanding becomes clearer as the Apostle Paul writes to the church

---

[8] John 14:16-17.
[9] John 14:26.

THE DOCTRINE OF THE HOLY SPIRIT | 75

in Corinth and says, "Now we have received, not the spirit of the world, but the Spirit who is from God, that we might know the things freely given to us by God, which things we also speak, not in words taught by human wisdom, but in those taught by the Spirit, combining spiritual thoughts with spiritual words." [10]

The phrase *the Spirit who is from God* tells us two things. First, we understand the Holy Spirit to be a person when associated with the word *who*, and second, this person can express God's thoughts to us. The concept that someone could know the thoughts of God is significant and explained to us this way. "For who among men knows the thoughts of a man except the spirit of the man, which is in him? Even so the thoughts of God no one knows except the Spirit of God." [11] This passage reveals that only someone coexisting in God's nature can know and share God's thoughts with others. This evidence points us to the conclusion that the Holy Spirit is God by nature and possesses authority with the weight of deity.

From this point in our understanding of who the Holy Spirit is, we can now move into a discussion on the purpose behind his existence.

THE WORK OF THE HOLY SPIRIT

The examples that follow reflect the work the Holy Spirit does on behalf of the *body of Christ*, as directed by God the Father and God the Son. The Scriptures reveal the work of the Holy Spirit as reflected through the following actions.

To Bear Witness—John 16:13-14 states, "But when He, the Spirit of truth, comes, He will guide you into all the truth; for He will not speak on His own initiative, but whatever He hears, He will speak; and He will disclose to you what is to come. He shall glorify Me; for He shall take of Mine, and shall disclose it to you." The Apostle John continues this theme by writing,

---

[10] 1 Cor. 2:12-13.
[11] 1 Cor. 2:11.

> This is the one who came by water and blood, Jesus Christ; not with the water only, but with the water and with the blood. And it is the Spirit who bears witness, because the Spirit is the truth. For there are three that bear witness, the Spirit and the water and the blood; and the three are in agreement. If we receive the witness of men, the witness of God is greater; for the witness of God is this, that He has borne witness concerning His Son. The one who believes in the Son of God has the witness in himself; the one who does not believe God has made Him a liar, because he has not believed in the witness that God has borne concerning His Son. And the witness is this, that God has given us eternal life, and this life is in His Son. He who has the Son has the life; he who does not have the Son of God does not have the life. [12]

To Baptize Believers—The prophet John the Baptist introduced the concept of the *baptism of the Holy Spirit* in Matthew 3:11. "As for me, I baptize you with water for repentance, but He who is coming after me is mightier than I, and I am not fit to remove His sandals; He will baptize you with the Holy Spirit and fire."

Acts 1:4-5 records Jesus' words on the topic this way, "And gathering them together, He commanded them not to leave Jerusalem, but to wait for what the Father had promised, 'Which,' He said, 'you heard of from Me; for John baptized with water, but you shall be baptized with the Holy Spirit not many days from now.'"

God promised the baptism of the Holy Spirit through Christ's declaration to them in Acts 1:5. But there is another aspect to what God promised to them through the New Covenant which is also tied to the baptism of the Holy Spirit.

The promise God the Father made comes in the form of the New Covenant made to Israel, to which the Gentiles were later grafted into (Romans 11:11-32). The New Covenant reads:

---

[12] 1 John 5:6-12.

'Behold, days are coming,' declares the Lord, 'when I will make a new covenant with the house of Israel and with the house of Judah, not like the covenant which I made with their fathers in the day I took them by the hand to bring them out of the land of Egypt, My covenant which they broke, although I was a husband to them,' declares the Lord. 'But this is the covenant which I will make with the house of Israel after those days,' declares the Lord, 'I will put My law within them, and on their heart I will write it; and I will be their God, and they shall be My people. And they shall not teach again, each man his neighbor and each man his brother, saying, Know the Lord, for they shall all know Me, from the least of them to the greatest of them,' declares the Lord, 'for I will forgive their iniquity, and their sin I will remember no more.' [13]

This covenant promises several things. First, that God will place within his people his laws, and they will know him personally. This conveys the impression that knowledge will come directly from God instead of outside sources, as previously required. This promise goes on to state that God will become their teacher, while simultaneously forgiving their sins, and that this forgiveness will be permanent (forever).

The answer to the second question of what is the Holy Spirit's relationship to the New Covenant comes through understanding how God is going to accomplish all that he promised. God fulfills his New Covenant by applying Christ's death, burial, and resurrection to believers' lives as they demonstrate repentance and faith (Acts 20:21).

The result of this action is the indwelling of the Holy Spirit in the believer through the actions of the baptism of the Holy Spirit. The result of the Holy Spirit's actions, of changing our status from being dead in our sins to being alive in Christ, is that we become a new creature in Christ (2 Corinthians 5:17), thus becoming adopted sons and daughters

---

[13] Jer. 31:31-34.

of God, which is expressed as being baptized by the Holy Spirit of God (Romans 8:15-17; 2 Corinthians 6:18; Joel 2:28-32; Acts 2:16-21).

There are other facets to this work that get confused with water baptism and the transitioning from John's baptism of repentance to Jesus' baptism of the Holy Spirit, as recorded in the book of Acts. We should understand that the baptism of the Holy Spirit occurs on the day a believer exercises repentance and faith, and because the New Covenant is unconditional and forever, the baptism of the Holy Spirit occurs only once and is forever (Ephesians 4:4-6; Acts 19:2).

If one teaches that the baptism of the Holy Spirit is not connected to the New Covenant or can be rescinded or is temporary, then the New Covenant becomes invalid and God's promise becomes a lie. For it is through the baptism of the Holy Spirit that we become God's adopted children, both metaphysically and spiritually, and are placed into the family of God. It is through Christ's work on the cross that we are forgiven of our sins—permanently!

Some within the body of Christ believe the baptism of the Holy Spirit is a second work of grace that provides an extra measure of God's power. This is based on Acts 2:4, Ephesians 5:18, and Acts 19:1-7, where there is a transition from John the Baptist's baptism of repentance to baptism in Christ's name.

We find in verse 2 the Apostle Paul's question, "Did you receive the Holy Spirit when you believed?" This question came with the expectation of an answer of yes! The reason for this is that this is how it worked for many others (Acts 10:44-48). But when they responded no, Paul baptized them as believers but also laid hands on them to bless them with God's gift of the Holy Spirit. The point to be made here is the normal intended pattern of the baptism of the Holy Spirit comes at the time of repentance and faith. That was Paul's expectation for everyone. But because of the need to transition from John's baptism to Christ's baptism, for those alive at the time, this extra step was taken, leading to some confusion on the subject.

To Empower the Believer—Acts 1:8 reads, "... but you shall receive power when the Holy Spirit has come upon you; and you shall be My witnesses both in Jerusalem, and in all Judea and Samaria, and even to the remotest part of the earth." These are the words Christ gave to his disciples just after informing them that the coming of God's Kingdom will come at a time which only God the Father knows.

When understood in context, the power Jesus is offering comes from the Holy Spirit who lives in all believers in Christ. The purpose of this power is to accomplish the work of the ministry or help the *body of Christ* (the church) evangelize or spread the good news of the gospel message. This internal power manifests itself in each believer's life through spiritual strength to overcome physically, mentally, and sometimes, supernaturally as God heals, controls one's circumstances, and event happenings. God can calm our spirits, troubled minds, or he can even control our environments to his glory. And the list could go on.

The key to seeing the power of God in one's life comes through prayer and obedience to the word of God. Through this process comes the filling of the Holy Spirit to overcome the powers of evil and to be unified with God in the spirit as a result (Ephesians 5:18-21).

We see evidence of this in the lives of the Apostles as they went into the world to be God's witnesses. Though this promise was made directly to Christ's disciples, God has demonstrated that this power works for all believers, because the same Holy Spirit that lived in the Apostles also lives in all believers in Christ. When we fellowship together as a church community, it is the testimony of many that what is being said here is true, and a confirmation from the Holy Spirit who resides in all believers. (Romans 8:15-28; Luke 4:1-13)

To Guide the Believer—In the first century of the church, God's guidance came directly from the Holy Spirit's interaction with believers (Acts 10:19-20; 21:10-11) because the New Testament Scriptures were still being written, and the Apostle's letters, though widely circulated, were not available to all; for the gospel was spreading rapidly and outpacing the organizing of Christ's church in local communities.

Today, the Scriptures are complete, and the question of the Canon has been settled since the sixteenth century among the *body of Christ* worldwide. These facts lead us to the question, How does the Holy Spirit guide believers today?

Second Timothy 3:16-17 reads, "All Scripture is inspired by God and profitable for teaching, for reproof, for correction, for training in righteousness; that the man of God may be adequate, equipped for every good work." The Apostle Peter expands on this concept by saying, "But know this first of all, that no prophecy of Scripture is a matter of one's own interpretation, for no prophecy was ever made by an act of human will, but men moved by the Holy Spirit spoke from God." [14] As reflected in these verses, we should understand that the primary source of the Holy Spirit's guidance today comes through a correct interpretation of the Scriptures, in which he is the influencing authority and power behind its words.

This leaves the question, does God still speak directly to believers verbally for us to hear and understand? Some in the *body of Christ* believe the answer is an emphatic no! But in reality, by the testimony of many other members of the *body*, the answer is yes! So, how should the question be settled? As with all questions of faith and practice, we should settle all our questions through a proper understanding of the Scriptures as a whole.

First John 4:1-3 reads, "Beloved, do not believe every spirit, but test the spirits to see whether they are from God; because many false prophets have gone out into the world. By this you know the Spirit of God: every spirit that confesses that Jesus Christ has come in the flesh is from God; and every spirit that does not confess Jesus is not from God; and this is the spirit of the antichrist, of which you have heard that it is coming, and now it is already in the world."

Not only can God communicate to us verbally as he has done through the Old and New Testament times, but Satan and demons can do the same. Therefore, we are told to test the spirits and the attitudes and teachings that come through false prophets and teachers that are considered antichrist.

The standard test all believers should use is the written word of God. We should understand that there are no contradictions within the Scriptures, therefore, for biblical truth to be true, it must agree with all

---

[14] 2 Peter 1:20-21.

other biblical truths. This same principle applies to the Holy Spirit with relation to the spoken or living Word versus the written word of God. The Holy Spirit will never speak words to anyone in direct contradiction to the written word of God, the Holy Scriptures. We know this because the Scriptures tell us so once we understand several concepts.

The Old Testament writings are the only means to know God the Father's words and thoughts. The New Testament is the only means we have to know the words and thoughts of Jesus Christ, the living Word of God. From this understanding, we are told two things. One, that Jesus only speaks the words his Father instructed him to convey (John 12:49-50). And second, the Holy Spirit only conveys what the Father and the Son have instructed him to reveal (John 14:15-26; 16:13-15). Therefore, if the Holy Spirit provides direct verbal instructions to any believer, it will never contradict what the Father and the Son have already said or instructed us to be or do within the Scriptures. But to say the Holy Spirit cannot verbally instruct any believer to go to a particular place or follow a course of action that will ultimately save their life or glorify God in a non-contradictory way of the Scriptures would be presumptuous on our part; especially when there is no Scriptural evidence speaking to the contrary.

Therefore, we test the spirits by comparing what the Scriptures teach to what a spirit or attitude behind an action is telling us to be or do.

To Provide Spiritual Gifting—In First Corinthians 12 God provides us an introduction to spiritual gifts with an opening statement in verse 1 that reads, "Now concerning spiritual gifts, brethren, I do not want you to be unaware."

This chapter explains what some gifts are and why they exist. Within the context of this chapter, we learn that every believer is a member of the *body of Christ*, and each member is given at least one gift to edify each other in the building up of this body (the church). The gifts in this chapter are wisdom, knowledge, faith, healing, effecting of miracles, prophecy, distinguishing of spirits, various kinds of tongues, interpretation of tongues, teaching, administration, and helps. Romans 12:3-8 also speaks to this subject by adding additional information such as more than one gift may be given to individuals, listing additional gifts like serving, exhortation, liberally giving, diligently leading, and cheerfully showing mercy. Ephesians 4:1-16 also speaks to this subject, providing five gifts given to some for carrying out God's ministry to his church and outreach to the world. These are sometimes referred to as the speaking gifts. These additional gifts are that of apostles, prophets, evangelists, pastors, and teachers.

The emphasis behind spiritual gift teachings should lie with the fact that the Holy Spirit is the one who determines who gets what gift or gifts, and that no one gift is more important than the other, just as no member of the *body of Christ* is more important than another. This understanding is in harmony with the statement found in Romans 2:11, which states, "For there is no partiality with God."

Within the context of First Corinthians Chapter 13, we learn that no gift has any value apart from being accompanied by LOVE—God's agape love.

Some believe this text supports the idea that the gifts of tongues and prophecy have ended and are no longer being given out by the Holy Spirit. They root this idea in First Corinthians 13:8, which reads, "Love never fails; but if there are gifts of prophecy, they will be done away; if there are tongues, they will cease; if there is knowledge, it will be done away." When evaluating this verse in the context of both chapters 12 and 13, we can see that the overall message is that LOVE is superior to any of the gifts provided and that all gifts are temporary with relation to LOVE. This is true because LOVE is eternal and is part of God and his adopted children, but gifts like prophecy, tongues, and knowledge will all end. When will the need for these gifts end? At the end of the church age and before the millennial kingdom.

It is also interesting to note that those who believe prophecy and tongues have ended never speak about the end of knowledge, which is spoken of in the same sentence.

To Bring Assurance of Salvation to the Believer—Jesus states in John 14:16-17, "And I will ask the Father, and He will give you another Helper, that He may be with you forever; that is the Spirit of truth, whom the world cannot receive, because it does not behold Him or know Him, but you know Him because He abides with you, and will be in you." The key point is that the Holy Spirit who is our helper (John 14:26), will be with us and in us FOREVER. This alone brings us assurance of God's commitment to our salvation.

The Apostle Paul expands on this concept by saying, "The Spirit Himself bears witness with our spirit that we are children of God, and if children, heirs also, heirs of God and fellow heirs with Christ, if indeed we suffer with Him in order that we may also be glorified with Him." [15] The writer of Hebrews explains the foundational element to this teaching by writing,

> And the Holy Spirit also bears witness to us; for after saying,
>
> *'This is the covenant that I will make with them
> After those days, says the Lord: I will put My laws
> upon their heart, And upon their mind I will write them,'*
>
> He then says,
>
> *'And their sins and their lawless deeds
> I will remember no more.'* [16]

The foundational principle behind salvation and its permanency is based on the New Covenant referenced by this passage in Hebrews. Salvation is forever because the New Covenant promise is unconditional and forever. And this is one more work the Holy Spirit does for those who have faith in God's promise, by being the internal teacher and reminder of God's laws as Christ's work on the cross becomes the completed task required for the permanent forgiveness of sins.

To Seal the Believer—Second Corinthians 1:21-22 reads, "Now He who establishes us with you in Christ and anointed us is God, who also

---

[15] Rom. 8:16-17.
[16] Heb. 10:15-17.

sealed us and gave us the Spirit in our hearts as a pledge." The pronoun *He* refers to the Holy Spirit, who seals us in Christ as pledged or promised through the New Covenant. The apostle Paul reinforces this teaching by saying, "In Him, you also, after listening to the message of truth, the gospel of your salvation—having also believed, you were sealed in Him with the Holy Spirit of promise, who is given as a pledge of our inheritance, with a view to the redemption of God's own possession, to the praise of His glory." [17]

Here Paul is telling us that the *body of Christ* (the Church) is sealed in *Him* (Christ) through the actions of the Holy Spirit, who was promised by Christ in John Chapter 14, in fulfillment of the New Covenant, as a pledge of our inheritance; understood to mean that all believers will be spiritually preserved until their future rapture or resurrection to be with Christ, thus providing their inheritance of heaven and Christ's eternal kingdom, as granted through their faith in Christ (John 14:1-3).

We know when our inheritance comes, as Paul writes, "And do not grieve the Holy Spirit of God, by whom you were sealed for the day of redemption." [18] The day of redemption occurs at the time of the *body of Christ's* resurrection or catching away, which is referenced as the rapture of the church (1 Thessalonians 4:13-18).

To Teach the Believer—John 14:25-26 states, "These things I have spoken to you, while abiding with you. But the Helper, the Holy Spirit, whom the Father will send in My name, He will teach you all things, and bring to your remembrance all that I said to you."

The Apostle John continues this concept by writing, "And as for you, the anointing which you received from Him abides in you, and you have no need for anyone to teach you; but as His anointing teaches you about all things, and is true and is not a lie, and just as it has taught you, you abide in Him." [19]

The wording of John's writings fits that of a similar concept spoken of in the New Covenant, "And they shall not teach again, each man

---

[17] Eph. 1:13-14.
[18] Eph. 4:30.
[19] 1 John 2:27.

his neighbor and each man his brother, saying, 'Know the Lord,' for they shall all know Me, from the least of them to the greatest of them,' declares the Lord, 'for I will forgive their iniquity, and their sin I will remember no more'" (Jeremiah 31:34).

To Bring Wisdom and Understanding to the Believer—We read in First Corinthians 2:10-16:

> For to us God revealed them through the Spirit; for the Spirit searches all things, even the depths of God. For who among men knows the thoughts of a man except the spirit of the man, which is in him? Even so the thoughts of God no one knows except the Spirit of God. Now we have received, not the spirit of the world, but the Spirit who is from God, that we might know the things freely given to us by God, which things we also speak, not in words taught by human wisdom, but in those taught by the Spirit, combining spiritual thoughts with spiritual words. But a natural man does not accept the things of the Spirit of God; for they are foolishness to him, and he cannot understand them, because they are spiritually appraised. But he who is spiritual appraises all things, yet he himself is appraised by no man. For who has known the mind of the Lord, that he should instruct Him? But we have the mind of Christ.

The Holy Spirit causes us to understand the revelation God brings us concerning himself. This is accomplished through the wisdom God gives us as believers. This teaching becomes clear as we read James 3:13-17:

> Who among you is wise and understanding? Let him show by his good behavior his deeds in the gentleness of wisdom. But if you have bitter jealousy and selfish ambition in your heart, do not be arrogant and so lie against the truth. This wisdom is not that which comes down from above, but is earthly, natural, demonic. For where jealousy and selfish

ambition exist, there is disorder and every evil thing. But the wisdom from above is first pure, then peaceable, gentle, reasonable, full of mercy and good fruits, unwavering, without hypocrisy.

It is here we learn that wisdom comes from two separate sources; represented as human wisdom, which is part of our human nature, and God's wisdom, which is part of God's nature. Not until the Holy Spirit provides his wisdom can anyone truly understand God's truth as revealed in the Scriptures.

We find this truth reinforced in Old Testament wisdom literature as we read, "The beginning of wisdom is: Acquire wisdom; And with all your acquiring, get understanding." [20] The same writer also declares, "For the Lord gives wisdom; From His mouth come knowledge and understanding." [21]

When we put these concepts together, we can create a formula that reads like this: God's wisdom + knowledge = understanding.

To Convict the World of Sin—John 16:7-11 reads, "But I tell you the truth, it is to your advantage that I go away; for if I do not go away, the Helper shall not come to you; but if I go, I will send Him to you. And He, when He comes, will convict the world concerning sin, and righteousness, and judgment; concerning sin, because they do not believe in Me; and concerning righteousness, because I go to the Father, and you no longer behold Me; and concerning judgment, because the ruler of this world has been judged."

We are told the Helper, *He*, as in the Holy Spirit, will come and convict the world of sin, righteousness, and judgment. This text is ultimately telling us the Holy Spirit will be the spiritual conscience for all of humanity.

---

[20] Prov. 4:7.
[21] Prov. 2:6.

OTHER NAMES FOR THE HOLY SPIRIT

Spirit of the Lord—2 Corinthians 3:17
Spirit of Truth—John 14:17
Spirit of Glory—1 Peter 4:14
Holy Ghost—King James Version usage for the term Holy Spirit.

{ CHAPTER DISCUSSION NOTES }

The subject of the doctrine of the Holy Spirit is one of the most controversial subjects in the Christian faith today. This is because of how the *body of Christ* interprets the Scriptures concerning salvation, eternal security, baptism, anointing, spiritual gifts, and how the Holy Spirit relates to these subjects overall.

Because of the great diversity within the *body of Christ* and each member's interpretations of the subjects mentioned, there remains much disagreement with how the Holy Spirit works in the world today. Despite the Church's agreement on the doctrine of a triune God, difficulties come when we try to understand how the Holy Spirit works within the *body*, then reconciling that with one's interpretation of the Scriptures.

These differences exist mainly because of the different methods of hermeneutics used in making interpretations. Some use a Grammatico-Historical (literal) method, while others use the Allegorical (spiritualizing) method. The outcome can be very different for each member of the *body*. Therefore, it is important to choose early in one's studies which hermeneutical method to use. Regarding this work, the Grammatical-Historical Method is used.

We should always remember that there are no contradictions in Scripture, therefore, for biblical truth to be true, it must agree with all other biblical truths.

Personal Notes

Four

THE DOCTRINE OF THE SCRIPTURES

THE UNIQUENESS OF THE SCRIPTURES

The collective claims the Scriptures make about its contents make these writings stand alone in the entirety of the literary world. No other collection of writings has ever made such claims with any real validity.

THE CLAIM TO BEING TRUE

From the Old Testament, the Psalmist states, "The sum of Thy word is truth, And every one of Thy righteous ordinances is everlasting." [1] Jesus reinforces these words as he prays, "Sanctify them in the truth; Thy word is truth." [2]

These claims testify to the words of Moses as he wrote, "God is not a man, that He should lie, Nor a son of man, that He should repent; Has He said, and will He not do it? Or has He spoken, and will He not make it good?" [3] The Apostle Paul continues this support for the claim of truthfulness when he wrote to Titus, his brother, and child in Christ, about the very nature of the Scriptures and the character of God, who is the true author of the Scriptures. Paul writes, "Paul, a bond-servant of God, and an apostle of Jesus Christ, for the faith of those chosen of God and the knowledge of the truth which is according to godliness, in the hope of eternal life, which God, who cannot lie, promised long ages ago, but at the proper time manifested, even His word, in the

---

[1] Ps.119:160.
[2] John 17:17.
[3] Num. 23:19.

proclamation with which I was entrusted according to the commandment of God our Savior." [4]

Within Paul's letter to Titus, he confirms the Scriptures as true based on God's promises in the Old Testament, to which God cannot lie, and confirms Moses' assessment that what God speaks is true and will come to pass.

Truthfulness Defined—When someone confirms truth, how should we understand it, or how should that even be defined? Within the context of the Scriptures, truth should be understood as knowledge without contradiction of the true nature of the facts. This then leads to the question of how should facts be established or proven out?

Within the scientific community, facts are proven by conducting experiments to gain proof of one's thesis. We then find proof in the consistency of the thesis. The laws of thermodynamics have been proven true because of the fact of the consistency of the laws. The first law of thermodynamics states that energy can change form but cannot be created or destroyed. We know this to be true because of the law's consistency with other knowledgeable science without contradiction. The second law of thermodynamics says that the result of working energy within our current world will always be less than 100% efficient. We could express this by saying there is no such thing as perpetual motion!

When we take these concepts and apply them to the Scriptures, we can say when there is no contradiction within the writings of the Scriptures as a whole, then truth has been verified. So our thesis statement would be, "There are no contradictions within the Scriptures, therefore, for biblical truth to be true, it must agree with all other biblical truths."

We can say then that facts within Scripture are proven when each claim or piece of knowledge is true without contradicting other proven facts.

When this definition applies to God's words, as written in the Scriptures, we find great overwhelming consistency between all parts of the Scriptures, both in the New and Old Testaments. We see

---

[4] Titus 1:1-3.

examples of this concept in the prophecies given throughout the Scriptures, having a 100% consistent record. We prove this out in the messianic prophecies foretelling Christ's incarnation through his ascension recorded in Acts Chapter 1. We should understand the validity of this proofing example to be equated with the truthfulness of God himself. The Scriptures state that no prophecy comes through the will of man but through God (2 Peter 1:20-21). Therefore, if any prophecy does not come true, it would make God a liar, which the Scriptures state that God cannot do—lie (Titus 1:2; Proverbs 12:22).

The Claim to be Inspired

Understanding the inspirational concept of the Scriptures has been elusive over the centuries. This debate over inspiration has been tied to reasoning through the concept of inspiration and what that looks like from a human perspective. When an author of a good book states they were inspired to write their work, we understand this to mean they were highly motivated and encouraged to write something they care about and look forward to writing about. But when we speak about the inspiration of the Holy Scriptures, the meaning becomes blurred by our human and cultural biases that influence our thinking on this subject.

We should understand the inspiration of the Scriptures to mean that human authors were guided by God's Spirit on what to write, conveying God's spoken words and thoughts. It is through this understanding that the debate concerning inspiration arises, with such questions as, how does God convey his words to the human author, and does God allow for human creativity in writing style?

The concept of the *Inspiration of the Scriptures* comes from within the Scriptures themselves. It is not some claim made by outside sources such as the church or from its readership. It is a claim made by God through His chosen human authors. This is true of both the Old and New Testaments.

New Testament Proofs

The Apostle Paul writes, "All Scripture is inspired by God and profitable for teaching, for reproof, for correction, for training in righteousness; that the man of God may be adequate, equipped for every good work." [5] This supports what the Apostle Peter wrote in Second Peter 1:20-21. "But know this first of all, that no prophecy of Scripture is a matter of one's own interpretation, for no prophecy was ever made by an act of human will, but men moved by the Holy Spirit spoke from God."

The key concept of this debate is not what it means to *move* or *inspire* someone to do something, but that the author's motivation and thought process was influenced by the Holy Spirit. It was God who started and guided the entire act of writing the Scriptures. This makes God the true author of the content, although he used human beings to put on paper what God wanted to convey to the world.

Theologians have held discussions of inspiration under theories such as Natural Inspiration, Universal Christian Inspiration, Mechanical or Dynamic Inspiration, Concept or Thought Inspiration, Verbal Inspiration, Partial Inspiration, and Plenary or Full Inspiration. [6] Regardless of how one understands the process of inspiration, we should note that the verbal, plenary inspiration of the Holy Scriptures is how Second Timothy presents this subject and would be the wisest choice or position to embrace from a scriptural perspective.

Doctrinal statements affirming the inspiration of the Scriptures generally state it this way, "We believe the Holy Scriptures to be verbal, plenary, and inerrant;" where *verbal* means the *word* was first spoken by God, then communicated in written form (2 Peter 3:1-7); *plenary*, meaning complete, as in nothing to be added or removed from the original Scriptures; *inerrant*, meaning the original writings to be without error.

Old Testament Proofs

Moses' writings are the historical foundation behind the rest of the Old Testament books, as reflected in the Pentateuch or books of the Law.

---

[5] 2 Tim. 3:16-17.
[6] William Evans, *The Great Doctrines of the Bible*, enlarged ed (Chicago: Moody Press, 1974), 199-201.

These would be the first five books written of the Old Testament and consists of Genesis, Exodus, Leviticus, Numbers, and Deuteronomy.

When we speak about the inspiration of the Scriptures, we must look at the life of Moses and his relationship with God. We read in Numbers 12:5-8,

> Then the Lord came down in a pillar of cloud and stood at the doorway of the tent, and He called Aaron and Miriam. When they had both come forward, He said,
>
> *Hear now My words:*
> *If there is a prophet among you,*
> *I, the Lord, shall make Myself known to him in a vision.*
> *I shall speak with him in a dream.*
> *Not so, with My servant Moses,*
> *He is faithful in all My household;*
> *With him, I speak mouth to mouth,*
> *Even openly, and not in dark sayings,*
> *And he beholds the form of the Lord.*
> *Why then were you not afraid*
> *To speak against My servant, against Moses?*

The significance of this passage is found in God revealing to the world that Moses is on direct speaking terms with the creator GOD. Not only is God speaking to Moses, but He also is speaking to him in a clear and understandable vernacular, not in visions or dreams apt to being misinterpreted by others like the writings of Nostradamus. God is then telling us that Moses received direct revelation from his creator, the true author of what Moses wrote, and we see this confirmed in Moses' writings (Exodus 4:10-15, 34:27; Numbers 17:2-3). Jesus affirms the authorship of the Pentateuch writings by saying, "But regarding the fact that the dead rise again, have you not read in the book of Moses, in the passage about the burning bush, how God spoke to him, saying, 'I am the God of Abraham, and the God of Isaac, and the God of Jacob'?" [7]

The concept of God conveying his words and thoughts to humanity also reached other prophets in the Old Testament as we see in Isaiah 8:1, 11, 12; Jeremiah 1:7, 7:27, 13:12, 30:1-2, 36:1, 2, 4, 11, 27-32; Ezekiel 2:7, 3:10, 11, 24:2, 37:15-16; Habakkuk 2:2, and Zechariah 7:8-12.

It would appear that in the Old Testament it was not so much a question of inspiration and how it all worked, as it was direct revelation and communications with the prophet writers of old. Here again, the key is not how God communicated to his writers, but that the writers, without question, were speaking for God.

THE CLAIM TO BE ETERNAL

The Psalmist writes, "Forever, O Lord, Thy word is settled in heaven."[8] Isaiah the prophet states, "The grass withers, the flower fades, But the word of our God stands forever." [9] Jesus, in a comparative format, states, "But it is easier for heaven and earth to pass away than for one stroke of a letter of the Law to fail." [10] The Apostle Peter sums up this concept of eternalness by saying, "Since you have in obedience to the truth purified your souls for a sincere love of the brethren, fervently love one another from the heart, for you have been born again not of seed which is perishable but imperishable, that is, through the living and abiding word of God. For,

> *All flesh is like grass,*
> *And all its glory like the flower of grass.*
> *The grass withers,*
> *And the flower falls off,*
> *But the word of the Lord abides forever.*

---

[7] Mark 12:26.
[8] Ps. 119:89.
[9] Isa. 40:8.
[10] Luke 16:17.

And this is the word which was preached to you." [11]

THE CLAIM THAT JESUS CHRIST IS THE WORD OF GOD

It is through the Apostle Peter's writings found in First Peter 1:22-25 that we come to fully understand the claim of the Scriptures that Jesus Christ is "the living and abiding Word of God." This is first introduced to us through the teachings of the Apostle John when he writes, "In the beginning was the Word, and the Word was with God, and the Word was God. He was in the beginning with God. All things came into being by Him, and apart from Him nothing came into being that has come into being... And the Word became flesh, and dwelt among us, and we beheld His glory, glory as of the only begotten from the Father, full of grace and truth." [12] Jesus supports John's claim by stating, "Heaven and earth will pass away, but My words shall not pass away." [13]

The writer of Hebrews reinforced this understanding of Christ being the Word of God when he writes, "By faith we understand that the worlds were prepared by the word of God, so that what is seen was not made out of things which are visible." [14] This passage reinforces what Moses wrote concerning God's creation in Genesis 1:3, "Then God said, 'Let there be light'; and there was light." God spoke (the words of God) representing "what was not seen," "and there was light" representing what then became visible.

This concept is reinforced by the writers of the New Testament forty-one times as they use the phrase, *word of God* to express the authority behind their writings.

Since the New Testament was not fully written or widely circulated at the time of these writings, what were the writers referencing by using this phrase? The most logical answer that fits the context of the writings and the historical times is, they are referring to all the Old Testament writings and their relationship to the words of Jesus Christ and

---

[11] 1 Peter 1:22-25.
[12] John 1:1-3, 14.
[13] Matt. 24:35.
[14] Heb. 11:3.

his teachings. Thus, showing us that the words of Christ are equivalent to the words of God. Later, as the New Testament writings were completed, we come to understand how the New Testament as a whole is considered the word of God, as the Apostles of Jesus Christ the living word of God mostly wrote it. (John 2:22)

We see in Second Peter 3:14-16 how the Apostle Peter suggests to his readers that whatever Paul wrote should be considered part of the Scriptures. This followed Peter's earlier statement suggesting that what the prophets, Christ, and the apostles have said are important, as he writes, "This is now, beloved, the second letter I am writing to you in which I am stirring up your sincere mind by way of reminder, that you should remember the words spoken beforehand by the holy prophets and the commandment of the Lord and Savior spoken by your apostles." [15] The Apostle Paul supports this theme by writing, "And for this reason we also constantly thank God that when you received from us the word of God's message, you accepted it not as the word of men, but for what it really is, the word of God, which also performs its work in you who believe." [16]

It is through these comments and others that the early church Fathers concluded that what the Apostles wrote should be considered part of the Holy Scriptures.

THE SCRIPTURES REPRESENT REVELATION FROM GOD

Revelation is defined for us through the words of the Apostle John, as he writes, "The Revelation of Jesus Christ, which God gave Him to show to His bond-servants, the things which must shortly take place; and He sent and communicated it by His angel to His bond-servant John, who bore witness to the word of God and to the testimony of Jesus Christ, even to all that he saw. Blessed is he who reads and those who hear the words of the prophecy and heed the things which are written in it; for the time is near." [17]

---

[15] 2 Peter 3:1-2.
[16] 1 Thess. 2:13.
[17] Rev. 1:1-3.

Based on this passage, we could say that the concept of *Revelation* is a product of God; or to be more specific, knowledge imparted from God to the world. Another way to express this is, Revelation is *knowledge* only known to God, who then communicates it to the world.

This differs from inspiration to the degree that things God inspires could be *information* already known or revealed in the world, whereas, Revelation is knowledge no one knows but God, who chose to share it with others.

Examples in Scripture that represent Revelation are the accounts of creation, God's written laws and commandments, Christ's incarnation, the origins of good and evil; and the list could go on. *Inspiration* is illustrated through the spoken words of Christ to his disciples. Although Jesus spoke many words known only to the disciples, it was through the inspiration of the Holy Spirit that some of those words were selected with purpose, to be written for others to read and gain knowledge and understanding (John 20:30-31).

LANGUAGES OF THE SCRIPTURES

The Old Testament Scriptures were written in Hebrew and Aramaic, while the New Testament was written in Greek. The number of human authors who took part in the writing of the Scriptures is debated, but it is generally agreed that there were about 40 different authors, with this authorship taking place over a period of about 1,500 years (1446 B.C. to A.D. 96). These dates would cover the time of Moses' adult life, who wrote the Pentateuch, to the approximate time at the end of the Apostle John's life, when he wrote the last book of the Scriptures, the Revelation to John.

Aramaic was the language used in parts of the book of Danial and Ezra due to the necessity of the times. Aramaic was also used in the times and places of these prophets. Ezra wrote some letters that required locals to have the ability to read, thus he wrote part of his book in Aramaic. It is not clear why Danial wrote part of his book in Aramaic, but some believe it was also out of some necessity to convey that part of the book in Aramaic, to allow a certain group of people (non-Hebrews) to learn what was said to the Hebrew people to whom it was originally written. [18]

Historical accounts reflect that the Gospel of Matthew was written in Hebrew as well as in Greek. This was attested to by early church Fathers like Papias, who wrote five books, to which only several fragments have been preserved. It was written that "Papias, who is now mentioned by us, affirms that he received the sayings of the apostles from those who accompanied them, and he moreover asserts that he heard in person Aristion and the presbyter John. Accordingly, he mentions them frequently by name, and in his writings gives their traditions." [19] Papias (A.D. 70) says, "Matthew put together the oracles [of the Lord] in the Hebrew language, and each one interpreted them as best he could." [20]

Irenaeus of Lyons (A.D. 180) wrote, "Matthew also issued a written Gospel among the Hebrews in their own dialect, while Peter and Paul were preaching at Rome, and laying the foundations of the Church. After their departure, Mark, the disciple and interpreter of Peter, did also hand down to us in writing what had been preached by Peter. Luke also, the companion of Paul, recorded in a book the Gospel preached by him. Afterwards, John, the disciple of the Lord, who also had leaned upon His breast, did himself publish a Gospel during his residence at Ephesus in Asia." [21]

---

[18] Benjamin Shaw, "Aramaic Thoughts," [article online]; available from https://www.studylight.org/language-studies/aramaic-thoughts.html; Internet; accessed 6 August 2020.

[19] Fragments of Papias vi. *Ante-Nicene Fathers*, Vol. 1. ed. Alexander Roberts, James Donaldson, and A. Cleveland Coxe, trans. Alexander Roberts and James Donaldson (Buffalo, NY: Christian Literature Publishing Co., 1885.) Revised and edited for New Advent by Kevin Knight. http://www.newadvent.org/fathers/0125 .htm.

[20] Ibid.

[21] Irenaeus of Lyons Against Heresies 3.1.1. *Ante-Nicene Fathers*, Vol. 1. ed. Alexander Roberts, James Donaldson, and A. Cleveland Coxe, trans. Alexander Roberts and William Rambaut (Buffalo, NY: Christian Literature Publishing Co., 1885.) Revised and edited for New Advent by Kevin Knight. http://www.newadvent.org/fathers/ 0103301.htm.

IMPORTANCE OF THE SCRIPTURES

The Psalmist writes, "For the word of the Lord is upright; And all His work is done in faithfulness. He loves righteousness and justice; The earth is full of the lovingkindness of the Lord.

By the word of the Lord the heavens were made, And by the breath of His mouth all their host." [22]

From within the Scriptures, we see not only the character behind God's words but the power of God's words, showing us that what God speaks is equivalent to our reality. This is true of both the natural and spiritual worlds in which we live.

This reality is evident through the witness of creation and by the testimony of our human nature, as evident by the writings of the Apostle Paul, who warned, "For the wrath of God is revealed from heaven against all ungodliness and unrighteousness of men, who suppress the truth in unrighteousness, because that which is known about God is evident within them; for God made it evident to them. For since the creation of the world His invisible attributes, His eternal power and divine nature, have been clearly seen, being understood through what has been made, so that they are without excuse." [23]

Jesus supports the concept that the Scriptures are important through several comments he made during his time on earth. When Jesus spent forty days in the wilderness before being confronted by Satan with three separate temptations (Matthew 4:1-7), Jesus' response to each confrontation was, *it is written*, as he quoted the word of God and stayed obedient to those words. Later we find Jesus teaching in the temple and using a parable to provide instruction to the history behind his life and ministry (Matthew 21:33-42). Within the telling of the parable, Jesus asked this question, "Did you never read in the Scripture...?" Jesus' question was intended to reveal the fact that the word of God (the Scriptures) held the key to understanding who He was, in relation to who we are, and that we are to search these things out for ourselves. The Scriptures reveal that Jesus is the chief cornerstone, the foundation the

---

[22] Ps. 33:4-6.
[23] Rom. 1:18-21.

church (the body of Christ) is built on, and the Messiah—the King of the promised kingdom to come (2 Samuel 7:4-17).

The Gospel of Mark records Jesus' response to a question on marriage and the resurrection of the dead by saying, "Is this not the reason you are mistaken, that you do not understand the Scriptures, or the power of God?" [24] Through this response we see Jesus placing a premium on the Scriptures for answers to living and afterlife issues. This response also supports the Old Testament teaching that *the word of the Lord* is both right and has the power to uphold that morality.

The Gospel of Luke and John also support the idea that the Scriptures speak to who and why Jesus exists. Regarding Jesus, Luke 24:27 reads, "And beginning with Moses and with all the prophets, He explained to them the things concerning Himself in all the Scriptures." Jesus continues this theme by stating, "You search the Scriptures because you think that in them you have eternal life; and it is these that bear witness of Me; and you are unwilling to come to Me, that you may have life." [25] It is through Christ's comment we can learn that the Scriptures have no saving power, but brings us the message of the person who can save us—Jesus Christ.

Jesus summarizes the importance of the word of God by speaking as the living Word of God when he states,

> Therefore everyone who hears these words of Mine, and acts upon them, may be compared to a wise man, who built his house upon the rock. And the rain descended, and the floods came, and the winds blew, and burst against that house; and yet it did not fall, for it had been founded upon the rock. And everyone who hears these words of Mine, and does not act upon them, will be like a foolish man, who built his house upon the sand. And the rain descended, and the floods came,

---

[24] Mark 12:24-25.
[25] John 5:39-41.

and the winds blew, and burst against that house; and it fell, and great was its fall. [26]

{ CHAPTER DISCUSSION NOTES }

THE UNIQUENESS OF THE SCRIPTURES

The Scriptures are not unique solely based on their claims, but also because of the history behind their preservation. With about 50 complete copies and over 5,000 partial manuscripts of the New Testament, the claim of remarkable preservation becomes valid. Within the literary world, there are no other known books or pieces of writings with as many known copies to testify of their validity and existence.

We do not cover the discussion on biblical translations within this book because of the vastness of its subject, requiring the need for study under two separate course disciplines.

The first discipline would be Textual Criticism, the study of writings to determine their origin and content from their conception. And the second is Translation Studies, which involves a study of translation techniques and the inherent issues involved in translating from one language to another. Understanding the full dynamics of this topic requires independent studies under these two-course disciplines. For those looking for a quicker path regarding a basic understanding of this subject, two books may prove helpful. (1) *Journey from Texts to Translations: The Origin and Development of the Bible* by Paul D. Wegner. (2) *The King James Version Debate: A Plea for Realism* by D.A. Carson.

---

[26] Matt. 7:24-27.

The Importance of the Scriptures

Reasons reflecting the importance of the Scriptures could not be stated plainer than through the words of the Apostle Paul.

> Until I come, give attention to the public reading of Scripture, to exhortation and teaching. Do not neglect the spiritual gift within you, which was bestowed upon you through prophetic utterance with the laying on of hands by the presbytery. Take pains with these things; be absorbed in them, so that your progress may be evident to all. Pay close attention to yourself and to your teaching; persevere in these things; for as you do this you will ensure salvation both for yourself and for those who hear you. [27]

Herein lies the importance of this passage, to give attention to the public reading of the Scriptures, from which comes exhortation and teaching of those words, resulting in the salvation to all who hear the Word. Paul continues this theme in Romans 10:14-15 as he writes, "How then shall they call upon Him in whom they have not believed? And how shall they believe in Him whom they have not heard? And how shall they hear without a preacher? And how shall they preach unless they are sent? Just as it is written, How beautiful are the feet of those who bring glad tidings of good things!"

Thus, reading and exhortation of the Word produce salvation in the hearer's ear, which is the most important benefit of the Scriptures among the many others such as encouragement, correction of incorrect thinking and behavior, and instruction on rightful living (2 Timothy 3:15).

The Apostle Peter writes, "As obedient children, do not be conformed to the former lusts which were yours in your ignorance, but like the Holy One who called you, be holy yourselves also in all your behavior; because it is written, 'You shall be holy, for I am holy.'" [28] And

---

[27] 1 Tim. 4:13-16.
[28] 1 Peter 1:14-16.

what are we to be obedient to? That which the Holy Scriptures conveys to its readers, the revelation of God and his Son Jesus Christ.

> Personal Notes

Five

THE DOCTRINE OF HUMANITY

THE CREATION OF HUMANITY

The biblical creation of humanity is recorded in Genesis1:26-27 and reads, "Then God said, 'Let Us make man in Our image, according to Our likeness; and let them rule over the fish of the sea and over the birds of the sky and over the cattle and over all the earth, and over every creeping thing that creeps on the earth.' And God created man in His own image, in the image of God He created him; male and female He created them." There are two key elements to this passage that require closer evaluation, these are the concepts of image and likeness.

THE IMAGE AND LIKENESS OF GOD

The Scripture states that humanity was created in the image of God, according to God's likeness. The very structure of the sentence suggests a difference between image and likeness based on the prepositional phrase, *according to*. Many theologians believe these two terms are parallelisms, meaning they are similar or mean the same thing. "If we follow the normal grammatical sentence structure of the English language, when God states, 'Let us make man in Our image, according to Our likeness,' we should understand the key phrase to be 'according to,' which is a preposition preceding the noun 'likeness.' The word 'according' is a technical term meaning to be consistent with, or to be in harmony with, some known pattern. The image being spoken of must be consistent with, or in harmony with, God's pattern or metaphysical structure." [1]

The likeness of God refers to God's metaphysical makeup; where the image of God refers to the moral character or nature of God.

These distinctions can be described this way. God's moral character or nature comprises God's Holiness, righteousness, goodness, wisdom, and love, to mention a few. The likeness of God is speaking about the attributes of God's personhood, as represented in God's emotion, intellect, and will functionality. Genesis 1:26 could be interpreted this way, "Let Us, the triune God, make humanity in Our image, that reflects our nature's attributes of Holiness, righteousness, goodness, wisdom, and love, *according to* our likeness that is reflected in Our personhood's intellect, emotion, and will." When understood in this light, we come to know that after humanity's fall, mankind lost the image of God but we never lost the likeness of God (Genesis 3:22). Fallen humanity can still demonstrate intellect, emotion, and will, but lacks in the ability to be Holy, as God is Holy.

After the fall of humanity into sin, God's image, represented by all the characteristics tied to God's Holiness, was lost, but humanity continued to be like, or in the likeness of God through our ability to still function like God in emotion, intellect, and will, with one additional ability, to know good and evil.

Because of long-standing disagreements between theologians on this point, it will require additional research to explore such interpretations.

THE CREATION OF SEXES (GENDER)

In the 21st century, gender identity has become a huge topic within world culture. Genesis 1:26 provides the definitive answer from a biblical perspective on God's position on this issue by informing us that God created humanity not only in His likeness and image but also in

---

[1] Reid A. Ashbaucher, *Made in the Image of God: Understanding the Nature of God and Mankind in a Changing World*, 3 rev. ed (Toledo, Ohio: Reid Ashbaucher Publications, 2020), 146.

the form of only two sexes, with a gender identity called male and female. Moses, the writer of Genesis, tells us the purpose of this difference was to unite the two into one through the bond of marriage, providing a support system and moral path for the procreation of children to populate the earth (Genesis 1:28; 2:24). This has always been God's plan from the very beginning.

Throughout world history, humanity operated and functioned according to this biblical basis. The human body, combined with the human spirit, makes up what we call human nature. We make this assessment through understanding the concepts presented in First Thessalonians 5:23; First Corinthians 15:35-39, and James 2:26. Within this understanding of what the nature of humanity is, we can assess the proper function of that nature. The Apostle Paul expressed in his writings what is abnormal behavior from God's perspective, as we read.

> For the wrath of God is revealed from heaven against all ungodliness and unrighteousness of men, who suppress the truth in unrighteousness, because that which is known about God is evident within them; for God made it evident to them. For since the creation of the world His invisible attributes, His eternal power and divine nature, have been clearly seen, being understood through what has been made, so that they are without excuse. For even though they knew God, they did not honor Him as God, or give thanks; but they became futile in their speculations, and their foolish heart was darkened. Professing to be wise, they became fools, and exchanged the glory of the incorruptible God for an image in the form of corruptible man and of birds and four-footed animals and crawling creatures.
>
> Therefore God gave them over in the lusts of their hearts to impurity, that their bodies might be dishonored among them. For they exchanged the truth of God for a lie, and worshiped and served the creature rather than the Creator, who is blessed forever. Amen.
>
> For this reason God gave them over to degrading passions; for their women exchanged the natural function for that

which is unnatural, and in the same way also the men abandoned the natural function of the woman and burned in their desire toward one another, men with men committing indecent acts and receiving in their own persons the due penalty of their error. [2]

As we read in this passage, humanity rejected God and the way he created things, instead pursued after what was not natural concerning their nature. Thus, God allowed them to continue with a great penalty to their bodies. This speaks not only of homosexuality but transgender identity issues as well. Because of the complexity and amount of information available on this issue, another book would be required for a more comprehensive understanding of this subject.

The conclusion one comes to from reading and understanding in the proper context of the Scriptures is that God created humanity in His image and likeness to function as a biological male and female, and have children within the bond of marriage, to which this cycle is designed to repeat over and over until God changes the purpose behind these relationships. Only through sin in the world does this process become altered or disrupted to operate in some other fashion. To function any other way is to deny the very nature God designed for humanity and creates chaos within the world, to which Satan shouts, "I am succeeding!"

THE NATURE OF HUMANITY

Theologians have defined human nature through two models. Through the following discussion, we will introduce these models and provide insight into how the Scriptures represent the doctrine of humanity.

HUMAN NATURE AS A DICHOTOMY

Human nature, composed of a body and spirit, represents the Dichotomy Model; with the *body* representing the natural while the *spirit*

---

[2] Rom. 1:18-27.

represents physical and spiritual life. They build this model on the belief soul and spirit are the same things, based on how one interprets the Scriptures. Therefore, understanding the term *soul* and *spirit* to mean the same thing results in arriving at a differing theological conclusion than the person who sees them as separate things.

HUMAN NATURE AS A TRICHOTOMY

Human nature composed of *body*, *soul*, and *spirit* represents the Trichotomy Model. The key to holding such a position is found in defining the difference between *soul* and *spirit*. To do this, one must study the Scriptures for a proper word usage of these terms from Genesis to Revelation, to which a completed study has already been done with the following results. [3]

The soul is that part of humanity that represents personhood, as demonstrated through our intellect, emotion, and will. Therefore, our soul is what makes a person a person. The spirit of humanity represents our nature, that part of us that generates attitudes and where physical life resides. It is also that part of us that comprises our old sinful nature.

The body/spirit combination makes up our human nature and is where our soul or personhood resides and interacts with our nature. For a quick illustration of this assessment, let us reference the following passages.

Hebrews 4:12 states, "For the word of God is living and active and sharper than any two-edged sword, and piercing as far as the division of soul and spirit, of both joints and marrow, and able to judge the thoughts and intentions of the heart." This verse not only expresses the fact that God recognizes a difference between soul and spirit, it even defines their differences.

Applying the completed study's defining definitions to this passage reveals that the word of God can judge both the thoughts, which represents intellect, a function of the soul, and the intent, representing an attitude, a function of the spirit. Within the study, it has been shown

---

[3] *Made in the Image of God: Understanding the Nature of God and Mankind in a Changing World* by Reid A. Ashbaucher (Third Revised Edition)

that attitude and motive can represent the same thing. Thus, the word *intent* in this passage represents motives. [4]

When this understanding of the terms is applied to the Scriptures, a better understanding of their intended meaning becomes clearer. First Thessalonians 5:23 reads, "Now may the God of peace Himself sanctify you entirely; and may your spirit and soul and body be preserved complete, without blame at the coming of our Lord Jesus Christ." The keywords here are *entirely* and *complete*.

Our *body*, *soul*, and *spirit* make up a complete person, for all three work together to comprise a complete human being. What Paul is praying for is our sanctification (to be set apart) as a whole person, which includes our intellect, emotion, and will that represents our soul, attitudes that represent our spirit, and body that represents the temple of the Holy Spirit.

We can also see this understanding in Luke 1:46, as it reads, "And Mary said: 'My soul exalts the Lord, And my spirit has rejoiced in God my Savior.'" To "exalt" someone is an act of the will, a function of the soul, and to "rejoice" is an attitude, a function of the spirit. When this understanding is applied to the Scriptures as a whole, 99% of the time it will be found to be a true understanding of the usage of these two terms.

We should also note that within the study, the term *spirit* could be defined by several meanings and placed into nine separate categories. Therefore, reading the full study would be most beneficial in understanding this theological debate and how to understand your own conclusions about the Scriptures as a whole.

THE FALL OF HUMANITY

When we speak about the fall of humanity, this should be understood as referring to the falling away from, or the casting down from some esteemed position. From the beginning of time, humanity was created perfect and lived in a perfect state of existence in God's presence. Then, through the temptation of Satan—a fallen angel—humanity wanted to become equal in the area of God's knowledge and wisdom (Genesis

---

[4] Ashbaucher, *Made in the Image of God*, 64.

3:1-7), thus becoming sinful through the attitude of pride, which God hates (Proverbs 8:13). This event created humanity's fallen state of going from a state of being in perfect fellowship with God to a fallen sinful state separated from God (Genesis 3:22).

The Nature of the Fall

To understand the nature of humanity's fall, it is important to understand the true source of sin. We read in Ezekiel 28:13-17:

> You were in Eden, the garden of God; Every precious stone was your covering: The ruby, the topaz, and the diamond; The beryl, the onyx, and the jasper; The lapis lazuli, the turquoise, and the emerald; And the gold, the workmanship of your settings and sockets, Was in you.
>
> On the day that you were created They were prepared. You were the anointed cherub who covers, And I placed you there. You were on the holy mountain of God; You walked in the midst of the stones of fire.
>
> You were blameless in your ways From the day you were created, Until unrighteousness was found in you. By the abundance of your trade.
>
> You were internally filled with violence, And you sinned; Therefore I have cast you as profane From the mountain of God.
>
> And I have destroyed you, O covering cherub, From the midst of the stones of fire. Your heart was lifted up because of your beauty; You corrupted your wisdom by reason of your splendor. I cast you to the ground; I put you before kings, That they may see you.

Who is this created individual that existed in the garden of Eden? According to this passage, it was a created angel of the cherub class who fell from God's righteousness through pride. This is the first record of sin, and it occurred even before humanity's transgression. We later learn in Genesis 3:1-7 that Eve's sin was the same as this angel's, which was the sin of PRIDE! Within other parts of the Scriptures, we learn the name of this angel is Lucifer/Satan, also referred to as the "morning star" (Isaiah 14:12 KJV; NIV).

The connection of Satan to the serpent who tempted Eve to know what God knows is referenced in Revelation 20:2. "And he laid hold of the dragon, the serpent of old, who is the devil and Satan, and bound him for a thousand years …"

Through a parallel study of both Genesis and Ezekiel's writings, we can see that it was the PRIDE of appearance and losing the reason for existence that drove Satan into an attitude of rebellion against God. This was the same sin Satan talked Eve into, causing her to forget her place in the world and desire to become like God—knowing good and evil. Thus, after Eve's fall, Adam chose to follow her in this same prideful way, causing the entirety of humanity to be in a state of sin.

THE EFFECTS OF SIN ON HUMAN NATURE

Now, the natural state of the human condition is separation from God. An understanding of this separation is a topic of debate among the Christian community. Some hold to the concept that there is a great divide between God and Humanity, and we can cross it through Christ's sacrifice on the Roman cross. This suggests sin is a barrier between God and humanity, but Christ's work on the cross removed it through repentance and faith. If this scenario is true, it suggests that sinful humanity can be saved through natural reasoning ability. If I am given the right information, and I believe that information to be true, the sin barrier will be removed, and I will once again have access to God.

Instead, the Scriptures seem to reflect a different scenario. The Scriptures teach that the wages of sin is death (Romans 6:23). James 5:20 further suggests that the soul can die, while Revelation 20:14 refers to the death of the soul as the second death.

Throughout the Scriptures, death, both physical and spiritual is a state of blindness toward our spiritual nature, resulting in separation from God. John 9:39-41 reads, "And Jesus said, 'For judgment I came into this world, that those who do not see may see; and that those who see may become blind.' Those of the Pharisees who were with Him heard these things, and said to Him, 'We are not blind too, are we?' Jesus said to them, 'If you were blind, you would have no sin; but since you say, 'We see,' your sin remains.'" Jesus is teaching that humans are naturally blind—spiritually. This means that apart from some outside help, humanity cannot see or understand the spiritual things of God.

This assessment is supported through Jesus' actions as recorded in Luke 24:45 which says, "Then He opened their minds to understand the Scripture;" this statement of Christ reflects that humans are in a natural state of spiritual blindness, resulting in the inability to understand spiritual truths. The Apostle Paul supports this concept by stating, "But a natural man does not accept the things of the Spirit of God; for they are foolishness to him, and he cannot understand them, because they are spiritually appraised." [5]

Sin not only brings physical and spiritual death it also places humans in a state of spiritual blindness. Therefore, salvation can only come through the GRACE of God, who must give humanity the ability to see spiritual truth before they can have faith and believe the message of the Gospel. This is why the prophet Jonah tells us that salvation comes from the Lord (Jonah 2:9).

Other effects that sin has on the human condition is that of attitudes, as reflected in several Scripture passages.

Psalm 53:1-3 states, "The fool has said in his heart, 'There is no God,' They are corrupt, and have committed abominable injustice; There is no one who does good. God has looked down from heaven upon the sons of men, To see if there is anyone who understands, Who seeks after God. Every one of them has turned aside; together they have become corrupt; There is no one who does good, not even one." The Apostle Paul quotes the Psalmist and writes, "What then? Are we better than they? Not at all; for we have already charged that both Jews and Greeks are all under sin; as it is written,

---

[5] 1 Cor. 2:14.

> *There is none righteous, not even one;*
> *There is none who understands,*
> *There is none who seeks for God;*
> *All have turned aside, together they have become useless;*
> *There is none does good,*
> *There is not even one.*
> *Their throat is an open grave,*
> *With their tongues they keep deceiving,*
> *The poison of asps is under their lips;*
> *Whose mouth is full of cursing and bitterness;*
> *Their feet are swift to shed blood,*
> *Destruction and misery are in their paths,*
> *And the path of peace have they not known.*
> *There is no fear of God before their eyes."* [6]

The book of James expresses how this affects the concept of human wisdom.

> Who among you is wise and understanding? Let him show by his good behavior his deeds in the gentleness of wisdom. But if you have bitter jealousy and selfish ambition in your heart, do not be arrogant and so lie against the truth. This wisdom is not that which comes down from above, but is earthly, natural, demonic. For where jealousy and selfish ambition exist, there is disorder and every evil thing. But the wisdom from above is first pure, then peaceable, gentle, reasonable, full of mercy and good fruits, unwavering, without hypocrisy. And the seed whose fruit is righteousness is sown in peace by those who make peace. [7]

Herein are reflected two types of wisdom—human and divine, with human wisdom being rooted in pride, while divine wisdom is

---

[6] Rom. 3:9-18.
[7] James 3:13-18.

rooted in holiness, as reflected in the statement "wisdom from above is first pure."

The other side of this discussion deals with a changed heart and the new concept of a new nature that is directly tied to the doctrine of salvation, which we will discuss in chapter seven.

{ CHAPTER DISCUSSION NOTES }

IMAGE AND LIKENESS

Why is this distinction between the concept of *image* and *likeness* important? The importance lies with the relationship these concepts have in supporting a distinction between *soul* and *spirit*. Proving these distinctions enables us to build a better model to help explain God and Human Nature, which then aids in obtaining a better understanding of various issues within the study of Theology and Anthropology.

From a practical standpoint, by better understanding the true nature of things, we can come to a greater knowledge of how God can be triune in nature, how Jesus can be both God and Man, and how humans can have a relationship with God on a metaphysical level.

Answers to these questions extend into other areas of theology that are able to provide answers to longstanding questions that have been debated for centuries. Thus, through a better understanding of spiritual questions, a better knowledgeable support system can be established to build up the believer for more effective faith-based living.

SEXES AND GENDER IDENTITY

By understanding what it means to be made in the *image* and *likeness* of God, we can come to a better understanding of the true nature of humanity and the purpose behind God's intentions for creating such beings.

It has been proven by science and testified to in California Superior Court on July 25, 1990, that genuine *sex change* is not surgically possible by leading experts in the medical field. [8] A person can socially and physically alter their sexual appearance, but they cannot alter, at the most basic level, the true sexual nature they were originally born into. Cutting off body parts or trying to alter one's hormone system can never change the true nature of an individual—male or female.

This is why, at the end of these attempted changes, denial, depression, regret and even suicide often take place. This has been documented by many experts in medical fields across the world.

There are those in the medical fields, primarily psychologists/sexologists, who will counsel individuals seeking sex changes that operations and drugs can help them. But theology and true science disagree. Most times, reversing the results of drug treatments and surgeries cannot be done. Thus, regret, depression, and suicide become a reality.

For a better understanding of these issues, the following book is suggested. *Irreversible Damage: The Transgender Craze Seducing Our Daughters* by Abigail Shrier.

HUMAN NATURE AS A TRICHOTOMY

The trichotomy model is the best one supporting the biblical evidence. It is also a better model supporting the differences between the terms, *soul,* and *spirit*. When understanding theology under this model, the Scriptures as a whole become more relevant in understanding human nature in all its complexities. This will be true over a student's lifetime of study.

---

[8] Walt Heyer, *The Daily Signal*, "'Sex Change' Isn't Surgically Possible, My Surgeon Testified in Court," [article online], available from https://www.dailysignal.com/2020/02/21/sex-change-isnt-surgically-possible-my-surgeon-testified-in-court/; Internet; accessed on 11 August 2020.

THE DOCTRINE OF HUMANITY | 117

Personal Notes

Six

THE DOCTRINE OF ANGELS

THE REALITY OF ANGELS

During the days of Christ, not everyone believed in the existence of angels or other spirit beings. Luke's gospel attests to this reality when he wrote, "For the Sadducees say that there is no resurrection, nor an angel, nor a spirit; but the Pharisees acknowledge them all." [1] This may be one reason for Jesus' acknowledgment of these beings' existence, to confirm the correct teaching in his day on this subject. Jesus made this direct statement establishing a truth: "See that you do not despise one of these little ones, for I say to you, that their angels in heaven continually behold the face of My Father who is in heaven." [2] Jesus makes another direct reference to angels as he comments on his return from heaven for his church: "But of that day and hour no one knows, not even the angels of heaven, nor the Son, but the Father alone." [3]

The Apostle Paul acknowledges the existence of angels as he writes, "… and to give relief to you who are afflicted and to us as well when the Lord Jesus shall be revealed from heaven with His mighty angels…" [4]

Angels are spoken of and presented in many ways throughout the Old and New Testaments (see Genesis 19:1; Psalm 91:11; Matthew 4:11, 24:31; 1 Corinthians 4:9; 1 Timothy 5:21).

---

[1] Acts 23:8.
[2] Matt. 18:10.
[3] Matt. 24:36.
[4] 2 Thess. 1:7.

Acknowledging that Angels exist in the twenty-first century is not a tall order. Those of the Christian faith believe Angels exist, along with people outside the faith such as those involved in the New Age movement. We do not include humanists in this discussion because they do not believe in the Supernatural, therefore they do not believe in gods, angels, or spirits of any kind. They claim to only rely on that which can be seen and proven through science. Thus, humanism is a religion to support all of humanity, as humans rely on one another to solve their problems with no need for a supernatural being of any kind.

Therefore, we will proceed to discuss factual information about angels as the Scriptures reveal them to us. We use the Scriptures because since angels are spirit beings, the only way one can learn factual truth about them is from God, the creator of all things, who through his revelation to us, reveals the facts about them.

THE NATURE OF ANGELS

Their Creation

We will look at three passages of Scripture that express the creation of angels. Nehemiah 9:6 states, "Thou alone art the Lord. Thou hast made the heavens, The heaven of heavens with all their host, The earth and all that is on it, The seas and all that is in them. Thou dost give life to all of them And the heavenly host bows down before Thee." Ezekiel 28:12-16 states,

> You had the seal of perfection, Full of wisdom and perfect in beauty. You were in Eden, the garden of God; Every precious stone was your covering: The ruby, the topaz, and the diamond; The beryl, the onyx, and the jasper; The lapis lazuli, the turquoise, and the emerald; And the gold, the workmanship of your settings and sockets, Was in you. On the day that you were created They were prepared. You were the anointed cherub who covers, And I placed you there. You were on the holy mountain of God; You walked in the midst of the stones of fire. You were blameless in your ways From the day you

were created, Until unrighteousness was found in you. By the abundance of your trade You were internally filled with violence, And you sinned; Therefore I have cast you as profane From the mountain of God.

The third passage is found in Colossians 1:16 which reads, "For by Him all things were created, both in the heavens and on earth, visible and invisible, whether thrones or dominions or rulers or authorities—all things have been created by Him and for Him." Here we see a definitive statement concerning God as being the creator of all things, whose nature is eternal. (see Exodus 3:14; Revelation 1:8, 21:6, 22:13)

These passages provide the biblical record and an eyewitness account of the creation of all angels, including Lucifer, who, according to the prophet Ezekiel, became full of PRIDE, transforming him into the fallen angel known as Satan—the devil.

THEIR NUMBERS

Although we do not know the actual number of angels represented within the Scriptures, we are given some inferences along the way. Jesus states in Matthew 26:53: "Or do you think that I cannot appeal to My Father, and He will at once put at My disposal more than twelve legions of angels?" Jesus' comment about the "legions" of angels should be understood in its historical context. A Roman legion in Christ's day was comprised of between 5,000 and 6,000 soldiers. Was Jesus referring to all the angels in heaven? Not likely. Jesus' comment reflects that he had at his disposal more than enough angels to get the job done. In Second Kings 19:35, a single angel killed 180,000 Assyrian soldiers in a single night, so 72,000 supernatural beings would have been more than adequate to set Christ free from Rome if He so chose.

Hebrews 12:22 refers to the many angels in the world, as it reads, "But you have come to Mount Zion and to the city of the living God, the heavenly Jerusalem, and to myriads of angels...." The term myriad used today can mean 10,000 or a number too high to count; such as the number of sands of the sea or a googolplex. In ancient Greece, a myriad was used to represent numbers to the power of ten, or it could represent a number too high to count; such as the number of sands of the sea. Thus, in the context of the passage with myriad being used in the plural, the number represents a number beyond counting.

Types of Angels

The Scriptures seem to reflect several classifications of angels, as listed below:

- Archangels
- Cherubim
- Seraphim
- Common Angels

Fallen or Sinful Angels

- The Devil
- Fallen Angels—acting out as demons

Archangel—Jude 9 states, "But Michael the archangel, when he disputed with the devil and argued about the body of Moses, did not dare pronounce against him a railing judgment, but said, 'The Lord rebuke you.'" First Thessalonians 4:16 reads, "For the Lord Himself will descend from heaven with a shout, with the voice of the archangel, and with the trumpet of God; and the dead in Christ shall rise first."

The word *arch*, when used as a prefix to another word means *Chief* or *Principle*. We see this term used within other parts of the religious community where they refer to Archbishops, meaning a chief bishop. Within the context of the scriptures referenced here, it seems to reflect that there is only one archangel, Michael (Jude 9), though some have suggested that Gabriel, whose duties seem to be delivering and interpreting messages (Luke 1:26-28; Daniel 8:16), versus one who guards and fights wars like Michael, is another option (Revelation 12:7). Daniel 10:13 seems to suggest there may be more than one archangel, as we read, "… Michael, one of the chief princes, came to help me." The key to this point is understanding what is meant by the term *prince*.

Jesus and King David are also referenced as being princes in God's realm (Acts 5:31; Ezekiel 34:24).

It would appear that only four angels are presented with proper names in the Scriptures and given descriptions of importance and their leadership roles. The same is true for the fallen angel Abaddon referenced in Revelation 9:11. "They have as king over them, the angel of the abyss; his name in Hebrew is Abaddon, and in the Greek, he has the name Apollyon." Michael is referenced in Daniel 10:13 and 12:1 as a chief or great prince in God's kingdom, whereas Apollyon is referenced as king of locusts, who are locked up in the abyss or Sheol (Proverbs 15:11), and he serves under the fourth angel, inferred too here as Satan, a cherub who is the prince of the power of the air and ruler over all fallen angels (Ephesians 2:2; Matthew 12:26).

We can say the archangel is the chief angel, reflecting some type of hierarchy or ranking among angels. This would also imply that the archangel carries the most authority and power of all the created angels in heaven under God.

Cherubim—The term *cherubim* is plural for the word *cherub*, and carries the connotation of Blessers, Mighty Ones, Approachers, or Internal Ones, as based on the Hebrew language. The Scriptures use this term about 100 times, but only refers to five such angels in Scripture, four referenced in these passages with Satan referenced as the fifth. Cherubim are referred to in Scripture as *living beings* or *creatures* in Ezekiel 10:15 and Revelation 4:6-8.

The lack of reference to the number of cherubim in the Scriptures does not mean more do not exist, only that we are only given details on five of them. Genesis Chapter 3 speaks about Cherubim who could also be the same ones spoken of in prophecy throughout the book of Ezekiel. From the descriptions found in Ezekiel Chapters 1 and 10, we learn about the physical characteristics of these angels. Ezekiel 1:5-14 reads,

> And within it there were figures resembling four living beings. And this was their appearance: they had human form. Each of them had four faces and four wings. And their legs were straight and their feet were like a calf's hoof, and they

gleamed like burnished bronze. Under their wings on their four sides were human hands. As for the faces and wings of the four of them, their wings touched one another; their faces did not turn when they moved, each went straight forward. As for the form of their faces, each had the face of a man, all four had the face of a lion on the right and the face of a bull on the left, and all four had the face of an eagle. Such were their faces. Their wings were spread out above; each had two touching another being, and two covering their bodies. And each went straight forward; wherever the spirit was about to go, they would go, without turning as they went. In the midst of the living beings there was something that looked like burning coals of fire, like torches darting back and forth among the living beings. The fire was bright, and lightning was flashing from the fire. And the living beings ran to and fro like bolts of lightning.

Seraphim—The term S*eraphim* only appears twice in the Scriptures in the same chapter of Isaiah, as the prophet writes,

> In the year of King, Uzziah's death, I saw the Lord sitting on a throne, lofty and exalted, with the train of His robe filling the temple. Seraphim stood above Him, each having six wings; with two he covered his face, and with two he covered his feet, and with two he flew. And one called out to another and said,

> 'Holy, Holy, Holy, is the Lord of hosts,
> The whole earth is full of His glory.'

> And the foundations of the thresholds trembled at the voice of him who called out, while the temple was filling with smoke. Then I said,

> 'Woe is me, for I am ruined!
> Because I am a man of unclean lips,

And I live among a people of unclean lips;
For my eyes have seen the King, the Lord of hosts.'

Then one of the seraphim flew to me, with a burning coal in his hand which he had taken from the altar with tongs. And he touched my mouth with it and said, 'Behold, this has touched your lips; and your iniquity is taken away, and your sin is forgiven.' [5]

From this passage, there is no hint as to the number of Seraphim, only that there are more than one, and most likely based on this text, there are many more than just two. This passage also suggests that the primary duties of the Seraphim are to be in the presence of God with continuous worship and praise.

Angels—The word *angel(s)* appears approximately 200 times in the English translations of the Scriptures. This number varies depending on the translation used. When angels are spoken of, their usual appearance is a human form in a glorified state of being, similar to Christ after his resurrection. This assessment seems supported by the author of Hebrews, who writes,

For He did not subject to angels the world to come, concerning which we are speaking. But one has testified somewhere, saying,

'What is man, that Thou rememberest him?
Or the son of man, that Thou art concerned about him?
"Thou hast made him for a little while lower than the angels; Thou hast crowned him with glory and honor,
And hast appointed him over the works of Thy hands;
Thou hast put all things in subjection under his feet.'

---

[5] Isa. 6:1-7.

> For in subjecting all things to him, He left nothing that is not subject to him. But now we do not yet see all things subjected to him. But we do see Him who has been made for a little while lower than the angels, namely, Jesus, because of the suffering of death crowned with glory and honor, that by the grace of God He might taste death for everyone. [6]

An analogy could be supported through this passage, that because Jesus took on a body subject to death, he became a little lower than the angels in bodily form only. Jesus is God by nature, while angels are created beings. After his resurrection, Jesus' body became a glorified one, and because he humbled himself before His heavenly Father, God exalted Jesus above all other created beings, as the Scriptures state in Acts 5:31. "He is the one whom God exalted to His right hand as a Prince and a Savior, to grant repentance to Israel, and forgiveness of sins."

As we continue our previous discussions, because of the tasks given angels, we can reasonably assume there are countless millions of them.

Tasks Performed by Angels

1. Angels stand in the presence of God to worship Him. (Genesis 28:12; Isaiah 6:3; Revelation 4:8; Hebrews 12:22)

2. Angels rejoice in God's works. (Luke 15:10)

3. Angels execute God's will. (Psalm 103:20)

4. Angels guard the affairs of nations. (Daniel 10:10-14, 20, 21)

5. Angels guide and guard God's elect. (Psalm 91:11; Daniel 6:22; Acts 8:26, 12:7)

---

[6] Heb. 2:5-9.

6. Angels minister, defend, and deliver God's elect. (Genesis 9:11; 1 Kings 19:5-8; Matthew 4:11; Hebrews 1:13-14)

7. Angels safeguard the dead Old Testament Saints. (Luke 6:22; Jude 9)

8. Angels will accompany Christ at his Second Advent return. (Matthew 25:31; 2 Thessalonians 1:7-8)

FALLEN ANGELS

Fallen angels followed the leadership of Satan over God's. At some point before the creation of human life, all the angels were conceivably created between Genesis 1:1 and 1:2.

The Devil—The name Lucifer appears in Isaiah 14:12 and translated from the Latin Vulgate meaning *a day star* that is bright and shining. The Hebrew word is translated in the King James Bible as Lucifer. Most other translations translate the term as *star of the morning*. The passage is interpreted to carry a parallel meaning, contrasting the similarities of Lucifer as a descriptive name for the king of Babylon to the prince of this world, Satan, as Isaiah shows the stark similarities of the rise and fall of the city of Babylon with the rise and fall of Satan. [7]

Throughout Scripture, the devil has been given several names, the most common being "Satan," used more than fifty times. The name Satan first appears in First Chronicles 21:1 and is the name Christ called him in Matthew 4:10. Other names for the devil in the Scriptures are The Dragon, The Serpent, the wicked one, the evil one, Beelzebul or Beelzebub, the god of this age, ruler of this world, prince of the power of the air, the tempter, the father of lies, and Belial.

---

[7] *A commentary, critical and explanatory, on the Old and New Testaments*, vol. 1, "Isaiah 14:12," by Rev. Robert Jamieson, Rev. A. R. Fausset and Rev. David Brown (New York: S.S. Scranton and company, 1873), 446; available from https://babel.hathitrust.org/cgi/ pt?id=miun.ajg3934.0001.001; Internet; accessed 22 September 2020.

There are other descriptive phrases for the devil, but these are the most common ones concerning his existence.

Ezekiel 28:11-19 records the event and reason for Satan's fall into sin, uncovering the devil's underlining sin of PRIDE. The Scriptures express God's attitude toward PRIDE this way, "The fear of the Lord is to hate evil; Pride and arrogance and the evil way, And the perverted mouth, I hate." [8]

Angel of the abyss—Revelation 9:11 reads, "They have as king over them, the angel of the abyss; his name in Hebrew is Abaddon, and in the Greek he has the name Apollyon." *They* refer to the locust-like creatures referenced in verses 3 and 4. These creatures are not the insect locusts referenced in Proverbs 30:27, who have no king or leader but still act in organized groups. The Scriptures also record the name Abaddon in Psalm 88:11 and Proverbs 15:11; 27:20. The collective context of these passages seems to reflect that Abaddon is a king over all the locust-like creatures imprisoned in the abyss, hell, or what it references as a part of Sheol. Abaddon is most likely not a reference to Satan; instead, it seems to be a position equivalent to an archangel, only in a fallen state under Satan.

Satan is the god and ruler over all fallen angels and of this current world system. His position regarding this world system will change, as reflected in Revelation 11:15. "The kingdom of the world has become the kingdom of our Lord, and of His Christ; and He will reign forever and ever."

This interpretation of Revelation 9:11 is also held by the writers of *Expository Notes on the Bible* by Thomas L. Constable; *Barnes' Notes,* by Albert Barnes; *A Commentary: Critical, Experimental, and Practical on the Old and New Testaments,* by Robert Jamieson, A.R. Fausset, and David Brown; *Adam Clarke's Commentary,* by Adam Clarke, and *Synopsis of the Bible* by John Nelson Darby.

---

[8] Prov. 8:13.

THE DOCTRINE OF ANGELS | 129

Demons—Fallen angels are referred to as demons throughout scripture more than seventy-five times, with three references appearing in the Old Testament (Leviticus 17:7; Deuteronomy 32:17, and Psalm 106:37). Many questions concerning demons are answered through the following passage.

> Then there was brought to Him a demon-possessed man who was blind and dumb, and He healed him, so that the dumb man spoke and saw. And all the multitudes were amazed, and began to say, 'This man cannot be the Son of David, can he?' But when the Pharisees heard it, they said, 'This man casts out demons only by Beelzebul the ruler of the demons.' And knowing their thoughts He said to them, 'Any kingdom divided against itself is laid waste; and any city or house divided against itself shall not stand. And if Satan casts out Satan, he is divided against himself; how then shall his kingdom stand? And if I by Beelzebul cast out demons, by whom do your sons cast them out?' [9]

Within this passage, we learn the Kingdom of God is not the same Kingdom as Satan's. We learn that the name Beelzebul is another name for Satan, who is the head of his kingdom with demons for subjects. We also learn that demons can possess humans, negatively affecting their lives.

Demons are intelligent, powerful spirits as reflected in Luke 4:41 which states, "And demons also were coming out of many, crying out and saying, 'You are the Son of God!' And rebuking them, He would not allow them to speak, because they knew Him to be the Christ.'"

We read in Luke 8:30-33, "And Jesus asked him, 'What is your name?' And he said, 'Legion;' for many demons had entered him. And they were entreating Him not to command them to depart into the abyss. Now there was a herd of many swine feeding there on the mountain; and the demons entreated Him to permit them to enter the swine.

---

[9] Matt. 12:22-27.

And He gave them permission. And the demons came out from the man and entered the swine; and the herd rushed down the steep bank into the lake, and were drowned."

The fallen spirit world is at war with God and humanity. We see this in Luke13:16 and Matthew 17:15-18. The Apostle Paul expresses this concept thusly: "For our struggle is not against flesh and blood, but against the rulers, against the powers, against the world forces of this darkness, against the spiritual forces of wickedness in the heavenly places. Therefore, take up the full armor of God, that you may be able to resist in the evil day, and having done everything, to stand firm." [10]

From these passages, we learn that God has total power over all demons and that more than one demon can possess a human being. We also see that God has equipped believers to fight the spiritual battles that confront them through the power of the Holy Spirit of God. (see Ephesians 6:10-17)

Through the following passages, we learn how God works in every believer's life for God's glory and the believer's spiritual success against evil forces (Josh.1:8; Ps. 138:3; 2 Cor. 12:9-10; Phil. 4:13; 2 Tim. 4:17; Eph. 1:18-21, 3:14-19, 6:10-17; Col. 1:9-14).

We are reassured of this truth as Paul writes, "For I am convinced that neither death, nor life, nor angels, nor principalities, nor things present, nor things to come, nor powers, nor height, nor depth, nor any other created thing, shall be able to separate us from the love of God, which is in Christ Jesus our Lord." [11]

THE QUESTION OF DEMON POSSESSION

This leaves open the question, can a person who is *born again* through the spirit of God become demon-possessed? The answer to that question is multi-layered based on the following scriptural concepts, as Jesus shows in Matthew 12:25-30.

---

[10] Eph. 6:12-13.
[11] Rom. 8:38-39.

And knowing their thoughts He said to them, 'Any kingdom divided against itself is laid waste; and any city or house divided against itself shall not stand. And if Satan casts out Satan, he is divided against himself; how then shall his kingdom stand? And if I by Beelzebul cast out demons, by whom do your sons cast them out? Consequently they shall be your judges. But if I cast out demons by the Spirit of God, then the kingdom of God has come upon you. Or how can anyone enter the strong man's house and carry off his property, unless he first binds the strong man? And then he will plunder his house. He who is not with Me is against Me; and he who does not gather with Me scatters.'

The concept presented here is that God is stronger than Satan, therefore anyone living in God's house is safe from thieves or those outside forces who want to come in to do harm. This passage states that the strongest person in the room wins, and both cannot exist in the same room at the same time. Therefore, the born-again believer (John 3:3), who is the temple of the Holy Spirit, possesses the stronger entity, the Holy Spirit of God. "Or do you not know that your body is a temple of the Holy Spirit who is in you, whom you have from God, and that you are not your own?" [12]

The ultimate question becomes, how long will the Holy Spirit be with us? Jesus states in John 14:16-17, "And I will ask the Father, and He will give you another Helper, that He may be with you forever; that is the Spirit of truth, whom the world cannot receive, because it does not behold Him or know Him, but you know Him because He abides with you, and will be in you."

The answer, as reflected in this passage, is FOREVER! Jesus backs up this concept in an earlier statement he made in John 8:34-36: "… Truly, truly, I say to you, everyone who commits sin is the slave of sin. And the slave does not remain in the house forever; the son does remain forever. If therefore the Son shall make you free, you shall be free

---

[12] 1 Cor. 6:19.

indeed." Jesus' statement reflects that He remains in our house FOREVER, thus making us FREE from sin, of which sin is the nature of the Kingdom of Satan.

THE JUDGMENT ON SATAN AND HIS DEMONS

The Apostle Peter sets up the day of Judgment this way,

> For if God did not spare angels when they sinned, but cast them into hell and committed them to pits of darkness, reserved for judgment; and did not spare the ancient world, but preserved Noah, a preacher of righteousness, with seven others, when He brought a flood upon the world of the ungodly; and if He condemned the cities of Sodom and Gomorrah to destruction by reducing them to ashes, having made them an example to those who would live ungodly thereafter; and if He rescued righteous Lot, oppressed by the sensual conduct of unprincipled men (for by what he saw and heard that righteous man, while living among them, felt his righteous soul tormented day after day with their lawless deeds), then the Lord knows how to rescue the godly from temptation, and to keep the unrighteous under punishment for the day of judgment, and especially those who indulge the flesh in its corrupt desires and despise authority. [13]

The writer of Jude continues this theme as he writes, "And angels who did not keep their own domain, but abandoned their proper abode, He has kept in eternal bonds under darkness for the judgment of the great day." [14]

The Apostle Paul tells us that God's people will take part in the day of judgment on these angels. Paul writes, "Do you not know that we shall judge angels? How much more, matters of this life?" [15]

---

[13] 2 Peter 2:4-10.
[14] Jude 6.
[15] 1 Cor. 6:3.

Revelation 20:1-3 speaks to Satan's temporary judgment as we read, "And I saw an angel coming down from heaven, having the key of the abyss and a great chain in his hand. And he laid hold of the dragon, the serpent of old, who is the devil and Satan, and bound him for a thousand years, and threw him into the abyss, and shut it and sealed it over him, so that he should not deceive the nations any longer, until the thousand years were completed; after these things he must be released for a short time."

THE ANGELS FINAL JUDGEMENT

Revelation 20:10 reads, "And the devil who deceived them was thrown into the lake of fire and brimstone, where the beast and the false prophet are also; and they will be tormented day and night forever and ever."

{ CHAPTER DISCUSSION NOTES }

Within the study of angels, a good rule to follow in any biblical research is this, there are no contradictions in Scripture, for biblical truth to be true, it must agree with all other biblical truths. The Apostle Paul encourages you to "Study to show thyself approved unto God, a workman that needeth not to be ashamed, rightly dividing the word of truth." [16]

I only considered facts that could be collaborated with the Scriptures or outside scholarly works on this subject. Speculations and things not supported through a Grammatico-Historical Method of interpretation were not presented here.

Though other details of this subject could be legitimately covered, I considered the information presented here to be essential factors one could use for a working foundation toward conducting a more in-depth study if they wished.

---

[16] 2 Tim. 2:15 KJV (King James Version).

Personal Notes

Seven

THE DOCTRINE OF SALVATION

THE NEED FOR SALVATION

Within our world, we see that evil exists. This is clear through human actions such as murder, rape, child molestation, human trafficking, spousal abuse, the telling of lies against others, adultery, and the list could go on. We can find the answer to this question of why evil exists in our world within the Scriptures.

Psalm 53:1-3 states, "The fool has said in his heart, 'There is no God,' They are corrupt, and have committed abominable injustice; There is no one who does good. God has looked down from heaven upon the sons of men, To see if there is anyone who understands, Who seeks after God. Every one of them has turned aside; together they have become corrupt; There is no one who does good, not even one." Jesus explains why this is true about humanity by saying, "But the things that proceed out of the mouth come from the heart, and those defile the man. For out of the heart come evil thoughts, murders, adulteries, fornications, thefts, false witness, slanders." [1]

Herein lie the issue and reason for the need for God's salvation. The human spirit and heart became corrupted and sinful before God. This corruption took place within the timeframe of Genesis Chapter 3, where we read,

> Now the serpent was more crafty than any beast of the field which the Lord God had made. And he said to the

---

[1] Matt. 15:18-19.

woman, 'Indeed, has God said, You shall not eat from any tree of the garden?' And the woman said to the serpent, 'From the fruit of the trees of the garden we may eat; but from the fruit of the tree which is in the middle of the garden, God has said, You shall not eat from it or touch it, lest you die.' And the serpent said to the woman, 'You surely shall not die! For God knows that in the day you eat from it your eyes will be opened, and you will be like God, knowing good and evil.' When the woman saw that the tree was good for food, and that it was a delight to the eyes, and that the tree was desirable to make one wise, she took from its fruit and ate; and she gave also to her husband with her, and he ate. Then the eyes of both of them were opened, and they knew that they were naked; and they sewed fig leaves together and made themselves loin coverings. [2]

This event, an exchange between God's enemy the devil and humanity, permitted sin or evil to gain entrance into the human heart, and thus, the results of bad human behavior in the world.

But this is not the only consequence of this interaction. The penalty for this violation of God's only rule is death. Not just physical death, but spiritual death. Revelation 20:14 calls this the second death. Therefore, the need to renew the human heart and save humans from this second death requires an act of salvation from God.

The process that takes place for salvation to happen becomes confused through the debate of human FREE WILL. Therefore, we will hold a brief discussion on this subject before moving on to the process that brings salvation to humanity.

FREE WILL

We will look at three views that frame this debate. The Calvinist view, the Arminian view, and an alternative view.

---

[2] Gen. 3:1-7.

THE DOCTRINE OF SALVATION

Calvinism—A theological teaching of John Calvin (A.D. 1509-1564), a French lawyer who changed his profession to become a pastor and theologian in the reformed church movement. John Calvin's teachings on the doctrine of salvation are summed up through the acronym **TULIP**, which represents the following theological perspectives.

- Total Depravity of Man—Sin has affected every aspect of human nature. This means there is nothing in humanity that can cause one to seek after God.

- Unconditional Election—God calls or draws people to himself, without conditions.

- Limited Atonement—Christ died only for the elect, those whom he has chosen.

- Irresistible Grace—God's calling, or drawing individuals to himself cannot be resisted. If you are chosen, you will be saved.

- Perseverance of the Saints—Salvation is for eternity. You cannot lose your salvation.

Arminianism—A theological teaching of Jacobus Arminius (A.D. 1560-1609). Arminius was a Dutch Reformed theologian, whose views on the doctrine of salvation are best expressed in the Five Articles of Remonstrance summarized below.

- Salvation is by God's enabled faith.

- Christ's atonement was for all people.

- Salvation comes through the work of the Holy Spirit. Humanity does not have the ability of faith through their own willpower.

- A believers' ability to do good only comes through the power of the Holy Spirit.

- Believers can resist sin through the grace of God, but their ability to resist or reject God's grace is still an unknown, needing further study.

We can find major differences between these teachings through the concept of the "Atonement," defined through Christ's life which was sacrificed on the cross for the forgiveness of sins. Then the question, is the atonement limited or unlimited? This, alongside the argument of whether God's grace can be resisted, speaks to the question of human choice. It should be noted that all these views believe faith is a gift of God toward salvation.

Alternative View—A theological perspective based on the trichotomy of humanity and a view that there are no contradictions in Scripture; for biblical truth to be true, it must agree with all other biblical truths. Consider the following perspectives.

- The total depravity of human nature. Sin has affected every aspect of human nature. (Psalm 53:1-3; Romans Chapter 3)

- Salvation comes only through the grace of God. (Ephesians 2:8-9)

- Christ died for the Atonement of all sin everywhere. (1 John 2:1-2)

- The conditions of salvation are repentance and faith. (Acts 20:18-21)

- Humanity has the ability to exercise faith within a fallen human nature. (Matthew 9:29, 15:28; Mark 10:52; Luke 7:50, 18:42; 2 Peter 1:5)

- We can only exercise faith toward God through God's enabled wisdom applied to the gospel message. (Luke 7:30-35; 1 Corinthians 2:6-16)

THE DOCTRINE OF SALVATION | 139

- Humanity's salvation is forever, based on the promises of the New Covenant, the work of Christ, and the Holy Spirit; all of which is unconditional and eternal. (John 14:16; Hebrews 7:23-25; 2 John 1-3)

To summarize this view, we could say:

- Humanity is sinful and under the condemnation of God.

- Christ died for the forgiveness of all sin.

- Humanity has the ability to choose to do anything within its nature's ability.

- Human nature does not have the ability to seek God on its own, without God's intervention.

- Humankind can exercise faith toward God only when God provides his wisdom to mankind's knowledge for a proper understanding of the gospel message.

- After God provides illumination to the truth of his Word, humanity still has the choice to exercise or not exercise faith in that truth.

- Salvation based on the indwelling of the Holy Spirit is forever and cannot be lost.

This view offers two different perspectives from the other views.

- Although saving faith is based on understanding God's gospel message, mankind cannot understand that message without possessing God-given wisdom, an attribute of God's nature. Therefore, by the grace of God, the gift of wisdom is provided in the salvation process so humanity can understand its knowledge and exercise individualized faith.

> Humanity's choice comes after receiving the grace of God's illumination of the truth of the gospel, because of the work of the Holy Spirit. This concept is illustrated in the life of King Solomon, who made wrong choices despite having God's wisdom provided to him in abundance.

THE PROCESS OF SALVATION

The elements that are part of the salvation process are threefold, knowledge, repentance, and faith.

Knowledge—The elements of repentance and faith cannot take place without understood knowledge. Knowledge provides us the information required to be aware of a problem, the reasons for the problem, and an answer to solve the problem. Thus, the Scriptures provide us information that tells us what the problem is, why there is a problem, and how to fix the problem. The Scriptures tell us we can also learn about God through his creation. Romans 1:16-20 reads,

> For I am not ashamed of the gospel, for it is the power of God for salvation to everyone who believes, to the Jew first and also to the Greek. For in it the righteousness of God is revealed from faith to faith; as it is written, 'But the righteous man shall live by faith.'
> For the wrath of God is revealed from heaven against all ungodliness and unrighteousness of men, who suppress the truth in unrighteousness, because that which is known about God is evident within them; for God made it evident to them. For since the creation of the world His invisible attributes, His eternal power and divine nature, have been clearly seen, being understood through what has been made, so that they are without excuse.

Knowledge also comes through the Word of God, as the Apostle Paul writes, "How then shall they call upon Him in whom they have not believed? And how shall they believe in Him whom they have not heard? And how shall they hear without a preacher?" [3] Luke supports this concept through his gospel concerning Christ, as he writes, "And beginning with Moses and with all the prophets, He explained to them the things concerning Himself in all the Scriptures." [4]

The Apostle John tells us that, "In the beginning was the Word, and the Word was with God, and the Word was God. He was in the beginning with God. All things came into being by Him, and apart from Him nothing came into being that has come into being.... And the Word became flesh, and dwelt among us, and we beheld His glory, glory as of the only begotten from the Father, full of grace and truth."[5]

Here, it is inferred that Jesus Christ is the living Word of God in the flesh. Because of this, the things Jesus spoke during his earthly ministry became part of the Scriptures—the written words of God. Jesus said, "Therefore everyone who hears these words of Mine, and acts upon them, may be compared to a wise man, who built his house upon the rock." [6]

Jesus' statement notes that humanity must act on the knowledge of Christ's words—the living Word—to establish a foundation for daily living. This teaching coincides with Jesus' definition of life: "Jesus said to him, 'I am the way, and the truth, and the life; no one comes to the Father, but through Me.'"

So, we learn that salvation comes through knowledge of Christ as the crucified, resurrected, and living Lord; but within this process just knowing these facts are not enough. The Scriptures also teach that salvation comes to us through an act of faith. Here lies the key to knowledge, which is the element of understanding. If one does not understand what the knowledge they possess means, their ability to act on that knowledge is limited. Understanding spiritual truth (knowledge), requires spiritual wisdom, which only comes from God (1 Corinthians 2:12-14). King Solomon, the wisest human who ever lived, expresses the concept this way: "For the Lord gives wisdom; From His mouth

---

[3] Rom. 10:14.
[4] Luke 24:27.
[5] John 1:1-3, 14.
[6] Matt. 7:24.

come knowledge and understanding." We could sum up this verse this way. Knowledge + Wisdom = Understanding.

Based on this assessment, repentance toward God and faith in Jesus Christ are now required for salvation to take place (Acts 20:21).

Repentance—Repentance of sin is an attitude of genuine regret and a turning away from those past actions that caused this regret. True repentance requires not just regret and being sorry about one's actions, but the added action of asking forgiveness from the one who was wronged.

When we talk about salvation for humanity, the offended or wronged one is God himself. Therefore, repentance is not just a recognition of one's personal sin against God, it also requests forgiveness from God for the sin itself. We know repentance is required by God through the command of Jesus himself, as we read, "And after John had been taken into custody, Jesus came into Galilee, preaching the gospel of God, saying, 'The time is fulfilled, and the kingdom of God is at hand; repent and believe in the gospel.'" [7] The Apostle Matthew reaffirms this command as he writes, "From that time Jesus began to preach and say, 'Repent, for the kingdom of heaven is at hand.'" [8]

Repentance can also mean *the changing of one's mind*, or just being *sorry* for one's choices. We see this illustrated in the parable of the two sons told in Matthew 21:28-32 where the King James Bible translates the concept as *repented*, and the New American Standard Bible translates it as a *changed mind*. We also see this concept in Genesis 6:6 concerning God himself, where the King James Bible translates it as *repented*, but the New American Standard Bible translates the concept as being *sorry*, as in being sorrowful over a decision made.

Within this discussion over human repentance, the question then becomes, can humanity repent on their own, or does it come through the enablement of God? This question exists because of the arguments over the issues of Free Will and is best answered through a scriptural analysis.

---

[7] Mark 1:14-15.
[8] Matt. 4:17.

The following are interpretations of this scriptural analysis and reflect differing viewpoints.

(A.) The Calvinist view would use Acts 11:15-18 to support its perspective, and reads,

> And as I began to speak, the Holy Spirit fell upon them, just as He did upon us at the beginning. And I remembered the word of the Lord, how He used to say, 'John baptized with water, but you shall be baptized with the Holy Spirit.' If God therefore gave to them the same gift as He gave to us also after believing in the Lord Jesus Christ, who was I that I could stand in God's way? And when they heard this, they quieted down, and glorified God, saying, 'Well then, God has granted to the Gentiles also the repentance that leads to life.'

The historical context of this passage is God giving the Holy Spirit to the newly formed church, who came to indwell them on the day of Pentecost, starting with the twelve Apostles, who, at this point, were messianic Jews. Being Jews—God's chosen people—they came to understand that God was now offering the Gentiles what He offered the Nation of Israel, which is permanent forgiveness of sins through the work of Christ and the indwelling of the Holy Spirit. This is the fulfillment of the New Covenant promise (Jeremiah 31:31-34), which was reemphasized by the prophet Ezekiel when he wrote, "Moreover, I will give you a new heart and put a new spirit within you; and I will remove the heart of stone from your flesh and give you a heart of flesh. And I will put My Spirit within you and cause you to walk in My statutes, and you will be careful to observe My ordinances." [9] And because God grafted the Gentiles into the New Covenant promise, this prophecy was extended to them as well. (see Romans Chapter 11)

This brings us back to how this relates to repentance. Within this context, repentance is God granting this ability as a gift, just as faith is

---

[9] Ezek. 36:26-27.

granted as a gift, for both are requirements for salvation. They would then see anything associated with salvation as a work of God's grace, which is a free gift, just as Ephesians 2:8-9 states.

(B.) From an Armenian point of view, their teaching suggests repentance is initially driven by the human fear of hell, which then becomes a sorrowful attitude of repentance based on the regret of sinning against God, resulting from one's knowledge of general and personal sin as it relates to God. [10] Thus, making it a natural ability that comes from within, a human act of the human will.

(C.) From the Alternative view, there are several factors to consider. God makes salvation available in the same way Satan made sin available to the human race, through an appeal to the soul and spirit of humanity. Satan first got Eve to doubt her knowledge of what God said through an appeal to her intellect; a function of her soul, then he appealed to her attitudes, a desire to be like God; a function of her spirit resulting in pride, the ultimate sin against God.

God, using the same process, brings about the conditions for reversing the decision made by a prideful act of sin. God appeals to our intellect by providing knowledge based on God's wisdom. Second Timothy 3:14-15 states, "You, however, continue in the things you have learned and become convinced of, knowing from whom you have learned them; and that from childhood you have known the sacred writings which are able to give you the wisdom that leads to salvation through faith which is in Christ Jesus." Knowledge speaks to our intellect, a part of our soul functionality.

Then we read in Romans 2:4, "Or do you think lightly of the riches of His kindness and forbearance and patience, not knowing that the kindness of God leads you to repentance?" God's attitude of love reaches out to our attitude of repentance, an attribute of our spirit. So like faith, repentance is a product of ourselves, but the key lies with the

---

[10] *The Society of Evangelical Arminians*, s.v. "Arminius on Repentance," by Roy Ingle; available from http://evangelicalarminians.org/arminius-on-repentance-2/; Internet; accessed 15 August 2020.

factor of understanding the knowledge presented. Here lies the factor of the grace of God, who provides us his wisdom, giving us the ability to see and understand God's gospel message, so we can respond with the attitude of repentance—a function of our spirit—and a willful act of faith, a function of our soul.

To conclude this part of our discussion, repentance involves an act of our intellect, emotion, willpower, and a changed attitude from PRIDE to HUMILITY in response to the attitude and action of God's LOVE. This brings about God's reward, the gift of the salvation of our souls.

Humility is the opposite of PRIDE, for the Scriptures state, "… and all of you, clothe yourselves with humility toward one another, for God is opposed to the proud, but gives grace to the humble." [11]

Faith—Hebrews 11:1 states, "Now faith is the assurance of things hoped for, the conviction of things not seen." The writer of Hebrews provides us examples of faith in action, eliminating a misunderstanding over what kind of faith God is looking for; examples like Noah, who was told by God to build an ark (an enormous boat), so when the rains came to the whole earth, God would save Noah and his family from impending death. Why was this an act of faith? Because Noah did not understand what rain was; since it had never rained before, nor did he know when this thing called rain would come. In this case, it was over 100 years later (Genesis 6:13-17).

We learn through the account of Abraham's life that through his son Isaac, God promised Abraham an inheritance that included becoming a great name and nation, the permanent possession of the land, and that inhabitants of the nations of the world who came after him would be blessed (Genesis 12:1-3, 15:18-21). A few years later, God told Abraham to take this same son and sacrifice him on an altar before God, at which point, just before Abraham was about to kill his own son, God stopped him and provided an alternative sacrifice; proving Abraham's faith through his obedience to God, knowing that even if he would have

---

[11] 1 Peter 5:5.

killed his only son, conceived through his wife Sarah, God would raise his son Isaac up from the dead to keep his promise (see Genesis 22:1-14; Hebrews Chapter 11).

This alternative view answers the question, if God gave Abraham his faith, did this truly represent an act of faith on the part of Abraham? Or would we see it as God orchestrating the entire event from both sides of the relationship for the benefit of His plan? This leaves an opening for an alternative perspective, that God allowed Abraham to understand what God was saying and truly meant, then believing what God said, Abraham exercised his own faith and was subsequently rewarded for that personal faith. The grace of God came by allowing Abraham to understand God's words from the beginning. When seen from this perspective, it seems to fit into the whole counsel of God without contradiction.

THE EFFECTS OF SALVATION

REGENERATION

Matthew 19:28 and Titus 3:5 are the only two places the word "regeneration" is found. *The Pulpit Commentary* provides us with this explanation on the term as found in Matthew 19:28.

> This may be but another name for the setting up of the kingdom of heaven. As the apostles were to be directly connected with it, the final 'restitution of all things' can hardly be meant. It is usual to refer such expressions to the 'second coming of Christ;' but he appears to have had in mind the starting of the Messianic kingdom at Pentecost. Understanding Christ to be using Eastern figures of speech, we may see his meaning to be simply this - Those who truly and self-sacrificingly

THE DOCTRINE OF SALVATION | 147

follow him shall occupy the chief places of influence in the new kingdom which he proposed soon to establish. [12]

This term, when used in Titus 3:5, carries a slightly different connotation as *The Pulpit Commentary* reads, "... describes the new birth in holy baptism, when the believer is put into possession of a new spiritual life, a new nature, and a new inheritance of glory. And the laver of baptism is called 'the laver of regeneration,' because it is the ordained means by or through which regeneration is obtained. And renewing of the Holy Ghost." [13]

In the end, we could say the regeneration referenced here is referring to the time of the baptism of the Holy Spirit that occurred at the moment of someone's salvation.

In summary, *regeneration* is a process that takes place through the Holy Spirit of God. It not only makes us new creatures in Christ by giving us a new nature (2 Corinthians 5:17, 2 Peter 1:4), it also places us in the presence of God at the end of the church age, and in the age to come, represented by the millennial kingdom. (Hosea 2:14-23; Revelation 4:4; 5:8-12)

JUSTIFICATION

When someone is born again (John 3:3), that person becomes justified before God. Justification means that as a result of one's salvation, the individual becomes forgiven of all sin, past, present, and future, becoming guiltless before God (Galatians 2:15-16). Another way to view this is by imagining someone standing before God the Judge, and upon their repentance of sin, and faith in Christ's finished work on the cross, the Judge declares that person not guilty, as if they had never sinned, and they will continue in this forgiven state from that day forward. It is

---

[12] *The Pulpit Commentary*, s.v. "Matthew 19:28," ed. H. D. M. Spence and Joseph S. Exell (New York: Funk & Wagnalls Co., 1880-1919) [Electronic Database] available from Biblesoft, Inc.

[13] *The Pulpit Commentary*, s.v. "Titus 3:5," ed. H. D. M. Spence and Joseph S. Exell.

being in a permanent state of forgiveness and being righteous or in right standing before God (Romans 5:9-11). Regeneration and justification are joined together as a single process.

The Apostle Paul, in his letter to Titus, sums up the concept this way, "But when the kindness of God our Savior and His love for mankind appeared, He saved us, not on the basis of deeds which we have done in righteousness, but according to His mercy, by the washing of regeneration and renewing by the Holy Spirit, whom He poured out upon us richly through Jesus Christ our Savior, that being justified by His grace we might be made heirs according to the hope of eternal life." [14]

Within this understanding, we see that through God's love, God extends his salvation that regenerates us as new creatures in Christ, which then makes us justified before God; bringing us hope in our current state of being and eternal life in our next life to come.

To many, the answer to the question of why all this is necessary becomes clear through the Apostle Paul, as he writes,

> And the gift is not like that which came through the one who sinned; for on the one hand the judgment arose from one transgression resulting in condemnation, but on the other hand the free gift arose from many transgressions resulting in justification. For if by the transgression of the one, death reigned through the one, much more those who receive the abundance of grace and of the gift of righteousness will reign in life through the One, Jesus Christ. So then as through one transgression there resulted condemnation to all men, even so through one act of righteousness there resulted justification of life to all men. For as through the one man's disobedience the many were made sinners, even so through the obedience of the One the many will be made righteous. And the Law came in that the transgression might increase; but where sin increased, grace abounded all the more, that, as sin reigned in

---

[14] Titus 3:4-7.

death, even so grace might reign through righteousness to eternal life through Jesus Christ our Lord. [15]

Through this passage, we come to learn that sin came into the world through one man called Adam, who brought condemnation to all of humanity. But, through God's grace, by one man—Jesus Christ—the gift of justification is offered to all of humanity. And this represents the good news of the gospel.

Jesus' actions in support of these concepts are through his commandments to everyone, everywhere, as he said, "The time is fulfilled, and the kingdom of God is at hand; repent and believe in the gospel."[16] It is through the gospel we are offered justification and regeneration, producing new life, starting with one's actions of repentance and faith.

ADOPTION

The Scriptures teach that through the salvation process believers are adopted into God's family. As children of God, they are provided a place of shared inheritance with Christ. Romans 8:14-17 teaches this concept, as we read, "For all who are being led by the Spirit of God, these are sons of God. For you have not received a spirit of slavery leading to fear again, but you have received a spirit of adoption as sons by which we cry out, 'Abba! Father!' The Spirit Himself bears witness with our spirit that we are children of God, and if children, heirs also, heirs of God and fellow heirs with Christ, if indeed we suffer with Him in order that we may also be glorified with Him."

The Apostle Paul gives us a fuller explanation of this concept by writing,

> Now I say, as long as the heir is a child, he does not differ at all from a slave although he is owner of everything, but he is under guardians and managers until the date set by the father. So also we, while we were children, were held in

---

[15] Rom. 5:16-21.
[16] Mark 1:15.

bondage under the elemental things of the world. But when the fulness of the time came, God sent forth His Son, born of a woman, born under the Law, in order that He might redeem those who were under the Law, that we might receive the adoption as sons. And because you are sons, God has sent forth the Spirit of His Son into our hearts, crying, 'Abba! Father!' Therefore you are no longer a slave, but a son; and if a son, then an heir through God. [17]

From these passages, we come to learn that through our salvation we are now adopted children of God and given the same attitude as Christ, to legitimately call God our Father.

We are reminded through the Scriptures why God is doing this on our behalf. The Scriptures read: "Blessed be the God and Father of our Lord Jesus Christ, who has blessed us with every spiritual blessing in the heavenly places in Christ, just as He chose us in Him before the foundation of the world, that we should be holy and blameless before Him. In love He predestined us to adoption as sons through Jesus Christ to Himself, according to the kind intention of His will, to the praise of the glory of His grace, which He freely bestowed on us in the Beloved."[18]

Adoption is a status given to all who have true faith in Christ, because of God's loving-kindness and grace.

SANCTIFICATION

Within the salvation of humanity comes the concept of *sanctification*. This concept is multi-tiered, requiring an explanation from the Scriptures as to how it all works.

Let us start our understanding by looking at the source of sanctification. First Corinthians 1:30-31 states, "But by His doing you are in Christ Jesus, who became to us wisdom from God, and righteousness

---

[17] Gal. 4:1-7.
[18] Eph. 1:3-6.

and sanctification, and redemption, that, just as it is written, 'Let him who boasts, boast in the Lord.'"

It is through our salvation that sanctification comes, which we later learn to mean, *to be set apart from something else*. We see this in our next passage. "For this is the will of God, your sanctification; that is, that you abstain from sexual immorality; that each of you know how to possess his own vessel in sanctification and honor, not in lustful passion, like the Gentiles who do not know God; and that no man transgress and defraud his brother in the matter because the Lord is the avenger in all these things, just as we also told you before and solemnly warned you. For God has not called us for the purpose of impurity, but in sanctification. Consequently, he who rejects this is not rejecting man but the God who gives His Holy Spirit to you." [19]

Within this passage, we learn that sanctification means to be separated from sinful behavior such as immoral lifestyles and sinful deeds, as described within the Scriptures.

Sanctification can also mean God setting us apart from the world as forgiven people who are no longer enslaved to sin. We see this where the Apostle Paul writes,

> But we should always give thanks to God for you, brethren beloved by the Lord, because God has chosen you from the beginning for salvation through sanctification by the Spirit and faith in the truth. And it was for this He called you through our gospel, that you may gain the glory of our Lord Jesus Christ. So then, brethren, stand firm and hold to the traditions which you were taught, whether by word of mouth or by letter from us.
>
> Now may our Lord Jesus Christ Himself and God our Father, who has loved us and given us eternal comfort and good hope by grace, comfort and strengthen your hearts in every good work and word. [20]

---

[19] 1 Thess. 4:3-8.
[20] 2 Thess. 2:13-17.

Through sanctification, we are set apart from the world system of sin and commanded to live a separated lifestyle from that sin. But because we still possess a sinful nature, being obedient in living a separated lifestyle becomes an ongoing battle, as expressed by the Apostle Paul in Romans 7:19-25.

> For the good that I wish, I do not do; but I practice the very evil that I do not wish. But if I am doing the very thing I do not wish, I am no longer the one doing it, but sin which dwells in me. I find then the principle that evil is present in me, the one who wishes to do good. For I joyfully concur with the law of God in the inner man, but I see a different law in the members of my body, waging war against the law of my mind, and making me a prisoner of the law of sin which is in my members. Wretched man that I am! Who will set me free from the body of this death? Thanks be to God through Jesus Christ our Lord! So then, on the one hand I myself with my mind am serving the law of God, but on the other, with my flesh the law of sin.

It is because of this ongoing war within us that this separation becomes a process, which in the theological world we call *progressive sanctification* because it is an ongoing process that we will always struggle with to some degree in this life. But when speaking in terms of Second Thessalonians Chapter 2, it refers to a sanctification process that is complete, representing our salvation as being a permanent separation from death unto life through the gospel of Jesus Christ.

INHERITANCE

The Scriptures present us with two concepts of God's covenant promise of inheritance. The first is an inheritance offered to the Nation of Israel, and the second concept of inheritance comes to all New Testament believers in Christ at the moment of salvation, a possession of the blessing of being with Christ forever (John 14:1-3; Ephesians 1:7-12). Continuing this discussion, we can say:

(A.) God established an inheritance for the Jewish people (the Nation of Israel) through the Abrahamic Covenant, which states in part, "And I will establish My covenant between Me and you and your descendants after you throughout their generations for an everlasting covenant, to be God to you and to your descendants after you. And I will give to you and to your descendants after you, the land of your sojournings, all the land of Canaan, for an everlasting possession; and I will be their God."[21]

The reinforcement of this covenant comes through another unconditional, everlasting covenant called the Davidic Covenant, which is presented in Second Samuel Chapter 7. This covenant states that God will establish, on the land grant promised, an everlasting Kingdom which will have no end.

The writer of Hebrews supports the concept of Israel's inheritance as he writes, "By faith Abraham, when he was called, obeyed by going out to a place which he was to receive for an inheritance; and he went out, not knowing where he was going. By faith he lived as an alien in the land of promise, as in a foreign land, dwelling in tents with Isaac and Jacob, fellow heirs of the same promise; for he was looking for the city which has foundations, whose architect and builder is God." [22]

Since the language of these covenants reflect unconditional, everlasting attributes, the question becomes, when will this inheritance become a reality? The answer is, it starts with the millennial Kingdom on earth. (see Luke 1:30-33; 1 Corinthians 15:22-26; Revelation 11:15; Daniel 7:13-14)

(B.) The inheritance for New Testament believers starts with John 14:2-3 which says, "In My Father's house are many dwelling places; if it were not so, I would have told you; for I go to prepare a place for you. And if I go and prepare a place for you, I will come again, and receive you to Myself; that where I am, there you may be also."

---

[21] Gen. 17:7-8.
[22] Heb. 11:8-10.

Jesus promised to return for his church (the body of Christ), and take them to live in a place Christ prepared for them where they will remain with Him forever.

The Apostle Paul supports an inheritance for the *body of Christ* in Ephesians 1:10-12, as it reads in part, "... In Him also we have obtained an inheritance, having been predestined according to His purpose who works all things after the counsel of His will, to the end that we who were the first to hope in Christ should be to the praise of His glory."

The Apostle Paul continues this theme in verses 13 and 14, by saying, "In Him, you also, after listening to the message of truth, the gospel of your salvation—having also believed, you were sealed in Him with the Holy Spirit of promise, who is given as a pledge of our inheritance, with a view to the redemption of God's own possession, to the praise of His glory."

Here, the Apostle Paul provides insight into the fact that our inheritance is directly tied to our salvation and is guaranteed through the indwelling of the Holy Spirit.

{ CHAPTER DISCUSSION NOTES }

FREE WILL

The subject of the *Free Will* of humanity can be an extremely large and divisive issue among Christian theologians and students of the various theological systems presented in churches and seminaries across all of Christendom.

The main issue is, how do we reconcile our understanding of theology and the complex questions of humanity in relation to God's sovereignty in a fallen world?

We find the differences between all three views presented here as having little to do with the reality of our salvation, instead it deals more with how we perceive God's actions within the salvation process. Regardless of what position anyone takes on this issue, it will not alter the facts that God loves us, provided a sacrifice to save us, and that we are saved through faith alone, apart from any works. Beyond this, our disagreements are over how one wants to view God in our lives, but this does not affect the salvation message or mission for the *body of Christ* in the world.

Therefore, let us follow the intent of Paul's instructions to Timothy, where he writes, "But the goal of our instruction is love from a pure heart and a good conscience and a sincere faith. For some men, straying from these things, have turned aside to fruitless discussion, wanting to be teachers of the Law, even though they do not understand either what they Are saying or the matters about which they make confident assertions." [23] The key to all our instructions or discussions should come from a motivation of love, not division within the Church. (1 Corinthians 12:20-25)

This is not to infer one cannot pick or live by any given position, only that we should be showing love and grace to those whom we disagree with as we interact with them within the *body of Christ*.

JUSTIFICATION AND SANCTIFICATION

When we enter into a discussion on Justification and Sanctification as it relates to personal salvation, there raises a debate within the *body of Christ* on eternal security or to the question, can one lose their salvation? The concern of some comes from possible attitudes of entitlement. Someone could view their salvation as a license to sin, maintaining an attitude of I have my salvation, now I can live as I please! What gets lost in this debate is the understanding of what happens in the process of one's salvation?

The Apostle Paul addresses this very question as he writes, "What then? Shall we sin because we are not under law but under grace? May it never be! Do you not know that when you present yourselves to someone as slaves for obedience, you are slaves of the one whom you obey, either of sin resulting in death, or of obedience resulting in righteousness? But thanks be to God that though you were slaves of sin, you

---

[23] 1 Tim. 1:5-7

became obedient from the heart to that form of teaching to which you were committed, and having been freed from sin, you became slaves of righteousness." [24]

This new position in Christ comes with new responsibilities that God oversees. The writer of Hebrews expresses this oversite this way, "You have not yet resisted to the point of shedding blood in your striving against sin; and you have forgotten the exhortation which is addressed to you as sons,

> *'My son, do not regard lightly the discipline of the Lord,*
> *Nor faint when you are reproved by Him;*
> *For those whom the Lord loves He disciplines,*
> *And He scourges every son whom He receives.'*

It is for discipline that you endure; God deals with you as with sons; for what son is there whom his father does not discipline? But if you are without discipline, of which all have become partakers, then you are illegitimate children and not sons." [25]

These are things to consider and aligns with the whole counsel of God.

> Personal Notes

---

[24] Rom. 6:15-18.
[25] Heb. 12:4-8.

Personal Notes

Eight

THE DOCTRINE OF THE CHURCH

INTRODUCTION

We will continue presenting biblical doctrine from a Biblicist perspective, not from any denominational viewpoint. This chapter presents what the Scriptures teach collectively on the subject of the church while following the Grammatical-Historical hermeneutical method of interpretation. It should be noted that some within the body of Christ interpret using an Allegorical method of interpretation, while others come from a traditional grammatical-historical perspective.

Therefore, we will provide what the Scriptures say, along with how various groups within the body of Christ have interpreted them. The chapter discussion notes will convey the author's opinion on any issue within this chapter.

THE CHURCH DEFINED

When we talk about how to define the church, we must start by putting aside our preconceived ideas of what the church is in our minds.

The concept of the church from a New Testament perspective is new. Not until Christ came into the world did we hear God's perspective on this concept.

From a word usage perspective, the concept of the church refers to an assembly of people and is used in both New and Old Testaments to portray a group of people assembling for various purposes. Milton S. Terry (Th.D.) expands on this thought by writing,

Take, for example, that commonly occurring New Testament word ἐκκλησία, commonly rendered church. Compounded of ἐκ, *out of*, and καλείν, to *call*, or summon, it was first used of an assembly of the citizens of a Greek community, summoned together by a crier, for the transaction of business pertaining to the public welfare.... The verb καλείν denotes that the assembly was legally called..., summoned for the purpose of deliberating in lawful conclave... the Septuagint translators generally render קהל by ἐκκλησία, and thus by an obvious process, ἐκκλησία came to represent among the Hellenists the Old Testament concept of "the congregation of the people of Israel," as usually denoted by the Hebrew word קהל. Hence it was natural for Steven to speak of the congregation of Israel, which Moses led out of Egypt, as "the ἐκκλησία in the wilderness" (Acts vii, 38), and equally natural for the word to become the common designation of the Christian community of converts from Judaism and the world. Into this New Testament sense of the world, it was also important that the full force of ἐκ and καλείν (κλήσις, κλητός) should continue. [1]

THE CHURCH ESTABLISHED

The concept of the church, from a New Testament perspective, should derive its intended meaning from Christ and the Apostle's teachings on this topic to obtain a more complete picture.

Jesus pronounces the following in Matthew 16:18, "And I also say to you that you are Peter, and upon this rock I will build My church; and the gates of Hades shall not overpower it." Jesus' next comments are directed to his disciples after they came to him with a question about who is the greatest in the kingdom of heaven. Toward the end of Jesus' comments, he says, "And if your brother sins, go and reprove him in private; if he listens to you, you have won your brother. But if he does

---

[1] Milton S. Terry, *Biblical Hermeneutics* (New York: Eaton & Mains, 1890), 74-75.

THE DOCTRINE OF THE CHURCH | 161

not listen to you, take one or two more with you, so that by the mouth of two or three witnesses every fact may be confirmed. And if he refuses to listen to them, tell it to the church; and if he refuses to listen even to the church, let him be to you as a Gentile and a tax-gatherer." [2]

Within these passages, Jesus not only established a new concept of the church; He also issued his first commandment regarding church discipline that correlates with the follow-up teaching from the Apostle Paul found in First Timothy 5:19-21, which reads, "Do not receive an accusation against an elder except on the basis of two or three witnesses. Those who continue in sin, rebuke in the presence of all, so that the rest also may be fearful of sinning. I solemnly charge you in the presence of God and of Christ Jesus and of His chosen angels, to maintain these principles without bias, doing nothing in a spirit of partiality."

Other related passages on church discipline can be found in First Corinthians Chapter 5 and First Timothy 1:18-20.

THE TERM CHURCH DEFINED AS THE BODY

Jesus established a new concept called the church that was later defined by the Apostle Paul this way,

> Now I rejoice in my sufferings for your sake, and in my flesh I do my share on behalf of His body (which is the church) in filling up that which is lacking in Christ's afflictions. Of this church I was made a minister according to the stewardship from God bestowed on me for your benefit, that I might fully carry out the preaching of the word of God, that is, the mystery which has been hidden from the past ages and generations; but has now been manifested to His saints, to whom God willed to make known what is the riches of the glory of this mystery among the Gentiles, which is Christ in you, the hope of glory.[3]

---

[2] Matt. 18:15-18.
[3] Col. 1:24-27.

Through Paul's explanation, we base the church Christ established on the concept of "Christ in you, the hope of glory." Paul reinforces this concept in Ephesians 3:1-13 by expressing Christ's church as a *mystery*.

> For this reason I, Paul, the prisoner of Christ Jesus for the sake of you Gentiles—if indeed you have heard of the stewardship of God's grace which was given to me for you; that by revelation there was made known to me the mystery, as I wrote before in brief. And by referring to this, when you read you can understand my insight into the mystery of Christ, which in other generations was not made known to the sons of men, as it has now been revealed to His holy apostles and prophets in the Spirit; to be specific, that the Gentiles are fellow heirs and fellow members of the body, and fellow partakers of the promise in Christ Jesus through the gospel, of which I was made a minister, according to the gift of God's grace which was given to me according to the working of His power. To me, the very least of all saints, this grace was given, to preach to the Gentiles the unfathomable riches of Christ, and to bring to light what is the administration of the mystery which for ages has been hidden in God, who created all things; in order that the manifold wisdom of God might now be made known through the church to the rulers and the authorities in the heavenly places. This was in accordance with the eternal purpose which He carried out in Christ Jesus our Lord, in whom we have boldness and confident access through faith in Him. Therefore I ask you not to lose heart at my tribulations on your behalf, for they are your glory.

THE BODY DEFINED AS MANY MEMBERS

We define the church as the *body of Christ*. The Apostle Paul continues his teaching as he explains how the *body* and the *church* are the same entity. First Corinthians 12:12-31 reads,

For by one Spirit we were all baptized into one body, whether Jews or Greeks, whether slaves or free, and we were all made to drink of one Spirit. For the body is not one member, but many. If the foot should say, 'Because I am not a hand, I am not a part of the body,' it is not for this reason any the less a part of the body. And if the ear should say, 'Because I am not an eye, I am not a part of the body,' it is not for this reason any the less a part of the body. If the whole body were an eye, where would the hearing be? If the whole were hearing, where would the sense of smell be? But now God has placed the members, each one of them, in the body, just as He desired. And if they were all one member, where would the body be? But now there are many members, but one body. And the eye cannot say to the hand, 'I have no need of you;' or again the head to the feet, 'I have no need of you.' On the contrary, it is much truer that the members of the body which seem to be weaker are necessary; and those members of the body, which we deem less honorable, on these we bestow more abundant honor, and our unseemly members come to have more abundant seemliness, whereas our seemly members have no need of it. But God has so composed the body, giving more abundant honor to that member which lacked, that there should be no division in the body, but that the members should have the same care for one another. And if one member suffers, all the members suffer with it; if one member is honored, all the members rejoice with it. Now you are Christ's body, and individually members of it. And God has appointed in the church, first apostles, second prophets, third teachers, then miracles, then gifts of healings, helps, administrations, various kinds of tongues. All are not apostles, are they? All are not prophets, are they? All are not teachers, are they? All are not workers of miracles, are they? All do not have gifts of healings, do they? All do not speak with tongues, do they? All do not interpret, do they? But earnestly desire the greater gifts.

To summarize, Christ established this new entity called the *Church*, now referenced as the *body of Christ* or the *body*. The *body* is represented by all saved individuals baptized by the Holy Spirit into this *body*, making individual believers members of the *body of Christ*, of which Christ is the head (1 Corinthians 12:12; Colossians 1:18).

THE UNIVERSAL CHURCH

When we speak about the universal church, we are speaking about the *body of Christ* worldwide. As expressed in the summary of our last segment, this body, consisting of individual members baptized by the Holy Spirit, makes up the universal church.

The term *universal church* is used to distinguish the difference between a worldwide universal church and a New Testament local church. The universal church comprises all born-again believers (John 3:3).

This teaching means the first-century church was represented as a single church body, unified by the Holy Spirit and under the apostles' leadership as they were guided by the Holy Spirit.

As time passed, the Scriptures were completed, replacing the now-deceased apostles, who were inspired by the Holy Spirit to write God's words to his church and the world, providing sound doctrine, instructions, and guidance to the church regarding how it should move forward. Church history reflects how the single first-century church changed from a universal church into the many groups represented within the *body of Christ* of today. These groups are represented by the Eastern and Western local Churches around the world and are comprised mainly of the Eastern Orthodox, Catholic, and Protestant groups.

Religious cults are not considered part of the *body of Christ* because they deny the biblical doctrine that God is triune in nature and that Jesus Christ shares in the same nature as God the Father and God the Holy Spirit. They deny the virgin birth of Christ, as a result of the work of the Holy Spirit. The top three groups placed under this category would be Mormons, Jehovah Witnesses, and Christian Science (see 1 John 2:18-23, 4:1-3, 5:20; 2 John 7-9) [4]

The vast majority of today's Christian local churches accept in principle the statement of the Nicene/Constantinople Creed of A.D. 381, which affirms the teaching of a triune God and that Christ is equal in nature with his Father, and not as a created being.

The Scriptures have always taught the concept of a local church, but over time this understanding has become more complicated, thus requiring additional explanation.

THE NEW TESTAMENT LOCAL CHURCH

We base the concept of a local church in the New Testament, where it expresses groups of believers coming together in various sizes and differing places. The church was formed and empowered in the city of Jerusalem on the day of Pentecost (Acts 2:1-4). It was to fellowship, to be taught by the apostles, to break bread—sharing the Lord's Supper—and to prayer (Acts 2:42). From the beginning, the church was persecuted by Jewish authorities led by Saul of Tarsus, resulting in some members fleeing from the city of Jerusalem (Acts 8:1-4).

Saul's conversion to Christianity (Acts 9:1-19) began a great missionary movement that went on to spread the gospel of Jesus Christ around the known world. Saul took on his gentile name of Paul (Acts 13:9), then became an apostle who was personally taught by Christ (Galatians 1:11-18) and sent out to be a missionary to the Gentile world (Acts 9:15).

Christianity, a new religious sect, went pretty much unnoticed by the Roman government until the days of Nero (A.D. 54-68). According to Tacitus—a Roman senator and historian, following the burning of Rome in A.D. 64, Nero blamed the Christians. Roland Bainton writes, "But what is meant by saying that they were convicted of *odium humani*

---

[4] For further research on this subject read Walter Martin, *The Kingdom of the Cults: The Definitive Work on the Subject,* 6th Edition (Minneapolis: Bethany House Publishers, 2019).

generis, hatred of the human race? With the emergence of Christianity in the pagan world, two intensely religious cultures came in conflict." [5]

It was during this time in history that the church responded to this intense persecution by spreading out among the gentile world, forming numerous local churches, as the Scriptures informs us of the many groups and locations of their existence. (see 1 Corinthians 1:1-3; Romans 16:1-15, and Acts 13:1-3)

To summarize this history, we can see that the first-century universal church became divided into smaller individual churches, all under the teaching and authority of the apostles. This apostolic authority was then transferred into the written format of the Scriptures (the Bible). From a Roman Catholic perspective, the apostolic authority of the first-century church was transferred to the Pope [6] through the verbal and traditional teachings of the Apostles, alongside the Catholic canon of the Scriptures. During the start of the Reformation in A.D. 1517, Martin Luther (a German Catholic theologian) showed through his interpretation of the Scriptures where he believed Papal authority lied concerning faith and practice in the Christian life. We find his conclusions in the sola statements from which came the teaching of *Sola Scriptura*, Latin for "by Scripture alone." This teaching was one of many dividing points between the Roman Catholic Church and the Protestant movement that resulted in the starting of numerous denominations represented by New Testament local churches.

THE PURPOSE OF THE CHURCH

The Scriptures seem to imply several purposes behind the message of the universal church, which should be the same message for all local New Testament churches.

---

[5] Roland H. Bainton, *Christendom: A Short History of Christianity and Its Impact on Western Civilization*, vol 1 (New York: Harper & Row Publishers, 1966), 52.

[6] *The Catholic Encyclopedia*, vol. 1, "Apostolic Succession," by Wilhelm, Joseph (New York: Robert Appleton Company, 1907.) 26 Apr. 2010 http://www.newadvent.org/cathen/01641a.htm

THE DOCTRINE OF THE CHURCH | 167

Matthew 28:18-20 reads, "And Jesus came up and spoke to them, saying, 'All authority has been given to Me in heaven and on earth. Go therefore and make disciples of all the nations, baptizing them in the name of the Father and the Son and the Holy Spirit, teaching them to observe all that I commanded you; and lo, I am with you always, even to the end of the age.'"

Here we see the first purpose of the church, to make disciples of Christ, baptizing them in the name of the Holy Trinity.

First Timothy 3:14-15 reads, "I am writing these things to you, hoping to come to you before long; but in case I am delayed, I write so that you may know how one ought to conduct himself in the household of God, which is the church of the living God, the pillar and support of the truth." Within this passage, we learn that the church should be the *pillar* and *support* of the truth. Jesus defines truth through his prayer recorded in John 17:17. "Sanctify them in the truth; Thy word is truth." Jesus' prayer supports the Psalmists words who wrote, "The sum of Thy word is truth, And every one of Thy righteous ordinances is everlasting." [7]

Truth is defined as the Word of God, which the church should be defending in the world. Here we find the Apostle Paul defining another concept that the church should be embracing; that the word of God and truth are synonymous.

To summarize, the church is to make disciples of Christ, baptizing them while supporting the Word of God as truth in the world. This is the true mission of the church; resulting in loving, caring people who are working in the world, performing good works toward humanity at God's direction for His glory and honor (Matthew 5:16; 1 Timothy 6:18-19).

ORDINANCES OF THE CHURCH

Protestant churches observe two ordinances, defined as an act of obedience to Christ's command. Matthew 28:18-20 reflects Christ's commandment to baptize all believers in the name of the Holy Trinity

---

[7] Ps. 119:160.

(Father, Son, and Holy Spirit). And second, to observe Christ's instructions to observe the Lord's table or serve communion among the believing church (Luke 22:19).

The Eastern Orthodox and Catholic groups observe sacraments, defined as "... outward signs of inward grace, instituted by Christ for our sanctification (Catechismus council. Trident., n. 4, ex St. Augustine, 'De Catechizandis rudibus')." [8] Daniel Kennedy expresses the Catholic position on sacraments this way:

> Almighty God can and does give grace to men in answer to their internal aspirations and prayers without the use of any external sign or ceremony. This will always be possible, because God, grace, and the soul are spiritual beings. God is not restricted to the use of material, visible symbols in dealing with men; the sacraments are not necessary in the sense that they could not have been dispensed with. But, if it is known that God has appointed external, visible ceremonies as the means by which certain graces are to be conferred on men, then in order to obtain those graces it will be necessary for men to make use of those Divinely appointed means. This truth theologians express by saying that the sacraments are necessary, not absolutely but only hypothetically, i.e., in the supposition that if we wish to obtain a certain supernatural end we must use the supernatural means appointed for obtaining that end. In this sense the Council of Trent (Sess. VII, can. 4) declared heretical those who assert that the sacraments of the New Law are superfluous and not necessary, although all are not necessary for each individual. It is the teaching of the Catholic Church and of Christians in general that, whilst God was nowise bound to make use of external ceremonies as symbols of things spiritual and sacred, it has pleased Him to do so, and this is the ordinary and most suitable manner of dealing

---

[8] *The Catholic Encyclopedia*, vol. 13, s.v. "Sacraments," by Daniel Kennedy (New York: Robert Appleton Company, 1912) April 26, 2010 from New Advent: http://www.newadvent.org/cathen/13295a.htm

with men. Writers on the sacraments refer to this as the *necessitas convenientiae*, the necessity of suitableness. It is not really a necessity, but the most appropriate manner of dealing with creatures that are at the same time spiritual and corporeal. In this assertion all Christians are united: it is only when we come to consider the nature of the sacramental signs that Protestants (except some Anglicans) differ from Catholics. [9]

The Catholic Church recognizes seven sacraments: baptism, confirmation, holy communion, confession, marriage, holy orders, and the anointing of the sick.

As noted by the above article, Protestants differ on this point regarding the very nature of the sacraments listed. Protestants practice confession by serving as their own priests before God (1 Peter 2:4-10), marriage is per the instruction given by God (Genesis 2:22-24), and anointing of oil on the sick as instructed by the Apostles (James 5:14). It is the nature of salvation to come through repentance toward God and faith in Jesus Christ (Acts 20:21).

Salvation is not a sanctification process through which humanity earns additional grace to gain or maintain access to the kingdom of God, instead, it is a gift granted by God through the sacrificial death of Jesus Christ on a Roman cross. This makes salvation not a work of grace through a progressive sanctification process, but a one-time work of grace through the life of Jesus Christ alone. As the writer of Hebrews tells us, Christ's death on the cross was a one-time sanctification event and not part of a progressive sanctification process. (see Hebrews 10:10-18)

This was the key difference between Protestant and Catholic doctrine on the issue of Christ's sacrifice on the cross and the way of salvation being progressive in nature. At the council of Trent (A.D. 1545-1563) the following line of reasoning concerning (faith) in Christ's sacrifice on the cross was adopted. "At the same time, it does not at once blot out individual sin, but only procures the means thereto, and these

---

[9] *The Catholic Encyclopedia*, vol. 13, s.v. "Sacraments," by Daniel Kennedy.

means are not restricted only to the predestined or to the faithful, but extend to all men (1 John 2:2; 1 Timothy 2:1-4)." [10]

Within the context of this statement, under the Catholic doctrine of the sixteenth-century faith alone is not sufficient for salvation, but a necessary starting point for salvation to take place, with the exception of dying declarations of faith.

This position changed in the twentieth century with the *Joint Declaration on the Doctrine of Justification* on October 31, 1999, between the Roman Catholic Church and the Lutheran World Federation. Their newly formed agreement on the issue of (faith) reads in part,

> [3.15] In faith we together hold the conviction that justification is the work of the triune God. The Father sent his Son into the world to save sinners. The foundation and presupposition of justification is the incarnation, death, and resurrection of Christ. Justification thus means that Christ himself is our righteousness, in which we share through the Holy Spirit in accord with the will of the Father. Together we confess: By grace alone, in faith in Christ's saving work and not because of any merit on our part, we are accepted by God and receive the Holy Spirit, who renews our hearts while equipping and calling us to good works. [11] [11]

Though it is true that there now seems to be an agreement on the careful wording and concept of justification, the agreement does not settle fundamental ideas on how that works out in one's salvation. It

---

[10] *The Catholic Encyclopedia*, vol. 6, s.v. "Sanctifying Grace," by Joseph Pohle, (New York: Robert Appleton Company, 1909.) April 26, 2010 http://www.newadvent.org/ cathen/ 06701a.htm.

[11] JOINT DECLARATION ON THE DOCTRINE OF JUSTIFICATION, by the Lutheran World Federation and the Catholic Church [document on-line]; available from http://www.vatican.va/roman_curia/pontifical_councils/chrstuni/documents/rc_pc_chrstuni_doc_31101999_cath-luth-joint-declaration_en.html; Internet; accessed 18 October 2020.

THE DOCTRINE OF THE CHURCH | 171

continues to be the Catholic position that (faith) in Christ is proven out through one's works.

> [4.30] Catholics hold that the grace of Jesus Christ imparted in baptism takes away all that is sin "in the proper sense" and that is "worthy of damnation" (Rom 8:1). [16] There does, however, remain in the person an inclination (concupiscence) which comes from sin and presses toward sin. Since, according to Catholic conviction, human sins always involve a personal element and since this element is lacking in this inclination, Catholics do not see this inclination as sin in an authentic sense. They do not thereby deny that this inclination does not correspond to God's original design for humanity and that it is objectively in contradiction to God and remains one's enemy in lifelong struggle. Grateful for deliverance by Christ, they underscore that this inclination in contradiction to God does not merit the punishment of eternal death [17] and does not separate the justified person from God. But when individuals voluntarily separate themselves from God, it is not enough to return to observing the commandments, for they must receive pardon and peace in the Sacrament of Reconciliation through the word of forgiveness imparted to them in virtue of God's reconciling work in Christ. [See Sources for section 4.4]. [12]

The Catholic position seems to be rooted in the concept of James 2:14-26 which states in part, "What use is it, my brethren, if a man says he has faith, but he has no works? Can that faith save him? If a brother or sister is without clothing and in need of daily food, and one of you says to them, 'Go in peace, be warmed and be filled,' and yet you do not give them what is necessary for their body, what use is that? Even so faith, if it has no works, is dead, being by itself. But someone may

---

[12] JOINT DECLARATION ON THE DOCTRINE OF JUSTIFICATION, by the Lutheran World Federation and the Catholic Church.

well say, 'You have faith, and I have works; show me your faith without the works, and I will show you my faith by my works.'"

This concept of faith and works then becomes attached to the Catholic sacraments as a practice of good works.

This stands in stark contrast to the Protestant position found in Ephesians 2:8-10 which reads, "For by grace you have been saved through faith; and that not of yourselves, it is the gift of God; not as a result of works, that no one should boast. For we are His workmanship, created in Christ Jesus for good works, which God prepared beforehand, that we should walk in them."

The key to this debate is found in the balance of interpreting the Scriptures, by following the only rule of interpretation within this volume, "There are no contradictions in Scripture, for biblical truth to be true, it must agree with all other biblical truths." With this in mind, we can hold to the Protestant's belief in *Sola Fide*, Latin meaning, "by faith alone," as supported through the teaching of the Apostle Paul in Ephesians 2:8-9. We are then instructed by Christ and the Apostle Paul, to do good works, as a product of our faith, which James emphasizes as something we should be practicing every day (Matthew 5:16; 1 Timothy 6:18-19).

Thus, salvation is through faith alone, in Christ alone, and not by any form of works or faith-based actions such as baptism or joining the local church.

Although the changed Catholic position would agree with this in a technical sense, based on their understanding of sin and how that works concerning human nature and the salvation process, there remains a work element in their teaching on the doctrine of eternal security.

It should be noted that while some Protestant churches disagree on the observance of sacraments, they do agree with the Catholic line of thinking on maintaining their salvation through the actions of good works, which is contrary to Christ's teaching and proper scriptural interpretation of the doctrine of eternal security. (see John 6:37-40; Ephesians 1:13, 4:30)

The Apostle Paul argues against this very point as he warns,

> You foolish Galatians, who has bewitched you, before whose eyes Jesus Christ was publicly portrayed as crucified? This is the only thing I want to find out from you: did you receive the Spirit by the works of the Law, or by hearing with faith? Are you so foolish? Having begun by the Spirit, are you now being perfected by the flesh? Did you suffer so many things in vain—if indeed it was in vain? Does He then, who provides you with the Spirit and works miracles among you, do it by the works of the Law, or by hearing with faith? Even so Abraham believed God, and it was reckoned to him as righteousness. Therefore, be sure that it is those who are of faith who are sons of Abraham. And the Scripture, foreseeing that God would justify the Gentiles by faith, preached the gospel beforehand to Abraham, saying, 'All the nations shall be blessed in you.' So then those who are of faith are blessed with Abraham, the believer. For as many as are of the works of the Law are under a curse; for it is written, 'Cursed is everyone who does not abide by all things written in the book of the law, to perform them.' Now that no one is justified by the Law before God is evident; for, 'The righteous man shall live by faith.' However, the Law is not of faith; on the contrary, 'He who practices them shall live by them.' Christ redeemed us from the curse of the Law, having become a curse for us—for it is written, 'Cursed is everyone who hangs on a tree'—in order that in Christ Jesus the blessing of Abraham might come to the Gentiles, so that we might receive the promise of the Spirit through faith. [13]

Here Paul is arguing that salvation is by faith alone, not by works or observing the Law. The historical context of Paul's writings and primary audience are messianic Jews who were saved through faith but began drifting back to their old belief system of being under the Old Testament Law. This is similar to those today who believe they must

---

[13] Gal. 3:1-14.

maintain their salvation through continuous obedience to the Word through the observance of the sacraments, or proving one's salvation through good works.

The Apostle's exhortation is that since we are saved by faith, works demonstrated through obedience to the Law or any part of the Scriptures do not affect our salvation status.

James' exhortation is emphasizing that we demonstrate our salvation through good works we do in the name of Christ; not to maintain our salvation but as evidence of our salvation. Jesus said, "Even so, every good tree bears good fruit; but the bad tree bears bad fruit. A good tree cannot produce bad fruit, nor can a bad tree produce good fruit. Every tree that does not bear good fruit is cut down and thrown into the fire. So then, you will know them by their fruits." [14]

James supports Christ's teaching through his point about faith and works (James 2:17-18), but we should remember that salvation is not secured through our efforts, but in Christ's efforts alone. Otherwise, as Paul expresses it, we make Christ's sacrifice pointless (Romans 4:14; 6:15-18).

CHURCH POLITY

Church polity is a branch within ecclesiology (the study of the church) that addresses the understanding behind the governance and hierarchal structure of the church.

TYPES OF LOCAL CHURCH GOVERNMENT

Episcopal—Is the polity of Eastern Orthodox, Coptic, Roman Catholic, Anglican, Methodist, and (some) Lutheran Churches. [15]

> The episcopal form of government has been the polity of the Church catholic as early as Ignatius of Antioch, all the way

---

[14] Matthew 7:17-20

[15] Theopedia, s.v. "Church Government," [online encyclopedia]; available from https://www.theopedia.com/church-government; Internet; accessed 27 August 2020.

down to the time of the Reformation. Advocates for an episcopal form of church government argue that the sheer fact that it went virtually uncontested until the time of the Reformation testifies to its claims of apostolicity, although not all contemporary episcopalian apologists argue from history rather than Scripture. A notable example is Ray Sutton, the Suffragan Bishop in the Diocese of Mid-America of the Reformed Episcopal Church, who has produced work arguing that the episcopal system is biblical. [16]

Presbyterian—This is a polity practiced in Presbyterian and Reformed churches with its church government commonly described as *Elder-run* or *Presbyter-run*.

"Typically, original authority—that is the authority that the church believes Christ gave to it—is said to reside at the local elder level in this model of polity. Thus the 'highest' authority in a Presbyterian or Reformed church (after Christ) is said to be the Elders of the church. Those elders are typically elected by the congregation on a periodic basis (usually a term lasts about 3 years). Sometimes elders are elected by the drawing of lots." [17]

Congregational—A polity that draws its independent governance from local congregations versus the authority and control of other religious bodies. "Paige Patterson has summarized congregational polity as follows: The Oxford Dictionary of the Christian Church defines 'congregationalism' as 'that form of Church polity which rests on the independence and autonomy of each local church.' According to this source, the principles of democracy in church government rest on the belief that Christ is the sole head of his church, the members are all

---

[16] Theopedia, s.v. "Church Government," [online encyclopedia]; available from https://www.theopedia.com/church-government.
[17] Ibid.

priests unto God, and these units are regarded each as an outcrop and representative of the church universal." [18]

BIBLICAL OFFICES OF CHURCH LEADERSHIP

The Greek word ἐπισκοπή (episcope) has been translated in the King James Bible as *bishop*, while the New American Standard Bible translates the word as *overseer*. When evaluating this office, we find that the term *bishop* is not used when speaking to appointments to these positions worldwide. Because of this, it would seem reasonable to say that the term *overseer* (elder) is a better interpretation of this word in the context of its usage.

This assessment is supported by Hubert Ahaus, who writes, "The union between bishops and presbyters [elders] was close, and the names remained interchangeable long after the distinction between presbyters and bishops was commonly recognized, e.g., in Irenaeus, Against Heresies IV.26.2. Hence it would seem that already, in the New Testament, we find, obscurely no doubt, the same ministry which appeared so distinctly afterwards." [19]

The qualifications to the office of *overseer* are explained in First Timothy 3:1-7, which reads,

> It is a trustworthy statement: if any man aspires to the office of overseer, it is a fine work he desires to do. An overseer, then, must be above reproach, the husband of one wife, temperate, prudent, respectable, hospitable, able to teach, not addicted to wine or pugnacious, but gentle, uncontentious, free from the love of money. He must be one who manages his own household well, keeping his children under control with all dignity (but if a man does not know how to manage his

---

[18] Theopedia, s.v. "Church Government," [online encyclopedia]; available from https://www.theopedia.com/church-government.

[19] *The Catholic Encyclopedia*, vol. 11, "Holy Orders," by Hubert Ahaus (New York: Robert Appleton Company, 1911.) 26 Apr. 2010 http://www.newadvent.org/cathen/11279a.htm.

own household, how will he take care of the church of God?); and not a new convert, lest he become conceited and fall into the condemnation incurred by the devil. And he must have a good reputation with those outside the church, so that he may not fall into reproach and the snare of the devil.

Within the context of this passage, it appears that the *overseer* is one who oversees the affairs of the local church; a person who is put in charge of an organized local church. When we read other Scriptures on this subject, they provide a more detailed description. Titus 1:5-9 is such an example.

> For this reason I left you in Crete, that you might set in order what remains, and appoint elders in every city as I directed you, namely, if any man be above reproach, the husband of one wife, having children who believe, not accused of dissipation or rebellion. For the overseer must be above reproach as God's steward, not self-willed, not quick-tempered, not addicted to wine, not pugnacious, not fond of sordid gain, but hospitable, loving what is good, sensible, just, devout, self-controlled, holding fast the faithful word which is in accordance with the teaching, that he may be able both to exhort in sound doctrine and to refute those who contradict.

Within this passage, we see the roles of elder and overseer expressed as being equal in both requirements and function. Because of this, it would be reasonable to assume that both titles represent the same offices. This passage seems to suggest that the elders need to have an ability to exhort and know what the Scriptures teach so they can defend or refute wrong teachings by others within and without the local church.

First Timothy 5:17-19 provides further details about this role as we read, "Let the elders who rule well be considered worthy of double honor, especially those who work hard at preaching and teaching. For the Scripture says, 'You shall not muzzle the ox while he is threshing,' and 'The laborer is worthy of his wages.' Do not receive an accusation against an elder except on the basis of two or three witnesses."

Through the expanded details of this passage, we can conclude that although not all elders must be preachers, they all must be knowledgeable of the Scriptures to the point of being able to recognize false teachers and doctrine in their midst. It also suggests that those elders who take on the role of teacher and preacher are worthy of being paid or compensated for their time in the study and delivery of these areas.

This brings us to the question of other terms used within the church that represent leadership roles. The dictionary definition for pastor means overseer or can mean herdsman. The Apostles Paul and Peter referred to the office of overseer or elder, as ones that should shepherd the church, thus the term pastor became another term for overseer or elder. (Acts 20:17, 28; 1 Peter 5:1-2)

Historically, "It is clear from Ignatius' letters that John's church leaders did not have the same roles as Paul and Peter's church leaders. Antioch, Ignatius' home church, and the churches to whom Ignatius wrote (except Rome, which both Paul and Peter helped establish) each had one overseer and multiple elders. Their elders were not all bishops. Only one church leader was the overseer.

By the mid-2nd century or so, it seems clear that every well-organized church functioned this way, and almost all Christian writers of the 2nd century and later seem to have forgotten that there was ever a time when churches had multiple overseers." [20]

We later learn that by the third century, as the Scriptures were being translated into Latin, the Latin term for *elder* could also be interpreted to mean *priest*, which then interjected a new concept into church history. [21]

For additional information on the history behind church leadership and their offices, refer to footnote 20.

The Scriptures provide the church guidance regarding what is expected of its leaders and how the church can fill its leadership roles under a local church polity.

---

[20] Paul Pavao, "Bishops, Elders, Pastors in Scripture and History," [article online]; available from https://www.christian-history.org/bishops-elders-pastors.html; Internet; Accessed 11 December 2020.

[21] Ibid.

A second office spoken of in the Scriptures is that of a *Deacon*. We find the details and qualifications of this office in First Timothy 3:8-13.

> Deacons likewise must be men of dignity, not double-tongued, or addicted to much wine or fond of sordid gain, but holding to the mystery of the faith with a clear conscience. And let these also first be tested; then let them serve as deacons if they are beyond reproach. Women must likewise be dignified, not malicious gossips, but temperate, faithful in all things. Let deacons be husbands of only one wife, and good managers of their children and their own households. For those who have served well as deacons obtain for themselves a high standing and great confidence in the faith that is in Christ Jesus.

Paul presents the office of Deacon as being separate in terms of function, but similar in its moral character requirements of elders. Paul affirms there are two offices in the local church through his address to the church at Philippi, as he writes, "Paul and Timothy, bond-servants of Christ Jesus, to all the saints in Christ Jesus who are in Philippi, including the overseers and deacons: Grace to you and peace from God our Father and the Lord Jesus Christ." [22]

The church has used Acts 6:2-6 to express the role of the deacon, as we read here:

> And the twelve summoned the congregation of the disciples and said, 'It is not desirable for us to neglect the word of God in order to serve tables. But select from among you, brethren, seven men of good reputation, full of the Spirit and of wisdom, whom we may put in charge of this task. But we will devote ourselves to prayer, and to the ministry of the word.' And the statement found approval with the whole congregation; and they chose Stephen, a man full of faith and of

---

[22] Phil. 1:1-2.

the Holy Spirit, and Philip, Prochorus, Nicanor, Timon, Parmenas and Nicolas, a proselyte from Antioch. And these they brought before the apostles; and after praying, they laid their hands on them.

As expressed here, the deacon's role was not to minister through the study and teaching of the word; but to serve the church through other duties that the elders did not have time for. Within today's culture that would include administrative duties such as overseeing building maintenance, caring for legal issues, finances, and for the needs of widows indeed, among many other things the local church needs outside the duties of the elders.

To summarize these biblical concepts, the elders are to care for the spiritual affairs of the local church, while the deacons care for the church's physical needs. Together, they form a team that allows the local church to function for the benefit of the whole body attending the local church. We then plug these understandings into local church polity to form church governing bodies for the benefit of *the body of Christ* as a whole.

Local Church Membership

As reflected earlier in this chapter, membership into the universal church (the body of Christ) is based on individual acts of repentance and faith toward God, who grants access into his *body*.

Local Church membership works a little differently. Every local body has a particular process for granting membership status. This could involve a public confession of faith, baptism, personal interview process, new member classes, signing of documents, or any combination of these and more.

We should note that to gain membership into a local New Testament church being born-again (John 3:3) is still a requirement, but this membership is a human process and based on an honor system, relying on the integrity of one's testimony of spiritual conversion. Personal testimonies can be fabricated for various reasons outside of personal faith, such as the need to belong to something, emotional support, the desire to do the right thing, or less honorable reasons such as infiltrating a local entity for the express purpose of harming the *body of Christ*. Jesus warned, "Not everyone who says to Me, 'Lord, Lord,' will enter the kingdom of heaven; but he who does the will of My Father who is in heaven. Many will say to Me on that day, 'Lord, Lord, did we not prophesy in Your name, and in Your name cast out demons, and in Your name perform many miracles?' And then I will declare to them, 'I never knew you; depart from Me, you who practice lawlessness.'" [23]

The Apostle Paul warned the first-century church to, "Be on guard for yourselves and for all the flock, among which the Holy Spirit has made you overseers, to shepherd the church of God which He purchased with His own blood. I know that after my departure savage wolves will come in among you, not sparing the flock; and from among your own selves men will arise, speaking perverse things, to draw away the disciples after them." [24]

Within these statements, we know that not everyone who attends or is a member of a local church is a Christian or belongs to the *body of Christ*. Therefore, we should understand that all Christians are in a constant state of spiritual warfare at every level of life. The Apostle Peter encourages us, as the *body of Christ* to move forward in the knowledge and practice of Godly living according to the Scriptures.

> Grace and peace be multiplied to you in the knowledge of God and of Jesus our Lord; seeing that His divine power has granted to us everything pertaining to life and godliness, through the true knowledge of Him who called us by His own glory and excellence. For by these He has granted to us His precious and magnificent promises, in order that by them you might become partakers of the divine nature, having escaped the corruption that is in the world by lust. Now for this very reason also, applying all diligence, in your faith supply moral excellence, and in your moral excellence, knowledge; and in your knowledge, self-control, and in your self-control,

---

[23] Matt. 7:21-23.
[24] Acts 20:28-30.

perseverance, and in your perseverance, godliness; and in your godliness, brotherly kindness, and in your brotherly kindness, love. For if these qualities are yours and are increasing, they render you neither useless nor unfruitful in the true knowledge of our Lord Jesus Christ. For he who lacks these qualities is blind or short-sighted, having forgotten his purification from his former sins. Therefore, brethren, be all the more diligent to make certain about His calling and choosing you; for as long as you practice these things, you will never stumble; for in this way the entrance into the eternal kingdom of our Lord and Savior Jesus Christ will be abundantly supplied to you. [25]

CHURCH CREEDS

Not all local churches observe or use early church creeds. Nevertheless, we shall talk about them for educational purposes while speaking to their significant nature.

Early in the life of Christ's church, attacks on church teachings arose including arguments over what they should consider to be the Word of God (the canon of Scripture) from other writings. By the fourth-century, Creeds were being formulated and agreed upon to bring unity among the scattered church around the known world, representing a unified front on major church teachings such as on the belief in a triune God and the deity and humanity of Jesus Christ. These two doctrines are essential to the Christian faith. Those denying such doctrines would be considered non-Christian; for without the acceptance of these two doctrines, one could never be born-again (John 3:1-18).

The following Creeds reaffirmed these two teachings and bring unified support and agreement among those holding to such doctrines within the church.

Nicaea Creed— First Ecumenical Council was held in A.D. 325, with 300 to 318 bishops in attendance from around Christendom in response

---

[25] 2 Peter 1:2-11.

to the heresy of Arius—the teaching of Arianism. With only five dissenters, later reduced to two, the council agreed to the following statement in opposition to the teaching of Arianism. [26]

> We believe in one God the Father Almighty, Maker of all things visible and invisible; and in one Lord Jesus Christ, the only begotten of the Father, that is, of the substance [ek tes ousias] of the Father, God of God, light of light, true God of true God, begotten not made, of the same substance with the Father [homoousion to patri], through whom all things were made both in heaven and on earth; who for us men and our salvation descended, was incarnate, and was made man, suffered and rose again the third day, ascended into heaven and cometh to judge the living and the dead. And in the Holy Ghost. Those who say: There was a time when He was not, and He was not before He was begotten; and that He was made out of nothing (ex ouk onton); or who maintain that He is of another hypostasis or another substance [than the Father], or that the Son of God is created, or mutable, or subject to change, [them] the Catholic Church anathematizes. [27]

The purpose of this creed was to affirm the church's position that God the Father and Jesus Christ (as God the Son) are one in nature, emphasizing that Christ was not created, but is eternal along with the Father.

Amplified Nicaea Creed—Was approved in an amplified form at the Council of Constantinople in A.D. 381. "It is the profession of the Christian Faith common to the Catholic Church, to all the Eastern Churches separated from Rome, and to most of the Protestant denominations.

---

[26] *The Catholic Encyclopedia*, vol. 11, s.v. "The First Council of Nicaea," by Henri Leclercq (New York: Robert Appleton Company, 1911.) 26 Apr. 2010 http://www.newadvent.org/ cathen/11044a.htm.
[27] Ibid.

The following is a literal translation of the Greek text of the Constantinopolitan form, the brackets indicating the words altered or added in the Western liturgical form in present use:" [28]

> We believe (I believe) in one God, the Father Almighty, maker of heaven and earth, and of all things visible and invisible. And in one Lord Jesus Christ, the only begotten Son of God, and born of the Father before all ages. (God of God) light of light, true God of true God. Begotten not made, consubstantial to the Father, by whom all things were made. Who for us men and for our salvation came down from heaven. And was incarnate of the Holy Ghost and of the Virgin Mary and was made man; was crucified also for us under Pontius Pilate, suffered and was buried; and the third day rose again according to the Scriptures. And ascended into heaven, sits at the right hand of the Father, and shall come again with glory to judge the living and the dead, of whose Kingdom there shall be no end. And (I believe) in the Holy Ghost, the Lord and Giver of life, who proceeds from the Father (and the Son), who together with the Father and the Son is to be adored and glorified, who spoke by the Prophets. And one holy, catholic, and apostolic Church. We confess (I confess) one baptism for the remission of sins. And we look for (I look for) the resurrection of the dead and the life of the world to come. Amen. [29]

Chalcedonian Creed—The Fourth Ecumenical Council was held in A.D. 451 at Chalcedon (a city of Bithynia in Asia Minor). The principal

---

[28] *The Catholic Encyclopedia*, vol. 11, s.v. "The Nicene Creed," by Joseph Wilhelm (New York: Robert Appleton Company, 1911.) 26 Apr. 2010 http://www.newadvent.org/cathen/ 11049a.htm.

[29] *The Catholic Encyclopedia*, vol. 11, s.v. "The Nicene Creed," by Joseph Wilhelm.

purpose was to assert church orthodox doctrine against the heresy of Eutyches and the Monophysites. [30]

"This Council of Chalcedon is the fourth of the seven ecumenical councils accepted by Eastern Orthodox, Catholic, and many Protestant Christian churches. It is the first Council not recognized by any of the Oriental Orthodox churches." [31] An English translation of the Chalcedonian Creed reads,

> We, then, following the holy Fathers, all with one consent, teach men to confess one and the same Son, our Lord Jesus Christ, the same perfect in Godhead and also perfect in manhood; truly God and truly man, of a reasonable [rational] soul and body; consubstantial [coessential] with the Father according to the Godhead, and consubstantial with us according to the Manhood; in all things like unto us, without sin; begotten before all ages of the Father according to the Godhead, and in these latter days, for us and for our salvation, born of the Virgin Mary, the Mother of God, according to the Manhood; one and the same Christ, Son, Lord, Only-begotten, to be acknowledged in two natures, in confusedly, unchangeably, indivisibly, inseparably; the distinction of natures being by no means taken away by the union, but rather the property of each nature being preserved, and concurring in one Person and one Subsistence, not parted or divided into two persons, but one and the same Son, and only begotten, God the Word, the Lord Jesus Christ, as the prophets from the beginning [have declared] concerning him, and the Lord Jesus Christ himself has

---

[30] *The Catholic Encyclopedia*, vol. 3, s.v. " Council of Chalcedon," by Francis Schaefer (New York: Robert Appleton Company, 1908.) 26 Apr. 2010 http://www.newadvent.org/cathen/03555a.htm

[31] *Theopedia*, s.v. "Chalcedonian Creed," [online encyclopedia]; available from https://www.theopedia.com/chalcedonian-creed; Internet; accessed 28 August 2020.

taught us, and the Creed of the holy Fathers has handed down to us. [32]

The Chalcedonian Creed defended the doctrinal teaching that Christ has two natures, a divine, and a human nature, supported through the Scriptures and taught by the Apostles (Luke 1:26-33; Hebrews 1:1-3).

To summarize this segment, we can say that the creeds spoken of here were universally accepted by the organized Christian church—worldwide regarding the theological concepts being dealt with. Whether or not everyone agrees with the exact wording of these creeds, we should not deny that the theological concepts addressed within them should be fully supported by the body of Christ as a whole.

Denying these theological concepts as untrue or unbiblical would be to deny the very foundational truths of the Scriptures concerning the *salvation* of humanity, and the fulfillment of the New Covenant, requiring an act of a triune God, and the fulfillment of Old Testament Prophecies that requires a suffering human Messiah—a God/Man by nature.

{ CHAPTER DISCUSSION NOTES }

What has been expressed throughout this chapter is defining what the church is, and how it should be biblically structured. The various interpretations of the Scriptures within the context of church history are complicated. Thus, the reason for not going into depth on any topic or heading. For proper support or defense on any issue could take another book on any given topic within this chapter.

---

[32] *Christian Classics Ethereal Library*, s.v. "Creeds of Christendom, with a History and Critical notes. Volume II. The History of Creeds," by Philip Schaff [book online]; available from https://www.ccel.org/ccel/schaff/creeds2.iv.i.iii.html; Internet; accessed 28 August 2020.

The goal behind this chapter was to present certain facts about the church and how it works, while providing foundational information that causes the reader to want to seek out additional information, thus coming to conclusions based on facts and the working of the Holy Spirit in the student's life.

> Personal Notes

Nine

THE DOCTRINE OF HEAVEN AND HELL

With Supplemental Discussions on Good and Evil

HEAVEN

Introduction

The biblical teaching on heaven and hell is rooted in the concepts of good and evil as related to God's Holiness. Therefore, this chapter will focus on the subjects of heaven and hell, good and evil.

Heaven's Existence

Does heaven exist or is it simply an idea of goodwill within the human experience? Jesus starts his ministry on earth by proclaiming the following message. "Repent, for the kingdom of heaven is at hand." [1] Jesus' statement reflects on the reality of something more than just the cosmos reflected by the vast expanse of space that we sometimes call the heavens. Jesus referred to this type of heaven by saying, "Heaven and earth will pass away, but My words will not pass away." [2] His comment about the earth with the surrounding cosmos, and stating it is more likely for them to become non-existent than the very words spoken by

---

[1] Matt. 3:2.
[2] Mark 13:31.

God, shows a difference between the concept of heaven based on morality and the heavens that surround the earth.

So, is there a real place connected to God called heaven? Matthew 6:9-10 reflects part of a prayer Jesus was teaching his disciples that helps provide an answer to this question. "… Our Father who art in heaven, Hallowed be Thy name. Thy kingdom come. Thy will be done, On earth as it is in heaven."

Here Jesus distinguishes the difference between a place called earth and a place called heaven. This concept can be seen throughout the gospels. The Apostle Paul expands on this concept when he told of an experience he had. "I know a man in Christ who fourteen years ago—whether in the body I do not know, or out of the body I do not know, God knows— such a man was caught up to the third heaven. And I know how such a man—whether in the body or apart from the body I do not know, God knows—was caught up into Paradise, and heard inexpressible words, which a man is not permitted to speak." [3]

Paul's testimony concerning this third heaven tied to spiritual things makes a distinction between a place called heaven and the cosmos. It is from this reality that the concept of the kingdom of heaven resides.

THE KINGDOM OF HEAVEN

The phrase *kingdom of heaven* was introduced to us by John the Baptist (Matthew 3:2) and is only translated this way in the gospel of Matthew, appearing 32 times throughout the book. Jesus continued this message throughout his ministry (see Matthew 4:17, 25:1).

Some theologians believe the phrase was introduced to indicate the beginning of the fulfillment of the Old Testament prophets, as illustrated in Daniel 7:13-14 [4] which reads, "I kept looking in the night

---

[3] 2 Cor. 12:2-4.

[4] *A commentary, critical and explanatory, on the Old and New Testaments*, vol. 2, "Matthew 3:2," by Rev. Robert Jamieson, Rev. A. R. Fausset and Rev. David Brown (New York: S.S. Scranton and company, 1873), 10; available from http://hdl.handle.net/2027/miun.ajg3934.0002.001; Internet; accessed 31 August 2020.

visions, And behold, with the clouds of heaven One like a Son of Man was coming, And He came up to the Ancient of Days And was presented before Him. And to Him was given dominion, Glory and a kingdom, That all the peoples, nations, and men of every language Might serve Him. His dominion is an everlasting dominion Which will not pass away; And His kingdom is one Which will not be destroyed."

This prophecy illustrates the concept of a coming kingdom that was first offered to the Nation of Israel. Following an official national rejection of Christ in Matthew Chapter 12, it was then offered to the gentile peoples of the world (Romans 11). This becomes more evident when we notice that after this happens, Christ begins speaking of the kingdom of God (Matthew 12:28) alongside the concept of the kingdom of heaven, following his rejection by Israel's leadership in chapter 12. This is also evident in the fact that the phrase the kingdom of heaven does not appear in the other three gospels. The reason for this is because the gospel of Matthew was strictly written to the Jewish nation with an emphasis on the coming Messiah who was going to bring in the promised earthly kingdom.

From this understanding, we can reason that the kingdom of heaven was not just a spiritual concept but also a physical concept representing a real place where God's heaven would be duplicated on earth.

This understanding of the kingdom of heaven fits the pattern of God's working in the world, as God worked with the prophet Moses when he established His tabernacle on earth, replicating the original tabernacle in heaven with God (see Exodus 25:8-9; Hebrews 8:1-7, 9:11-13).

Summarizing this point, the phrase the *kingdom of heaven* was used as a concept the Jewish nation would naturally associate with the prophesied promised coming kingdom. When Christ's offer was rejected, a transition to a different phrase (*the kingdom of God*) was used to represent the same concept used with the Jewish nation but is now for the benefit of the gentile world.

Within the reality of these phrases, we see demonstrated a real place called heaven not in obscurity, but out in the open for all to see and understand.

The New Heaven and New Earth

Revelation Chapter 21 speaks to the subject of a new heaven and a new earth. This concept deals more with God's physical creation than the heaven or spiritual attributes associated with God. The new heaven and new earth deal more with remaking the current creation, similar to what occurred in Genesis 1:1-2, which states, "In the beginning, God created the heavens and the earth. And the earth was formless and void...." Revelation 21:1-6 expresses this new makeover.

> And I saw a new heaven and a new earth; for the first heaven and the first earth passed away, and there is no longer any sea. And I saw the holy city, new Jerusalem, coming down out of heaven from God, made ready as a bride adorned for her husband. And I heard a loud voice from the throne, saying, 'Behold, the tabernacle of God is among men, and He shall dwell among them, and they shall be His people, and God Himself shall be among them, and He shall wipe away every tear from their eyes; and there shall no longer be any death; there shall no longer be any mourning, or crying, or pain; the first things have passed away.' And He who sits on the throne said, 'Behold, I am making all things new.' And He said, 'Write, for these words are faithful and true.' And He said to me, 'It is done. I am the Alpha and the Omega, the beginning and the end.'

As we close out this section on the topic of heaven, we can see through this passage that a literal kingdom will exist and represent what the prophets foretold. This reality is said to come out of heaven from God, reemphasizing there is a real place called heaven where God is said to reside (Isaiah 66:1-2), and that our heaven will be created by God here on a new earth, with Christ ruling on his throne forever (see Luke 1:31-33; 2 Samuel 7:13-17).

HELL

HELL AS A PLACE

The term *hell* is introduced to us by Christ through his sermon on the Mount, where he refers to it as a place of punishment (Matthew 5:22, 29-30). Jesus later expands on this concept by saying, "You have heard that the ancients were told, 'You shall not commit murder' and 'Whoever commits murder shall be liable to the court.' But I say to you that everyone who is angry with his brother shall be guilty before the court; and whoever shall say to his brother, 'Raca,' shall be guilty before the supreme court; and whoever shall say, 'You fool,' shall be guilty enough to go into the fiery hell." [5] Jesus speaks about *hell* as a literal place of punishment, and not through allegory to mean something else.

Toward the end of Jesus' life on earth, He engaged in the following conversation with the Jewish religious rulers of his day, "Consequently you bear witness against yourselves, that you are sons of those who murdered the prophets. Fill up then the measure of the guilt of your fathers. You serpents, you brood of vipers, how shall you escape the sentence of hell?"

Here Jesus references hell as being a place to which one is sentenced, similar to a lengthy prison term, only to find out later that the term of the sentence is forever.

The Apostle Peter writes, "For if God did not spare angels when they sinned, but cast them into hell and committed them to pits of darkness, reserved for judgment.... then the Lord knows how to rescue the godly from temptation, and to keep the unrighteous under punishment for the day of judgment...." [6]

Here we learn that hell was first created to be a holding place for fallen angels before their final judgment, but has since been expanded to include humanity. This leads us to the ultimate question, what is God's final judgment on all sinful creatures? The answer is given by the Apostle John in Revelation 20:14-15. "And death and Hades were

---

[5] Matt. 5:21-22.
[6] 2 Peter 2:4, 9.

thrown into the lake of fire. This is the second death, the lake of fire. And if anyone's name was not found written in the book of life, he was thrown into the lake of fire."

We are also told by John as he states, "And the devil who deceived them was thrown into the lake of fire and brimstone, where the beast and the false prophet are also; and they will be tormented day and night forever and ever." [7] Through John's writings, we learn that those in hell will later be transferred to a place called *the lake of fire,* similar to being transferred from jail to prison. As an extension of this understanding, we can say that *hell* is ultimately forever.

With regard to this subject called *hell*, Jesus provides us this instruction: "And do not fear those who kill the body, but are unable to kill the soul; but rather fear Him who is able to destroy both soul and body in hell." [8]

THE PLACE CALLED SHEOL

The Old Testament explains the concept of Sheol as being a place for the dead. Another way to express this concept is by saying all created life in the form of humans and angels is eternal. Each of these beings will eventually live eternally in heaven or hell.

Before Christ's death, burial, and resurrection, all those who physically died went to *Sheol* because Christ had not yet gone to Calvary. One part of *Sheol* consisted of paradise, a place of comfort while the other part was *hell,* a place of torment. The Scriptures also used other names for Sheol such as *the Pit,* from which came the metonymy — *the pit of hell,* and *hades* as referenced by Christ in Matthew 16:18 and used nine other times in the New Testament.

When Old Testament saints died, they went to paradise (Abraham's Bosom) part of Sheol. When the wicked die, they go to a different part of Sheol called hell. Thus, before the cross, following physical death, the souls of all beings still lived in Sheol. This is what Sheol is, a place of the dead—spiritually alive, but physically dead.

---

[7] Rev. 20:20.
[8] Matt. 10:28.

THE DOCTRINE OF HEAVEN AND HELL | 195

After the cross, the scriptures tell us that Christ went to Sheol and took all those in paradise with him to heaven while those in hell remain there to this day until they eventually face their final judgment where they will be sentenced to the lake of fire, known as the second and final death—a final eternal separation from God, where those *inmates* will live in torment forever and ever.

The scriptural evidence of these claims are summarized through the following five points:

1. Sheol is mentioned in the Old Testament sixty-seven times, and first referenced in Genesis 37:35 with its final reference in Habakkuk 2:5.

2. The concept of Sheol being a divided place is suggested in Christ's account of a rich man and a poor man named Lazarus in Luke 16:19-31.

> Now there was a certain rich man, and he habitually dressed in purple and fine linen, gaily living in splendor every day. And a certain poor man named Lazarus was laid at his gate, covered with sores, and longing to be fed with the crumbs which were falling from the rich man's table; besides, even the dogs were coming and licking his sores. Now it came about that the poor man died and he was carried away by the angels to Abraham's bosom; and the rich man also died and was buried. And in Hades he lifted up his eyes, being in torment, and saw Abraham far away, and Lazarus in his bosom. And he cried out and said, 'Father Abraham, have mercy on me, and send Lazarus, that he may dip the tip of his finger in water and cool off my tongue; for I am in agony in this flame.' But Abraham said, 'Child, remember that during your life you received your good things, and likewise Lazarus bad things; but now he is being comforted here, and you are in agony. And besides all this, between us and you there is a great chasm fixed, in order that those who wish to come over from here to you may not be able, and that none may cross over from there to us.' And he said, 'Then I beg you, Father, that you send him

to my father's house—for I have five brothers—that he may warn them, lest they also come to this place of torment.' But Abraham said, 'They have Moses and the Prophets; let them hear them,' But he said, 'No, Father Abraham, but if someone goes to them from the dead, they will repent!' But he said to him, 'If they do not listen to Moses and the Prophets, neither will they be persuaded if someone rises from the dead.'

The prophet Isaiah seems to back this concept up where he writes,

> Sheol from beneath is excited over you to meet you when you come; It arouses for you the spirits of the dead, all the leaders of the earth; It raises all the kings of the nations from their thrones. They will all respond and say to you, 'Even you have been made weak as we, You have become like us. Your pomp and the music of your harps Have been brought down to Sheol; Maggots are spread out as your bed beneath you, And worms are your covering. How you have fallen from heaven, O star of the morning, son of the dawn! You have been cut down to the earth, You who have weakened the nations! But you said in your heart, I will ascend to heaven; I will raise my throne above the stars of God, And I will sit on the mount of assembly In the recesses of the north. I will ascend above the heights of the clouds; I will make myself like the Most High.' Nevertheless you will be thrust down to Sheol, To the recesses of the pit. [9]

Isaiah prophesied Satan's (star of the morning) destiny to be Sheol. Revelation 20:1-3 records the time when Isaiah's prophecy will be fulfilled. "And I saw an angel come down from heaven, having the key of the bottomless pit and a great chain in his hand. And he laid hold on the dragon, that old serpent, which is the Devil, and Satan, and bound him a thousand years, And cast him into the bottomless pit, and shut him up, and set a seal upon him, that he should deceive the nations no

---

[9] Isa. 14:9-15.

THE DOCTRINE OF HEAVEN AND HELL | 197

more, till the thousand years should be fulfilled: and after that he must be loosed a little season" (KJV).

3. The prophet Ezekiel confirms the location of Sheol (hell) as he writes, "For thus says the Lord God, 'When I shall make you a desolate city, like the cities which are not inhabited, when I shall bring up the deep over you, and the great waters will cover you, then I shall bring you down with those who go down to the pit, to the people of old, and I shall make you dwell in the lower parts of the earth, like the ancient waste places, with those who go down to the pit, so that you will not be inhabited; but I shall set glory in the land of the living.'" [10] Ezekiel continues this theme by writing, "Elam is there and all her multitude around her grave; all of them slain, fallen by the sword, who went down uncircumcised to the lower parts of the earth, who instilled their terror in the land of the living, and bore their disgrace with those who went down to the pit." [11]

4. Jesus tells us what will occur after his death, as Matthew writes, "But He answered and said to them, 'An evil and adulterous generation craves for a sign; and yet no sign shall be given to it but the sign of Jonah the prophet; for just as Jonah was three days and three nights in the belly of the sea monster, so shall the Son of Man be three days and three nights in the heart of the earth.'" [12]

The Apostle Paul then explains what Jesus was doing during this three-day time.

> There is one body and one Spirit, just as also you were called in one hope of your calling; one Lord, one faith, one baptism, one God and Father of all who is over all and through all and in all. But to each one of us grace was given according to the measure of Christ's gift. Therefore it says,

---

[10] Ezek. 26:19-20.
[11] Ezek. 32:24.
[12] Matt. 12:39-40.

> *'When He ascended on high,*
> *He led captive a host of captives,*
> *And He gave gifts to men.'*
>
> *(Now this expression, 'He ascended,' what does it mean except that He also had descended into the lower parts of the earth? He who descended is Himself also He who ascended far above all the heavens, that He might fill all things.)* [13]

These verses reflect the fact that Christ went to Sheol where the Old Testament saints were held captive, then ascended to heaven as he took them with him.

5. John goes on to tell us that Sheol (Hades) will come to an end at the end of the millennial age. "And the sea gave up the dead which were in it, and death and Hades gave up the dead which were in them; and they were judged, every one of them according to their deeds. And death and Hades were thrown into the lake of fire. This is the second death, the lake of fire. And if anyone's name was not found written in the book of life, he was thrown into the lake of fire." [14]

THE LAKE OF FIRE

The term *lake of fire* only appears five times in Scripture and is described this way. "… the lake of fire which burns with brimstone." [15] The lake of fire is believed to exist because of the creation of a new heaven and new earth, eliminating Sheol, thus requiring a final resting place for all the fallen angels and humanity (see Revelation 21:1-6; 20:10-15).

---

[13] Eph. 4:4-10.
[14] Rev. 20:13-15.
[15] Rev. 19:20.

GOOD AND EVIL

The concept of *good* and *evil* is first revealed to us by God in Genesis 2:9, and reads, "And out of the ground the Lord God caused to grow every tree that is pleasing to the sight and good for food; the tree of life also in the midst of the garden, and the tree of the knowledge of good and evil." According to this account in the Genesis record, God did not create the human race with knowledge or understanding of the concept of good and evil. God even commanded Adam and Eve not to seek after such understanding through his command not to eat of the one tree that would provide such knowledge (Genesis 2:16-17).

The question may arise as to why God even provided the option to obtain such knowledge? The answer may lie with the fact that evil had already come into existence through the fall of the devil (Satan) and his angels, known as demons (see Ezekiel 28:11-19; Isaiah 14:7-15).

One line of reasoning to the question may be found in the Scriptures, taking on the form of testing of humanity to check on their sincere loyalty to the God of heaven. It should be noted that the biblical concept of testing differs from the concept of temptation. Examples of this difference can be seen in the Scriptures. James 1:3 tells us that God tests our faith. This can be seen when a trial over personal finances comes. Do we solve the issue through ethical and legal methods, or do we seek out unethical or illegal methods?

Temptation comes when we are asked to sin against God. Example: Someone offers you a bribe to take some action against someone, or asks you to commit perjury against someone. These are not tests to see how one will respond, rather they are temptations to sin. The definitive answer to these differences can be found in James 1:13, which reads, "Let no one say when he is tempted, 'I am being tempted by God'; for God cannot be tempted by evil, and He Himself does not tempt anyone." The conclusion to this revelation is that God never entices anyone with a temptation to sin. Temptation comes from Satan, not God. This becomes evident in First Corinthians 7:5.

We see glimpses of the testing action of God in Deuteronomy 8:2. "And you shall remember all the way which the Lord your God has led you in the wilderness these forty years, that He might humble you, testing you, to know what was in your heart, whether you would keep His commandments or not."

God continues to use this tool called testing in the New Testament, as the Apostle Peter writes, "Beloved, do not be surprised at the fiery ordeal among you, which comes upon you for your testing, as though some strange thing were happening to you; but to the degree that you share the sufferings of Christ, keep on rejoicing; so that also at the revelation of His glory, you may rejoice with exultation." [16]

God even closes out human history using this format, which we can see in Revelation 3:10. "Because you have kept the word of My perseverance, I also will keep you from the hour of testing, that hour which is about to come upon the whole world, to test those who dwell upon the earth."

Within the context of this passage, Jesus is speaking to his church, referring to the seven-year period referred to as the tribulation period, which will be a time of testing for the whole world.

Here lies the defining issue of evil; evil comes through beings who disobey God's commands and revealed will.

THE NATURE OF GOOD AND EVIL

GOOD

Good can be defined through two concepts. The first one is illustrated this way, "And God saw all that He had made, and behold, it was very good. And there was evening and there was morning, the sixth day. Thus the heavens and the earth were completed, and all their hosts." [17]

From this illustration, *good* can be defined as anything God does that affects the natural world. The extension of this concept is that all of God's creation was good. We see the second concept illustrated in Genesis 2:18. "Then the Lord God said, 'It is not good for the man to be alone; I will make him a helper suitable for him.'"

---

[16] 1 Peter 4:12-13.
[17] Gen. 1:31-2:1.

Through this verse, we can conclude that anything that God does on behalf of himself or others is considered good. By extension we can say that God establishing the institution of marriage is good, God establishing the institution of government is good, and God establishing his Laws for humanity is good. These concepts are summed up by the Psalmist who writes, "The Lord is good to all, And His mercies are over all His works." [18] And, "For the Lord is good; His lovingkindness is everlasting, And His faithfulness to all generations." [19]

Jesus reaffirms these statements as Mark writes, "And Jesus said to him, 'Why do you call Me good? No one is good except God alone.'"[20] Jesus' statement was not denying his deity, but simply affirming that the very nature of goodness is found in God's nature. Therefore, anything God does or speaks should be considered good. The result of this discussion is that the concept of good is based on God's nature, and whatever comes through God's personhood or existence is always classified as good. This conclusion suggests that goodness is a result of God's presence, not by any efforts performed by angels or humanity.

Because goodness is defined by God's nature, it is required that we define God's nature through tangible attributes that affect humanity. These tangible attributes can be seen as a result of God's nature working in the world. Jesus expresses this concept this way,

> Either make the tree good, and its fruit good; or make the tree bad, and its fruit bad; for the tree is known by its fruit. You brood of vipers, how can you, being evil, speak what is good? For the mouth speaks out of that which fills the heart. The good man out of his good treasure brings forth what is good; and the evil man out of his evil treasure brings forth what is evil. And I say to you, that every careless word that men shall speak, they shall render account for it in the day of

---

[18] Ps. 145:9.
[19] Ps. 100:5.
[20] Mark 10:18.

judgment. For by your words you shall be justified, and by your words you shall be condemned. [21]

The context of the passage is Jesus speaking to the religious leaders of his day, who were accusing him of performing miracles through the power of Satan. Jesus used this parable to express the concept that good can only come from something that is by nature good, and similarly evil (bad) can only come from something that by nature is evil or bad. Therefore, by extension, Jesus concludes that any good that may come from humanity is the result of God's nature residing in them, and any evil or bad acts are likewise a result of Satan's nature working in them.

The Apostle Paul supports Jesus' teaching by saying, "... for the fruit of the light consists in all goodness and righteousness and truth..."[22] Paul continues this theme when he writes, "But the fruit of the Spirit is love, joy, peace, patience, kindness, goodness, faithfulness, gentleness, self-control; against such things there is no law." [23] The context of this passage reflects that the fruit of the Spirit is a product of God's nature.

The question then becomes, if all this is true how can humanity ever produce good fruit? The Apostle Peter provides the answer by saying, "For by these He has granted to us His precious and magnificent promises, in order that by them you might become partakers of the divine nature, having escaped the corruption that is in the world by lust."[24] Goodness is a product of God's nature, which can only be possessed by humanity through Christ's sacrificial work on the cross (Ephesians 2:8-9).

To summarize this section of the discussion, good is a product and the result of God's nature. Evil is a product and the result of Satan's nature. The Apostle John expresses the concept this way, "Beloved, do not imitate what is evil, but what is good. The one who does good is of

---

[21] Matt. 12:33-37.
[22] Eph. 5:9.
[23] Gal. 5:22-23.
[24] 2 Peter 1:4.

God; the one who does evil has not seen God." [25] These truths will become clearer in the next segment of the discussion.

Evil

Evil is the opposite of good. The Scriptures affirm God is good, therefore, evil must be the opposite of what God is. To understand the nature of evil we must understand why it is classified as evil. The best way to illustrate this is by reviewing the lives of those who originally fell out of the good graces of God.

Ezekiel 28:12-17 reads,

> Thus says the Lord God, 'You had the seal of perfection, Full of wisdom and perfect in beauty. You were in Eden, the garden of God; Every precious stone was your covering: The ruby, the topaz, and the diamond; The beryl, the onyx, and the jasper; The lapis lazuli, the turquoise, and the emerald; And the gold, the workmanship of your settings and sockets, Was in you. On the day that you were created They were prepared. You were the anointed cherub who covers, And I placed you there. You were on the holy mountain of God; You walked in the midst of the stones of fire. You were blameless in your ways From the day you were created, Until unrighteousness was found in you. By the abundance of your trade You were internally filled with violence, And you sinned; Therefore I have cast you as profane From the mountain of God. And I have destroyed you, O covering cherub, From the midst of the stones of fire. Your heart was lifted up because of your beauty; You corrupted your wisdom by reason of your splendor. I cast you to the ground; I put you before kings, That they may see you.'

---

[25] 3 John 11.

Within this account of Satan's fall from grace, we learn that before his fall, Satan had full access to the garden of Eden, and he is described as an angel of the cherub class, a high and prestigious position. Satan was created blameless and given the great privilege of being in the very presence of God.

Then the Scriptures state that unrighteousness was found in him. We are told that this unrighteousness came from within Satan himself, and by his own doing he took on an attitude of violence toward God, thus this attitude of Satan was labeled as *sin*. This passage then provides the root attitudinal cause behind all the other attitudes of Satan—PRIDE! "Your heart was lifted up because of your beauty; You corrupted your wisdom by reason of your splendor." This is the reason for Jesus' teaching on evil as something that comes from the heart or the very nature of any living being outside of God's grace.

From Satan's violent and prideful attitude toward God comes the first lie in human history, as told to Eve in the same garden they both had access to. This lie of Satan to Eve came from his internal attitude and is why Jesus referred to Satan as the father of all lies. In John 8:44 Jesus tells the religious leaders "You are of your father the devil, and you want to do the desires of your father. He was a murderer from the beginning, and does not stand in the truth, because there is no truth in him. Whenever he speaks a lie, he speaks from his own nature; for he is a liar, and the father of lies."

This concept was not just a reflection of who Jesus was directly speaking to but should be applied to all of humanity. We can conclude this because humanity committed the same sin Satan committed, as we read in Genesis 3:1-7.

> Now the serpent was more crafty than any beast of the field which the Lord God had made. And he said to the woman, 'Indeed, has God said, You shall not eat from any tree of the garden?' And the woman said to the serpent, 'From the fruit of the trees of the garden we may eat; but from the fruit of the tree which is in the middle of the garden, God has said, You shall not eat from it or touch it, lest you die.' And the serpent said to the woman, 'You surely shall not die! For God

knows that in the day you eat from it your eyes will be opened, and you will be like God, knowing good and evil.' When the woman saw that the tree was good for food, and that it was a delight to the eyes, and that the tree was desirable to make one wise, she took from its fruit and ate; and she gave also to her husband with her, and he ate. Then the eyes of both of them were opened, and they knew that they were naked; and they sewed fig leaves together and made themselves loin coverings.

Here we see Satan lying to Eve, planting in her heart and mind doubts that tempted her to view God as a liar, and a God who wanted to keep her from becoming equal to himself in wisdom and knowledge. This then becomes the nature of evil, to have PRIDE that gives us the motivation to become equal to God, thereby placing oneself in a position with no need of God at all. This would also be true for those who deny God's existence, displaying the attitude of the modern humanist who believes, "Man is at last becoming aware that he alone is responsible for the realization of the world of his dreams, that he has within himself the power for its achievement. He must set intelligence and will to the task." [26]

Here lies humanity's alignment to evil in the world, to see oneself with PRIDE as being self-sufficient, having no need of God. The Scriptures confirm this assessment of humanity's condition.

> As it is written, 'There is none righteous, not even one; There is none who understands, There is none who seeks for God; All have turned aside, together they have become useless; There is none who does good, There is not even one. Their throat is an open grave, With their tongues they keep deceiving, The poison of asps is under their lips; Whose mouth is full of cursing and bitterness; Their feet are swift to shed

---

[26] Spiritualpilgrim.net, "The Humanist Manifesto 1933," [article online]; available from http://spiritualpilgrim.net/07_Special-Documents/Historical-Documents/1933_Humanist-Manifesto.htm; Internet; accessed 4 September 2020.

blood, Destruction and misery are in their paths, And the path of peace have they not known. There is no fear of God before their eyes.' [27]

As Adam followed suit in attitude and action with Eve, human nature then became part of the evil classification that brings death to all. Romans 5:12 states, "Therefore, just as through one man sin entered into the world, and death through sin, and so death spread to all men, because all sinned..."

IN SUMMARY

God, in a conversation with Satan, confirms the reality of this discussion. "And the Lord said to Satan, 'Have you considered My servant Job? For there is no one like him on the earth, a blameless and upright man, fearing God and turning away from evil.'" [28] God declares evil as something not associated with himself. King Solomon affirms this when he writes, "The fear of the Lord is to hate evil; Pride and arrogance and the evil way, And the perverted mouth, I hate." [29] Solomon points out that PRIDE and arrogance is part of evil, and that God hates it all.

{ CHAPTER DISCUSSION NOTES }

The end result of good and evil in our lives is represented in James 4:1-7.

> What is the source of quarrels and conflicts among you? Is not the source your pleasures that wage war in your

---

[27] Rom. 3:10-18.
[28] Job 1:8.
[29] Prov. 8:13.

members? You lust and do not have; so you commit murder. And you are envious and cannot obtain; so you fight and quarrel. You do not have because you do not ask. You ask and do not receive, because you ask with wrong motives, so that you may spend it on your pleasures. You adulteresses, do you not know that friendship with the world is hostility toward God? Therefore whoever wishes to be a friend of the world makes himself an enemy of God. Or do you think that the Scripture speaks to no purpose: 'He jealously desires the Spirit which He has made to dwell in us'? But He gives a greater grace. Therefore it says, 'God is opposed to the proud, but gives grace to the humble.' Submit therefore to God. Resist the devil and he will flee from you.

It is from within us that good and evil wage war. As the believer is commanded to submit to God, the true source of what is good in us and the world; and to resist the devil, the source of such PRIDE.

This spiritual war raging within us expresses itself in two ways; James states,

> Who among you is wise and understanding? Let him show by his good behavior his deeds in the gentleness of wisdom. But if you have bitter jealousy and selfish ambition in your heart, do not be arrogant and so lie against the truth. This wisdom is not that which comes down from above, but is earthly, natural, demonic. For where jealousy and selfish ambition exist, there is disorder and every evil thing. But the wisdom from above is first pure, then peaceable, gentle, reasonable, full of mercy and good fruits, unwavering, without hypocrisy. And the seed whose fruit is righteousness is sown in peace by those who make peace. [30]

The source of our spiritual battles can be found in our new and old natures. Our new nature is the nature of God, brought to us by the Holy

---

[30] James 3:13-18.

Spirit of God (2 Peter 1:4; 2 Corinthians 5:17). And the old nature in us is our own human spirit, which is sinful and falls short of the glory of God (John 8:44; Romans 3:10-18, 3:23).

From the Scriptures referenced, we can say that good only comes from God, and his presence and influence; and evil only comes through Satan and his presence and influence. All of this is seen by the fruit produced in our lives. As Jesus expressed earlier, only a good tree can produce good fruit, represented by God's nature in us. Likewise, a bad tree can only produce bad fruit, represented by our old nature. And here lies the basis for the battle between good and evil in the world.

We should remember what good fruit looks like; it can be seen in the fruit of the Spirit, as expressed here: "But the fruit of the Spirit is love, joy, peace, patience, kindness, goodness, faithfulness, gentleness, self-control; against such things there is no law." [31]

This war between good and evil will never end until Christ defeats his last enemy once and for all. The Apostle Paul explains it this way,

> For since by a man came death, by a man also came the resurrection of the dead. For as in Adam all die, so also in Christ all shall be made alive. But each in his own order: Christ the first fruits, after that those who are Christ's at His coming, then comes the end, when He delivers up the kingdom to the God and Father, when He has abolished all rule and all authority and power. For He must reign until He has put all His enemies under His feet. The last enemy that will be abolished is death. For He has put all things in subjection under His feet. But when He says, 'All things are put in subjection,' it is evident that He is excepted who put all things in subjection to Him. And when all things are subjected to Him, then the Son Himself also will be subjected to the One who subjected all things to Him, that God may be all in all. [32]

---

[31] Gal. 5:22
[32] 1 Cor. 15:21-28.

Personal Notes

Ten

THE DOCTRINE OF ESCHATOLOGY

INTRODUCTION

We can define eschatology as the study of future things, with a specific emphasis on the end-time events within Christian Theology. This chapter will focus on the subject in an introductory format. For those wanting a more comprehensive study, I would suggest the author's book *Dispensational Theology: A Textbook on Eschatology in the Twenty-First Century*.

Eschatology has been written about for centuries and is one of the more hotly debated subjects within the Christian faith. This chapter will focus on information from a dispensational perspective while presenting other viewpoints to provide a better understanding of the subject.

TERMS USED IN ESCHATOLOGY[1]

Millennium—A term originating from Latin which means thousand. Within the context of Eschatology, it refers to a future period of one thousand years when Christ establishes his kingdom on earth to fulfill God's covenant promises to Israel.

Premillennialism—This view believes in a literal millennial period, with Christ returning to the earth before this period begins for the purpose of ruling and reigning over his Kingdom on earth.

---

[1] Reid A. Ashbaucher, *Dispensational Theology: A Textbook on Eschatology in the Twenty-First Century* (Toledo, Ohio: Reid Ashbaucher Publications, 2019), 20-22.

Postmillennialism—This view holds to a period labeled millennium in which the Gospel can be preached worldwide. After which, Christ will return at the end of this period.

Amillennialism—This term comes from the Greek—meaning no millennialism. This view denies a literal millennial kingdom on earth. It holds to a view that Old Testament promises for a future kingdom will be fulfilled as a spiritual kingdom. This view also holds this spiritual kingdom could manifest itself in one of two ways. One, the Church represents this kingdom between the first and Second Advent. Second, the Church is in heaven with Christ ruling.

Present or Realized Millennialism—A twentieth-century term that represents a belief in a millennial period currently being realized between the first and second advents. This view does not hold to no millennialism, but to a present or realized millennialism—taking place now—spiritually.

Many holding to the Reformed tradition of John Calvin also hold to Realized Millennialism.

Rapture—This term represents the concept of being taken or the catching away of living saints, along with the resurrection of the dead in Christ during the Church Age, with the Church Age represented as the time between the day of Pentecost and the future Rapture which takes place before the Second Advent.

The concept of the Church age is supported by interpreting the mysteries spoken of in the New Testament and the understanding of certain prophecies.

The Tribulation—A future seven-year period, which is considered an unprecedented time of trouble on earth when God will pour out his wrath in judgment upon the nations of the world.

The Great Tribulation—A reference to the last three and half years of the seven-year Tribulation period where God's judgment becomes more severe.

Pre-tribulation Rapture View—This view holds that the Rapture will take place before the seven-year tribulation period, thus protecting the Church, also referred to as the body of Christ, from God's coming wrath (God's wrath—Revelation 6:15-17; 14:19-20; 16:1; 19:15-16; 1 Thessalonians 1:9-10; Colossians 3:5-7).

The Partial Rapture View—This view holds to the belief that those actively looking for the Rapture will be taken at that time, and all other Christians will remain behind and live through the seven-year tribulation period.

Mid-tribulation Rapture View—This view believes that the Church will be raptured at the midpoint of the Tribulation period and be saved from the Great Tribulation that takes place during the final three-and-a-half years.

Post-tribulation Rapture View—This view holds to the Rapture taking place after the seven-year tribulation period with the Second Advent taking place immediately afterward.

Second Advent—This term represents the second coming of Jesus Christ to the earth with his saints at the end of the tribulation period.

The Revelation of Christ—This term is associated with the Greek word Apokalupsis (ἀποκάλυψις) and carries the idea to uncover or unveil, as used many times in the New Testament in both noun and verb form.

Within the context of Eschatology, the term The Revelation of Christ represents the unveiling of the Glory of Christ as it relates to both the Rapture and the Second Coming of Christ, also referred to as the Second Advent (Scriptural references to the second coming—1 Peter 4:13; 2 Thessalonians 1:7; Luke 17:30) (Scriptural references to the Rapture—1 Corinthians 1:7; Colossians 3:4; 1 Peter 1:7, 13).

This term is specifically referenced in First Corinthians 1:7-9, and reads: "so that you are not lacking in any gift, awaiting eagerly the

Revelation of our Lord Jesus Christ, who shall also confirm you to the end, blameless in the day of our Lord Jesus Christ."

Imminence—This term carries the meaning of impending. When this word is used regarding the Rapture, it means the event could take place at any time, versus the idea of something that could happen soon.

The Church—Within the context of Dispensational Theology, The Church is represented by all the saints who ever lived from the day of Pentecost to the time of a future Rapture. This period is also referenced as the Church Age.

Within other theological systems, the term Church may include Old Testament saints covering other periods.

Dispensation—Scripturally, we may define dispensations as an economy or stewardship implemented by God for his purpose at any point in human history—past, present, or future. These economies rarely overlap—but they do on occasion.

The term economy as expressed in the previous paragraph is defined by Merriam-Webster's 11th Collegiate Dictionary in three ways: (3 a: "The arrangement or mode of operation of something: Organization." b: "a system especially of interaction and exchange." (4: "The structure or conditions of economic life in a country, area, or period.")

When placing these three definitions into the discussion, they become helpful in aiding our understanding of dispensations by providing a clearer picture of purpose and functionality of the designated dispensational periods.

Chiliasm—The word itself means Millennialism. This word is used in older writings—pre-twentieth Century—when referencing the doctrine of the millennial kingdom based on Revelation 20:1-3.

BIBLICAL HERMENEUTICS

Hermeneutics is the art and science of Scripture interpretation. The discipline of hermeneutics is what holds the key to understanding Eschatology.

Bernard Ramm (Ph.D.) defines hermeneutics this way: "Hermeneutics is the science and art of Biblical interpretation. It is a science because it is guided by rules within a system; and it is an art because the application of the rules is by skill, and not by mechanical imitation. As such, it forms one of the most important members of the theological sciences." [2]

The Grammatico-Historical Method of interpretation is defined as the "Literal Interpretation—The art of explaining the original meaning of Scripture according to the normal and customary usages of its language." [3] This method was used for the first 300 years of the Christian church, only to be later abandoned by many in favor of the Allegorical Method until the sixteenth century when Martin Luther reestablished the literal interpretive approach to Scripture.

The second method of hermeneutics is called *The Allegorical Method* and came down through history from four allegorical schools of thought—Greek Allegorism, Jewish Allegorism, Christian and Patristic Allegorism, and Catholic Allegorism. [4]

Paul Lee Tan (Th.D.) defines the Allegorical Method this way: "Allegorization—A method of interpretation based on the assumption that the Scriptures contains multiple sense." [5]

These two methods bring about two vastly differing views of the Scriptures. Until one can agree on which method to use, there can never really be any actual agreement on the subject of Eschatology between these differing hermeneutical approaches.

---

[2] Bernard Ramm, *Protestant Biblical Interpretation*, 3 rev ed. (Grand Rapids: Baker Book House, 1970), 1.

[3] Paul Lee Tan, *The Interpretation of Prophecy* (Winona Lake, Indiana: Assurance Publishing, 1974), 367.

[4] Ramm, *Protestant Biblical Interpretation*, 23-38.

[5] Tan, *The Interpretation of Prophecy*, 363.

AMILLENNIALISM [6]

Amillennialism is primarily a view held by Roman Catholic, Lutheran, or Reformed perspectives, with some exceptions. The following are the pillar theological points of Amillennialism.

1. There is no <u>literal</u> millennial earthly kingdom.

2. The millennial period in Revelation 20 represents the time between the First and Second Advents.

3. The binding of Satan in Revelation 20 either took place at the time of Christ's First Advent or is currently taking place between the First and Second Advent.[7]

4. The Church of the New Testament has become the new spiritual Israel, or the Church has replaced Israel to fulfill God's plans moving forward.

5. The Abrahamic Covenant is <u>not</u> unconditional.[8]

6. The mysteries Paul spoke to are not new and are unknown truths representing the church age or the gap between Daniel's 69 and 70th week as prophesied in Daniel 9:24-27.

7. Man does not possess two natures through the salvation process as alluded to in the following passages, (Second Timothy 1:14; Second Peter 1:4; James 4:5; 5:17; Romans 7:19-23; 11:15-24;

---

[6] Ashbaucher, *Dispensational Theology*, 50-51.
[7] Anthony A. Hoekema, *The Bible and the Future* (Grand Rapids: Willian B. Eerdmans Publishing Company, 1979), 178.
[8] Oswald T. Allis, *Prophecy and the Church*, 3 ed. (The Presbyterian and Reformed Publication Company, 1955), 58.

Jeremiah 31:33).[9] Instead, the new man of the New Testament represents spiritual newness and growth through the sanctification process of the Holy Spirit.[10] This concept correlates to the idea in eschatology that the kingdom will continually grow, making things better and better over time as the Gospel is preached to the entire world.

8. There are two schools of thought in Amillennialism:

   a. Heavenly School
   b. Earthly School

(a) The heavenly school represents the view that the millennium is represented by the rule of Christ in heaven with the saints and takes place between the two Advents along with the binding of Satan taking place during the same time.[11]

(b) The earthly school represents the view that the millennium is represented by the kingdom of Christ and the kingdom of Satan coexisting side by side here on earth until the Second Advent. This is supported through the interpretation of Matthew 13: 36-43, with the parable of the Tares, while the binding of Satan took place at the first advent.[12]

POSTMILLENNIALISM [13]

This view holds to a period labeled millennium during which the Gospel can be preached worldwide; with Christ returning at the end of this period.

---

[9] Reid A. Ashbaucher, *Made in the Image of God: Understanding the Nature of God and Mankind in a Changing World*, 3 rev ed. (Toledo, Ohio: Reid Ashbaucher Publications, 2020), 127.
[10] Allis, *Prophecy and the Church*, 44.
[11] Hoekema, *The Bible and the Future*, 174.
[12] Ibid., 180.
[13] Ashbaucher, *Dispensational Theology*, 51-59.

Postmillennialism has a conservative and liberal approach to its positions and does not hold to a belief in the *imminent return* of Christ. Those associated with this perspective are Joachim of Floris (A.D. 1132-1203), Daniel Whitby (A.D. 1638-1726), Charles Hodge (A.D. 1797-1878), A. H. Strong (A.D. 1836-1921), B. B. Warfield (A.D. 1851-1921)—Warfield is sometimes associated with Amillennialism—, Loraine Boettner (A.D. 1901-1990), and Jousas J. Rushdoony (A.D. 1916-2001). Loraine Boettner is seen as one of the last defenders of this perspective, with many holding to this viewpoint having moved to an Amillennial perspective.

PREMILLENNIALISM [14]

There are four types of Premillennialism. Covenant Historical, Dispensational, Progressive or Revised Dispensationalism, along with Hyper or Ultra-Dispensationalism. Within these views is an additional perspective on the translation or rapture event of the saints. These views are pre-tribulation, mid-tribulation, and post-tribulation.

Covenant Historical Premillennialism—Holds to the following key views.[15]

1. Its belief in a literal kingdom is mostly based on a literal interpretation of Revelation 20:1-6.

2. This view does not necessarily support Old Testament prophecies being fulfilled by Israel.

3. This view makes no clear distinction between Israel and the church. This view strongly opposes Dispensationalism.

---

[14] Ashbaucher, *Dispensational Theology*, 78-96.
[15] Hodge, *Systematic Theology*, vol. 3, (New York: Scribner, Armstrong, and Company, 1873), 861-862, quoted in Ashbaucher, *Dispensational Theology: A Textbook on Eschatology in the Twenty-First Century*, 78-79.

4. Adherents of this view mostly hold to a post-tribulation rapture.

5. This view tends to be more optimistic than Amillennialism or Postmillennialism.

Dispensational Premillennialism—Holds to the following key views.[16]

1. The hermeneutical principle of a grammatical-historical interpretation of the Scriptures.

2. The literal fulfillment of Old Testament prophecies.

3. A clear recognized distinction between the Nation of Israel and the New Testament Church.

4. This view supports a pre-tribulation rapture.

5. This view supports a literal millennial kingdom.

6. Salvation is always by grace through faith and believes the various dispensations are rules of life, never the basis or cause of salvation.

Progressive or Revised Dispensationalism—Holds to the following key changes to Dispensationalism. [17]

1. Holds to the hermeneutical principle of a grammatical-historical-literary-theological or (complimentary hermeneutical) interpretation of the Scriptures.

2. Moving away from a recognized distinction between the Nation of Israel and the New Testament Church.

---

[16] Ashbaucher, *Dispensational Theology*, 81.
[17] Ibid., 89-90.

Hyper or Ultra-Dispensationalism—holds to the following key elements.

Dr. Roy L. Aldrich writes,

> This school makes a separate dispensation out of part or all of the book of Acts. There are two types of ultradispensationalism: (1) The extreme believe that the mystery church began after Acts 28, i.e., after Paul's imprisonment. (2) The moderate believe the mystery church began sometime (they are vague about the starting point) after Paul's conversion, or between Acts 9 and 13.
>
> Both the extreme and moderate types of ultradispensationalism agree on the following: (1) The great commissions in Matthew and Mark are Jewish. (2) The ministry of the Twelve was only a continuation of the ministry of Christ. (3) The church (mystery or body church) did not begin at Pentecost. (4) The sign gifts were Jewish and related to the kingdom period only. (5) Water baptism is not for this age. (6) That there is a distinction between Paul's early and later ministries. (7) That the mystery church began with Paul. (8) That Acts 2:38, Mark 16:16, Luke 7:30, etc., teach a legalistic plan of salvation different from the grace plan for this age.[18]
>
> Charles Ryrie adds to this list that ultra-dispensationalists believe the bride of Christ is represented by Israel not the Church.[19]

---

[18] R. L. Aldrich, "An Outline Study on Dispensationalism," *Bibliotheca Sacra* (1961): 118, 134–135; available from Theological Journal Library, Vol. 1-5, (Faithlife Corporation product available from Logos.com.), quoted in Ashbaucher, *Dispensational Theology*, 95-96.

[19] Charles C. Ryrie, *Dispensationalism*, (Chicago: Moody Publishers, 2007), 232, quoted in Ashbaucher, *Dispensational Theology*, 96.

UNDERSTANDING THE KINGDOM

Within eschatology, the kingdom of God is viewed in differing ways. Some hold that the kingdom will be established at the same time as the millennial kingdom. Others hold that the kingdom is progressive, meaning it will come upon us gradually as Jesus said, "The time is fulfilled, and the kingdom of God is at hand; repent and believe in the gospel;" [20] until it is fully consummated during the millennial kingdom. Still, others believe the kingdom is being realized now in some form and will be consummated at the time of the new heaven and new earth.

Because of these divergent views, multiple theological perspectives are expressed within the study of eschatology. How will the kingdom be experienced by the church, Israel, and the rest of the world? The answer to this question will shape one's theological views on the Scriptures as a whole, which will then go on to be reflected in one's eschatological views.

It is not the intent of this chapter to convince or persuade towards any particular viewpoint but to make the reader aware that there are such views in theology, and as we explore them we should stay obedient to the word of God, as it tells us to study to show ourselves approved unto God, to be a workman that need not be ashamed of one's interpretations before God as referenced in Second Timothy 2:15.

It is not about whether we all agree with one another, but whatever we believe should be based on the Scriptures, and found pleasing to God through its practical display in our lives.

THE TRIBULATION PERIOD

Based on Deuteronomy 4:29-31, there are several reasons behind the seven-year tribulation period. One purpose is to turn Israel back to God, and the second, to prepare them for the fulfillment of the Abrahamic Covenant. Other reasons include the fulfillment of Matthew 23:39 and to provide salvation to the nation's unbelieving gentiles (Revelation 7:9-14).

---

[20] Mark 1:15.

Based on Jeremiah 30:4-11 we can conclude that "(1) The tribulation induces terror and anguish on the part of those living. (2) The tribulation is distinct from any other time in Israel's history. (3) The tribulation destroys gentile dominion over Israel. (4) The tribulation is followed by the millennium, as seen with Israel restored to their land.

It should be noted that the *Eternal State* does not follow the *Time of Trouble*. Instead, Israel is restored to the land. This shows the necessity of a period such as the millennium to accomplish this and is an argument that would oppose an Amillennialism perspective." [21]

The tribulation period is also established in Daniel 7:7, 8, 19-28; 9:24-27. The minor prophets continue this theme in Zephaniah 1:14-18, Zechariah 13:8-14:5, and Amos 5:18-20. The timeframe of the Great Tribulation is spoken of in Daniel 11:36-45 and 12:11-13 and affirmed in Revelation 11:2 and 12:6.

Jesus speaks to this time frame in Matthew 24:14-30, where we can derive the following concepts.

> (1) The Olivet Discourse provides specific details presented as signs of the Lord's coming at his Second Advent. (2) Matthew 24:15 reads, 'Therefore when you see the abomination of desolation which was spoken of through Daniel the prophet, standing in the holy place (let the reader understand.)' This reflects back to Daniel 9:27, providing support for the concept that Jesus' comments in Matthew 24 are referencing Daniel's prophecy of the seventieth week. (3) Matthew 24:21 reflects on the fact that this period will be a time of unprecedented trouble. (4) Matthew 24:14, 20 indicates that the events of this period are influenced by divine control. (5) Luke 21:24 speaks to this same timeframe, which supports the concept that this period will be a time of final Gentile domination over the world, and ultimately over Israel. (6) Matthew 24:29-30 reads, 'But immediately after the tribulation of those days the sun will be darkened, and the moon will not give its light,

---

[21] Ashbaucher, *Dispensational Theology*, 174.

and the stars will fall from the sky, and the powers of the heavens will be shaken, and then the sign of the Son of Man will appear in the sky, and then all the tribes of the earth will mourn, and they will see the Son of Man coming on the clouds of the sky with power and great glory.' This passage reflects on the fact that the tribulation period will usher in the coming of the Lord at his Second Advent. [22]

The Apostle Paul speaks to four concepts associated with the tribulation period found in First Thessalonians 5:1-11. (1) No one knows the time of Christ's return, speaking of the coming kingdom. (2) Paul is now using the term *day of the Lord* reflecting on a time of judgment. (3) Paul indicates a coming time of sudden destruction that will occur during a prolonged period of world peace, using the term *they*, not *we*, as he makes the distinction between who he is writing to (Christians), as opposed to the rest of the world in verse 3. (4) Paul points out that the church (those of the light of day) will not be part of *the day of the Lord* when the wrath of God will be poured out upon the earth.

Ten characteristics represent the tribulation period. [23]

1. Wrath—Zephaniah 1:15-18; 1 Thessalonians 1:10, 5:9; Revelation 6:16-17.
2. Judgment—Revelation 14:7, 15:4, 16:5, 7, 19:2.
3. Indignation—Isaiah 26:20-21, 34:1-3.
4. Trial—Revelation 3:10.
5. Trouble—Jeremiah 30:7; Zephaniah 1:14-15; Daniel 12:1.
6. Destruction—Joel 1:15; 1 Thessalonians 5:3.
7. Darkness—Joel 2:2; Amos 5:18.
8. Desolation—Daniel 9:27; Zephaniah 1:14-15.
9. Overturning—Isaiah 24:1-4, 19-21.
10. Punishment—Isaiah 24:20-21.

---

[22] Ashbaucher, *Dispensational Theology*, 178.
[23] Ibid., 179-180.

THE SECOND ADVENT

The Second Advent encompasses four major themes associated with this future event and is defined as a literal, physical second return of Christ to the earth with his saints to establish His earthly kingdom.

JUDGMENT

Seven judgments are associated with the Second Advent: [24]

1. A judgment of the believer's works at the judgment seat of Christ (1 Corinthians 3:11-15).

2. A judgment against the anti-Christ and his forces at the Second Advent (2 Thessalonians 2:3-11; Revelation 19:19-20).

3. The judgment of the living nation of Israel (Ezekiel 20:37-38; Zechariah 13:8-9).

4. A judgment of the surviving gentile nations for how they treated the Jewish people during the tribulation. (Matthew 25:37-38; Isaiah 34:1-2; Joel 3:1-2).

5. The judgment on the fallen angels (Jude 6; 1 Corinthians 6:3). This judgment will take place on that great day, which is also known as the day of the Lord. The location and details of this place are unclear, but the Scriptures tell us the saints will participate in pronouncing these judgments in some capacity.

6. The judgment of Satan resulting in his being bound for 1,000 years. After which he will be released for a season to attempt one more final rebellion against God. Following his armies being consumed in an instant, his final sentence will be

---

[24] Ashbaucher, *Dispensational Theology*, 203.

pronounced and he will be thrown into the Lake of Fire for all eternity (Revelation 20:1-3, 10).

7. The judgment of the Great White Throne (Revelation 20:11-15).

Resurrections

The Second Advent of Christ will trigger the *first resurrection* event spoken of in the Scriptures (Revelation 20:4-6), affecting three distinct groups of people. The first group consists of the Old Testament saints (Hebrews 11:32-40). While the second group is represented by the judgment and resurrection of the entirety of the Nation of Israel who lived before the gospel of Christ (Daniel 12:1-3; Isaiah 26:19-21). The third group is represented by all the saints that died during the tribulation period (Revelation 20:4-5).

The Davidic Kingdom

This period will be the time of the re-establishment of the Davidic Kingdom promised in Second Samuel Chapter 7. The prophet Amos writes,

> 'In that day I will raise up the fallen booth of David, And wall up its breaches; I will also raise up its ruins, And rebuild it as in the days of old; That they may possess the remnant of Edom And all the nations who are called by My name,' Declares the Lord who does this.
> Behold, 'days are coming,' declares the Lord, 'When the plowman will overtake the reaper And the treader of grapes him who sows seed; When the mountains will drip sweet wine, And all the hills will be dissolved. Also I will restore the captivity of My people Israel, And they will rebuild the ruined cities and live in them, They will also plant vineyards and drink their wine, And make gardens and eat their fruit. I will also plant them on their land, And they will not again be

rooted out from their land Which I have given them,' Says the Lord your God. [25]

This passage is tied with the pronouncement of Christ's birth in Luke 1:31-33, where it links Amos' prophecy to a future kingdom with Christ as its final King. "And behold, you will conceive in your womb, and bear a son, and you shall name Him Jesus. He will be great, and will be called the Son of the Most High; and the Lord God will give Him the throne of His father David; and He will reign over the house of Jacob forever; and His kingdom will have no end."

The fulfillment of these passages will usher in the millennial kingdom promised to the Nation of Israel throughout the many prophecies of the Old Testament.

Not all eschatological views hold to a rapture event, resulting in their adherents coming to differing conclusions on the kingdom and its associated resurrections.

THE MILLENNIUM

This section will deal with the millennium from a Premillennial Pretribulational perspective and summarize many of the details involved with the subject.

Our summary will consist of the following five categorical topics. The purpose of the millennium; Christ's relationship to the millennium; characteristics of the millennium; the government of the millennium, and the events closing out the millennium.

THE PURPOSE OF THE MILLENNIUM

The primary purpose of the millennium is to fulfill the unconditional promises God made through the Abrahamic, Davidic, and New Covenants (Genesis Chapters 12, 15, 17; 2 Samuel Chapter 7; Jeremiah Chapter 31). Accomplishing this upholds the second reason, which is to maintain the truthfulness of God. Simply put, if God does not honor

---

[25] Amos 9:11-15.

all the promises he made to Israel, then by the nature of things, God becomes a liar which is something God cannot do (Titus 1:2). The prophet Moses expresses it this way. "God is not a man, that He should lie, nor a son of man, that He should repent; Has He said, and will He not do it? Or has He spoken, and will He not make it good?" [26]

We can see another reason for the millennium by what occurs at its end where it provides irrefutable and undeniable proof of the total depravity of humanity. Following an unprecedented time of total and complete global peace, something which all world leaders and people claim to desire, for 1,000 years under an incorruptible king and a perfect government, Satan is loosed for a short time. Into this perfect kingdom, he immediately finds a sizeable population gladly willing to follow him in a final rebellion against God (Revelation 20:7-9).

CHRIST'S RELATIONSHIP TO THE MILLENNIUM

Christ's relationship to the millennial kingdom can be summed up through two passages. The Apostle Paul writes, "For as in Adam all die, so also in Christ all shall be made alive. But each in his own order: Christ the first fruits, after that those who are Christ's at His coming, then comes the end, when He delivers up the kingdom to the God and Father, when He has abolished all rule and all authority and power. For He must reign until He has put all His enemies under His feet. The last enemy that will be abolished is death." [27]

The prophet Daniel supports this theme. "I kept looking in the night visions, And behold, with the clouds of heaven One like a Son of Man was coming, And He came up to the Ancient of Days And was presented before Him. And to Him was given dominion, Glory and a kingdom, That all the peoples, nations, and men of every language Might serve Him. His dominion is an everlasting dominion Which will not pass away; And His kingdom is one Which will not be destroyed."[28]

---

[26] Num. 23:19.
[27] 1 Cor. 15:22-26.
[28] Dan. 7:13-14.

Through this summary, we see that Jesus Christ will be the ruling king, exercising sole and final authority over his kingdom, just as was proclaimed in Luke 1:31-33: "And behold, you will conceive in your womb, and bear a son, and you shall name Him Jesus. He will be great, and will be called the Son of the Most High; and the Lord God will give Him the throne of His father David; and He will reign over the house of Jacob forever; and His kingdom will have no end."

Characteristics of the Millennium

Two aspects define the Characteristics of the millennium—the physical and the spiritual. We can define the physical nature of the millennium through the prophet Isaiah as he writes,

> And the wolf will dwell with the lamb, And the leopard will lie down with the kid, And the calf and the young lion and the fatling together; And a little boy will lead them. Also the cow and the bear will graze; Their young will lie down together; And the lion will eat straw like the ox. And the nursing child will play by the hole of the cobra, And the weaned child will put his hand on the viper's den. They will not hurt or destroy in all My holy mountain, For the earth will be full of the knowledge of the Lord As the waters cover the sea.[29]

Through this passage, we notice that this kingdom's peace extends to all of creation, between both human and animal life. People will also continue to be born during this period since there seem to be children present. And we see that there is water covering the sea. This is significant because we are told in Revelation 21:1 that there is no longer any sea, speaking to the time after the millennium of the new heaven and new earth—the eternal state. Since the Bible speaks of a sea during the millennium, this period could not be speaking of the time of eternity, in which there is no sea. This detail alone would work against an Amillennial perspective.

---

[29] Isa. 11:6-9.

The spiritual aspect of the kingdom is reflected in the prophet Isaiah's writings, which reads,

> Then a shoot will spring from the stem of Jesse, And a branch from his roots will bear fruit. And the Spirit of the Lord will rest on Him, The spirit of wisdom and understanding, The spirit of counsel and strength, The spirit of knowledge and the fear of the Lord. And He will delight in the fear of the Lord, And He will not judge by what His eyes see, Nor make a decision by what His ears hear; But with righteousness He will judge the poor, And decide with fairness for the afflicted of the earth; And He will strike the earth with the rod of His mouth, And with the breath of His lips He will slay the wicked. Also righteousness will be the belt about His loins, And faithfulness the belt about His waist.[30]

"This is the spirit by which Christ will rule the kingdom, steeped in righteousness, wisdom, knowledge, strength and faithfulness to his own holy nature. The spiritual atmosphere will be one of righteousness. (Matthew 25:37; Isaiah 60:21 and Psalm 72:7); of obedience (Jeremiah 31:33-34; Psalm 110:1-3); of holiness (Zechariah 14:20; Joel 3:17); of truth (John 14:6; Psalm 85:10; Zechariah 8:3), and full of the Holy Spirit (Ezekiel 36:27; 37:14; Jeremiah 31:33)"[31]

The occupation of the millennial kingdom will consist of all the Old Testament saints, all the New Testament saints, represented by the *body of Christ*, the church, and all the living saints that survived the tribulation period. (1 Corinthians 15:20-24; Hebrews 11:39; Danial 12:1-2; Isaiah 26:19-21; Revelation 20:4-6)

THE GOVERNMENT OF THE MILLENNIUM

The millennial kingdom will be a theocratic monarchy type government. We can see this through the following statement made in

---

[30] Isa. 11:1-5.
[31] Ashbaucher, *Dispensational Theology*, 215.

Revelation 11:5, "And the seventh angel sounded; and there arose loud voices in heaven, saying, The kingdom of the world has become the kingdom of our Lord, and of His Christ; and He will reign forever and ever." The prophet Isaiah writes,

> For a child will be born to us, a son will be given to us; And the government will rest on His shoulders; And His name will be called Wonderful Counselor, Mighty God, Eternal Father, Prince of Peace. There will be no end to the increase of His government or of peace, On the throne of David and over his kingdom, To establish it and to uphold it with justice and righteousness From then on and forevermore. The zeal of the Lord of hosts will accomplish this.[32]

"Isaiah later writes, 'For the Lord is our judge, The Lord is our lawgiver, The Lord is our king; He will save us.' [33] These proclamations tell us that the kingdom's government will be centered on one person, who will be the final authority on judicial, legislative and executive matters of the kingdom, and that person will be Jesus Christ the Son of God." [34]

EVENTS CLOSING OUT THE MILLENNIUM

Satan's revolt against God and his saints closes out the millennium as reflected in Revelation 20:1-3, 7-10. Upon the defeat of Satan's army, purging of the earth spoken of in Second Peter 3:10 will begin. "But the day of the Lord will come like a thief, in which the heavens will pass away with a roar and the elements will be destroyed with intense heat, and the earth and its works will be burned up."

The Apostle John supports this as he writes, "And I saw a great white throne and Him who sat upon it, from whose presence earth and

---

[32] Isa. 9:6-7.
[33] Isa. 33:22.
[34] Ashbaucher, *Dispensational Theology*, 216.

heaven fled away, and no place was found for them." [35] As expressed here the great white throne judgment follows the ending of the millennium. The Apostle John writes,

> And I saw the dead, the great and the small, standing before the throne, and books were opened; and another book was opened, which is the book of life; and the dead were judged from the things which were written in the books, according to their deeds. And the sea gave up the dead which were in it, and death and Hades gave up the dead which were in them; and they were judged, every one of them according to their deeds. And death and Hades were thrown into the lake of fire. This is the second death, the lake of fire. And if anyone's name was not found written in the book of life, he was thrown into the lake of fire.[36]

Revelation 20:12-15 summarizes the millennial kingdom; which is then followed by the final eternal states as expressed in Revelation 21:1-6, and reads,

> And I saw a new heaven and a new earth; for the first heaven and the first earth passed away, and there is no longer any sea. And I saw the holy city, new Jerusalem, coming down out of heaven from God, made ready as a bride adorned for her husband. And I heard a loud voice from the throne, saying, 'Behold, the tabernacle of God is among men, and He shall dwell among them, and they shall be His people, and God Himself shall be among them, and He shall wipe away every tear from their eyes; and there shall no longer be any death; there shall no longer be any mourning, or crying, or pain; the first things have passed away.' And He who sits on the throne said, 'Behold, I am making all things new.' And He said,

---

[35] Rev. 20:11.
[36] Rev. 20:12-15.

'Write, for these words are faithful and true.' And He said to me, 'It is done. I am the Alpha and the Omega, the beginning and the end. I will give to the one who thirsts from the spring of the water of life without cost.'

{ CHAPTER DISCUSSION NOTES }

The study of Eschatology is vast and broad, covering an area of Christian theology spanning all of Christendom worldwide. This is reflected in each of the various positions on the millennium and tribulation periods. It should be noted that the reason for these differences is equally numerous, which can be traced back to the progressive influence on the history of hermeneutics. This history is part of my book on Dispensational Theology, which most of this chapter content reflects.

As stated from the beginning, this chapter is intended to be a summary of the subject while providing a synopsis on the topic. Having completed two semesters on Premillennialism in college, I can understand why there are so many diverse views on the subject. I would like to encourage every student of the Word to seek out additional ways to learn more. This Chapter provides the minimal amount of information needed to lay a proper foundation to build upon.

> Personal Notes

Personal Notes

WORKS CITED

Ahaus, Hubert. "Holy Orders." *The Catholic Encyclopedia.* Vol. 11. Robert Appleton Company, 1911.

Aldrich, R. L. "An Outline Study on Dispensationalism." *Bibliotheca Sacra*, no. 118 (1961).

Allis, Oswald T. *Prophecy and the Church.* The Presbyterian and Reformed Publication Company, 1955.

Ashbaucher, Reid A. *Dispensational Theology: A Textbook on Eschatology in the Twenty-First Century.* Toledo: Reid Ashbaucher Publications, 2019.

—. *Made in the Image of God: Understanding the Nature of God and Mankind in a Changing World.* Third Revised Edition. Toledo: Reid Ashbaucher Publications, 2020.

Bainton, Roland H. *Christendom: A Short History of Christianity and Its Impact on Western Civilization.* Vol. 1. New York: Harper & Row Publishers, 1966.

"Church Government." *Theopedia.* n.d. https://www.theopedia.com/church-government (accessed August 27, 2020).

Economy. CD-ROM. Merriam-Webster's 11th Collegiate Dictionary, 2003.

Evans, William. *The Great Doctrines of the Bible.* Enlarged Edition. Chicago: Moody Press, 1974.

Finegan, Jack. *Handbook of Biblical Chronology: Principles of Time Reckoning in the Ancient World and Problems of Chronology in the Bible.* Princeton. NJ: Princeton University Press, 1964.

Fragments of Papias vi. Vol. 1, in *Ante-Nicene Fathers*, edited by James Donaldson, A. Cleveland Coxe Alexander Roberts, translated by James Donaldson Alexander Roberts. Buffalo, NY: Christian Literature Publishing Co., 1885.

Frame, John. *The Doctrine of God.* Phillipsburg: P & R Publishing Co., 2002.

"Genealogy of Jesus." *Complete-bible-genealogy.* n.d. https://www.complete-bible-genealogy.com/genealogy_of_jesus.htm (accessed July 13, 2020).

"Haggigah." Chap. Book 77, #4. Palestinian Talmud, n.d.

Hervey, Lord Arthur. *The Genealogies of Our Lord and Saviour Jesus Christ.* Cambridge: Macmillan and Co., 1853.

Heyer, Walt. "Sex Change' Isn't Surgically Possible, My Surgeon Testified in Court." *The Daily Signal.* n.d. https://www.dailysignal.com/ 2020/02/21/sex-change-isnt-surgically-possible-my-surgeon-testified-in-court/ (accessed August 11, 2020).

Hodge. *Systematic Theology.* Vol. 3. New York: Scribner, Armstrong and Company, 1873.

Hoekema, Anthony A. *The Bible and the Future.* Grand Rapids: Willian B Eerdmans Publishing Company, 1979.

Ingle, Roy. "Arminius on Repentance." *The Society of Evangelical Arminians.* n.d. http://evangelicalarminians.org/arminius-on-repentance-2/ (accessed August 15, 2020).

Irenaeus of Lyons Against Heresies 3, 21.10. Vol. 1, in *Ante-Nicene Fathers*, edited by Donaldson, and A. Cleveland Coxe Alexander Roberts, translated by Alexander Roberts and William Rambaut. Buffalo, NY: Christian Literature Publishing Co., 1885.

Irenaeus of Lyons Against Heresies 3.1.1. Vol. 1, in *Ante-Nicene Fathers*, edited by James Donaldson, A. Cleveland Coxe Alexander Roberts, translated by James Donaldson Alexander Roberts. Buffalo, NY: Christian Literature Publishing Co., 1885.

"Jesus Birth and When Herod the Great Really Died." *Complete-bible-genealogy.* n.d. https://strangenotions.com/jesus-birth-and-when-herod-the-great-really-died/ (accessed July 14, 2020).

"Joint Declaration on the Doctrine of Justification." *The Holy See.* Lutheran World Federation and the Catholic Church. October 31, 1999.

http://www.vatican.va/roman_curia/pontifical_councils/chrstu

ni/documents/rc_pc_chrstuni_doc_31101999_cath-luth-joint-declaration_en.html (accessed October 18, 2020).

Kennedy, Danial. *Sacraments.* Vol. 13, in *The Catholic Encyclopedia.* New York: Robert Appleton Company, 1912.

Leclercq, Henri. *The First Council of Nicaea.* Vol. 11, in *The Catholic Encyclopedia.* New York: Robert Appleton Company, 1911.

"Legion." *Encyclopedia Britannica.* n.d. https://www.britannica.com/topic/legion (accessed August 8, 2020).

Martin, Walter. *The Kingdom of the Cults: The Definitive Work on the Subject.* 6th Edition. Minneapolis: Bethany House Publishers, 2019.

Martindale, Cyril Charles. *Christmas.* Vol. 3, in *The Catholic Encyclopedia.* New York: Robert Appleton Company, 1908.

"Matthew 19:28." In *The Pulpit Commentary*, edited by Joseph S. Exell H.D.M. Spence. New York: Funk & Wagnalls Co., 1880-1919.

Morris, Thomas. *Our Idea of God.* Downers Grove: Intervarsity Press, 1991.

Nash, Ronald. *The Concept of God.* Grand Rapids: Zondervan Publishing House, 1983.

Pavao, Paul. "Bishops, Elders, Pastors in Scripture and History." *Christian History for Everyman.* n.d. https://www.christian-history.org/bishops-elders-pastors.html (accessed December 11, 2020).

Sanctifying Grace. Vol. 6, in *The Catholic Encyclopedia*, by Joseph Pohle. New York: Robert Appleton Company, 1909.

Pope, Charles. "150 Titles of Christ from the Scriptures." *Community in Mission.* n.d. http://blog.adw.org/2012/05/150-titles-of-christ-from-the-scriptures/ (accessed July 22, 2020).

Ramm, Bernard. *Protestant Biblical Interpretation.* 3 Revised Edition. Grand Rapids: Baker Book House, 1970.

"Isaiah 14:12." In *A Commentary, Critical and Explanatory, on the Old and New Testaments*, by A.R. Fausset, David Brown

Robert Jamieson. New York: S.S. Scranton and Company, 1873.

Matthew 3:2. Vol. 2, in *A Commentary, Critical and Explanatory, on the Old and New Testaments*, by A.R. Fausset, David Brown Robert Jamieson. New York: S.S. Scranton and Company, 1873.

Ryrie, Charles C. *Dispensationalism.* Chicago: Moody Publishing, 2007.

Schaefer, Francis. *Council of Chalcedon.* Vol. 3, in *The Catholic Encyclopedia.* New York: Robert Appleton Company, 1908.

Schaff, Philip. "Creeds of Christendom, with a History and Critical Notes. Volume II. The History of the Creeds." *Christian Classics Ethereal Library.* n.d. https://www.ccel.org/ccel/schaff/creeds2.iv.i.iii.html (accessed August 28, 2020).

—. *The Creeds of Christendom, with a History of Critical Notes.* Vol. 2. New York: Harper & Brothers, Franklin Square, 1877.

Shaw, Benjamin. "Aramaic Thoughts." *Studylight.org.* n.d. https://www.studylight.org/language-studies/aramaic-thoughts.html (accessed August 6, 2020).

Tacitus Annals xv, 44. n.d.

Tan, Paul Lee. *The Interpretation of Prophecy.* Winona Lake: Assurance Publishing, 1974.

—. *The Interpretation of Prophecy.* Winona Lake: Assurance Publishing, 1974.

"The Christ of John." In *New American Standard Bible.* Nashville: Thomas Nelson Publishers, 1985.

"The Christ of Mark." In *New American Standard Bible.* Nashville: Thomas Nelson Publishers, 1985.

"The Christ of Matthew." In *New American Standard Bible.* Nashville: Thomas Nelson Publishers, 1985.

"The Humanist Manifesto 1933." *Spiritualpilgrim.net.* n.d. http://spiritualpilgrim.net/07_Special-Documents/Historical-Documents/1933_ Humanist-Manifesto.htm (accessed September 4, 2020).

"Titus 3:5." In *The Pulpit Commentary*, edited by Joseph S. Exell H.D.M. Spence. New York: Funk & Wagnalls Co., 1880-1919.

Vallicella, William F. "Divine Simplicity." Vers. Spring 2019 Edition. *The Stanford Encyclopedia of Philosophy.* Edited by Edward N. Zalta. 2019. https://plato.stanford.edu/archives/spr2019/entries/divine-simplicity/ (accessed June 25, 2020).

Walvoord, John F. "New Testament Words for the Lord's Coming." *Bibliotheca Sacra*, no. 101 (July-September 1944).

"What Year was Jesus Born." *Strangenotions.* n.d. https://strangenotions.com/what-year-was-jesus-born-the-answer-may-surprise-you/ (accessed July 16, 2020).

Wilhelm, Joseph. "Apostolic Succession." *The Catholic Encyclopedia.* Vol. 1. New York: Robert Appleton Company, 1907.

—. "The Nicene Creed." *The Catholic Encyclopedia.* Vol. 11. New York: Robert Appleton Company, 1911.

SCRIPTURE INDEX

1

1 Chronicles 21:1 127
1 Corinthians 1:1-3 166
1 Corinthians 1:30-31 150
1 Corinthians 1:7 213
1 Corinthians 12:12 164
1 Corinthians 12:12-31 162
1 Corinthians 12:20-25 155
1 Corinthians 13:8 82
1 Corinthians 15:20-24 229
1 Corinthians 15:21-28 208
1 Corinthians 15:22-26 153
1 Corinthians 15:35-39 107
1 Corinthians 15:45 41
1 Corinthians 2:10-12 17
1 Corinthians 2:10-16 .... 10, 85
1 Corinthians 2:11 75
1 Corinthians 2:12-13 75
1 Corinthians 2:12-14 141
1 Corinthians 2:6-16 138
1 Corinthians 3:11-15 224
1 Corinthians 4:9 119
1 Corinthians 6:19 131
1 Corinthians 6:3 .... 132, 224
1 Corinthians 7:5 199
1 John 2:1-2 138
1 John 2:18-23 165
1 John 2:2 170
1 John 2:27 84
1 John 2:29 20
1 John 3:19 20 18
1 John 3:5 42
1 John 4:1-3 .... 80, 165
1 John 5:20 165
1 John 5:6-12 76
1 Kings 19:5-8 127
1 Kings 2:26 28
1 Peter 1:14-16 102
1 Peter 1:15-16 19
1 Peter 1:22-25 95
1 Peter 1:7, 13 213
1 Peter 2:24-25 30
1 Peter 2:4-10 169
1 Peter 4:12-13 200
1 Peter 4:13 213
1 Peter 4:14 87
1 Peter 5:10-11 17
1 Peter 5:1-2 178
1 Peter 5:5 145
1 Samuel 16:23 71
1 Thessalonians 1:10 223
1 Thessalonians 1:9-10 213
1 Thessalonians 2:13 96
1 Thessalonians 4:13-18 .... 82, 84
1 Thessalonians 4:3-8 151
1 Thessalonians 5:1-11 223
1 Thessalonians 5:23 .... 107, 110
1 Thessalonians 5:3 223
1 Thessalonians 5:9 223
1 Tim. 1:5-7 155
1 Timothy 1:18-20 161
1 Timothy 2:1-4 170
1 Timothy 3:14-15 167
1 Timothy 3:8-13 179
1 Timothy 4:13-16 102
1 Timothy 4:6-8 9
1 Timothy 5:17-19 177

1 Timothy 5:19-21 161
1 Timothy 5:21 119
1 Timothy 6:13-16 .... 39, 57
1 Timothy 6:18-19 .... 167, 172

2

2 Corinthians 1:21-22 83
2 Corinthians 12:2-4 190
2 Corinthians 12:9-10 130
2 Corinthians 3:17 87
2 Corinthians 3:17, 18 71
2 Corinthians 4:17-18 16
2 Corinthians 5:17 .... 21, 77, 147, 208
2 Corinthians 5:20-21 42
2 Corinthians 6:18 78
2 John 1-3 139
2 John 7-9 165
2 Kings 19:35 121
2 Peter 1:20-21 .... 49, 80, 91, 92
2 Peter 1:2-11 182
2 Peter 1:4 .... 147, 202, 208, 216
2 Peter 1:5 138
2 Peter 2:4, 9 193
2 Peter 2:4-10 132
2 Peter 3:10 230
2 Peter 3:1-2 96
2 Peter 3:14-16 96
2 Peter 3:1-7 92
2 Samuel 7:13-17 192
2 Samuel 7:14-18 64
2 Samuel 7:4-17 100
2 Thessalonians 1:5 20
2 Thessalonians 1:7 .... 119, 213
2 Thessalonians 1:7-8 127
2 Thessalonians 2:13-17 151
2 Thessalonians 2:3-11 224
2 Timothy 1:14 216
2 Timothy 2:13 .... 15, 38
2 Timothy 2:15 221
2 Timothy 2:15 KJV 133
2 Timothy 2:15; KJV 38
2 Timothy 3:14-15 144
2 Timothy 3:15 102
2 Timothy 3:16 49
2 Timothy 3:16-17 .... 80, 92
2 Timothy 4:17 130
2 Timothy 4:3-4 10

3

3 John 11 203

A

Acts 1:4-5 76
Acts 1:8 78
Acts 10:19-20 79
Acts 10:38 48
Acts 10:44-48 78
Acts 10:9-11:18 31
Acts 11:15-18 143
Acts 12:7 126
Acts 13:1-3 166
Acts 13:9 165
Acts 15:28 70
Acts 16:16 70
Acts 19:15 71
Acts 19:1-7 78
Acts 19:2 78
Acts 2:1-4 165
Acts 2:16-21 78
Acts 2:38 220
Acts 2:4 78
Acts 2:42 165
Acts 20:17, 28 178
Acts 20:18-21 138
Acts 20:21 .... 77, 142, 169
Acts 20:28-30 181
Acts 21:10-11 79
Acts 23:8 119
Acts 3:19-26 55

SCRIPTURE INDEX | 243

Acts 5:31 .... 123, 126
Acts 5:3-4 11
Acts 6:2-6 179
Acts 8:26 126
Acts 9:1-19 165
Acts 9:15 165
Amos 5:18 223
Amos 5:18-20 222

C

Colossians 1:15-17 16
Colossians 1:16 121
Colossians 1:18 164
Colossians 1:24-27 161
Colossians 1:9-14 130
Colossians 3:4 213
Colossians 3:5-7 213

D

Danial 12:1-2 229
Danial 9:24-27 54
Daniel 10:10-14, 20, 21 126
Daniel 10:13 123
Daniel 11:36-45 222
Daniel 12:1 .... 123, 223
Daniel 12:11-13 222
Daniel 12:1-3 225
Daniel 6:22 126
Daniel 7:13-14 .... 153, 190
Daniel 7:14 67
Daniel 7:7, 8, 19-28 222
Daniel 8:16 122
Daniel 9:24-27 .... 216, 222
Daniel 9:27 .... 222, 223
Deuteronomy 18:15 54
Deuteronomy 18:18-19 66
Deuteronomy 32:17 129
Deuteronomy 32:4 19
Deuteronomy 33:27 17

Deuteronomy 4:29-31 221
Deuteronomy 6:4-9 72
Deuteronomy 8:2 199

E

Ephesians 1:10-12 154
Ephesians 1:13 172
Ephesians 1:13-14 84
Ephesians 1:18-21 130
Ephesians 1:3-6 150
Ephesians 1:7-12 152
Ephesians 2:2 123
Ephesians 2:4-7 22
Ephesians 2:8-10 172
Ephesians 2:8-9 .... 138, 144, 172, 202
Ephesians 3:1-13 162
Ephesians 3:14-19 130
Ephesians 4:11-16 9
Ephesians 4:1-16 82
Ephesians 4:30 .... 70, 84, 172
Ephesians 4:4-10 198
Ephesians 4:4-6 78
Ephesians 5:18 78
Ephesians 5:18-21 79
Ephesians 5:27 19
Ephesians 5:9 202
Ephesians 6:10-17 130
Ephesians 6:12-13 130
Exodus 13:19 52
Exodus 15:26 27
Exodus 18:5, 6, 8 52
Exodus 25:17-22 22
Exodus 25:8-9 .... 66, 191
Exodus 3:14 .... 25, 52, 121
Exodus 32:11-14 18
Exodus 34:27 93
Exodus 4:10-15 93
Exodus 4:25, 26 52
Exodus 6:1-8 28
Exodus 8:24, 28, 58 52

Exodus 17:15 27
Ezekiel 1:5-14 123
Ezekiel 10:15 123
Ezekiel 2:7 94
Ezekiel 20:37-38 224
Ezekiel 24:2 94
Ezekiel 26:19-20 197
Ezekiel 28:11-19 .... 128, 199
Ezekiel 28:12-16 120
Ezekiel 28:12-17 203
Ezekiel 28:13-17 111
Ezekiel 3:10, 11 94
Ezekiel 32:24 197
Ezekiel 34:24 123
Ezekiel 36:26-27 143
Ezekiel 36:27 229
Ezekiel 37:14 229
Ezekiel 37:15-16 94

G

Galatians 1:11-18 165
Galatians 2:15-16 147
Galatians 3:1-14 173
Galatians 4:1-7 150
Galatians 5:22-23 21
Genesis 1:1-2 192
Genesis 1:2 70
Genesis 1:26 .... 11, 36, 106
Genesis 1:28 107
Genesis 1:3 95
Genesis 1:31-2:1 200
Genesis 11:7 .... 11, 36
Genesis 12:1-3 145
Genesis 15:18-21 145
Genesis 17:1 28
Genesis 17:7-8 153
Genesis 19:1 119
Genesis 2:16-17 199
Genesis 2:18 200
Genesis 2:22-24 169

Genesis 2:24 107
Genesis 2:4 27
Genesis 2:4-5 27
Genesis 22:14 27
Genesis 28:12 126
Genesis 3:14-15 53
Genesis 3:1-6 9
Genesis 3:1-7 .... 111, 136, 204
Genesis 3:22 .... 36, 106, 111
Genesis 41:38, KJV 71
Genesis 6:13-17 145
Genesis 9:11 127
Genesis 1:26-27 105

H

Habakkuk 2:2 94
Habakkuk 2:5 195
Hebrews 1:1-3 .... 37, 186
Hebrews 1:13-14 127
Hebrews 10:10-18 169
Hebrews 10:15-17 83
Hebrews 10:38 13
Hebrews 11:1 145
Hebrews 11:3 95
Hebrews 11:32-40 225
Hebrews 11:39 229
Hebrews 11:8-10 153
Hebrews 12:22 .... 121, 126
Hebrews 12:4-8 156
Hebrews 2:5-9 126
Hebrews 4:12 109
Hebrews 4:14-5:6 56
Hebrews 7:21 18
Hebrews 7:23-25 139
Hebrews 8:1-7 191
Hebrews 9:11-13 191
Hebrews 9:1-28 22
Hosea 2:14-23 147

I

Isaiah 1:18 17
Isaiah 11:1-5 229
Isaiah 11:6-9 228
Isaiah 14:12 127
Isaiah 14:12; KJV; NIV 112
Isaiah 14:7-15 199
Isaiah 14:9-15 196
Isaiah 24:1-4, 19-21 223
Isaiah 24:20-21 223
Isaiah 26:19-21 .... 225, 229
Isaiah 26:20-21 223
Isaiah 33:22 230
Isaiah 34:1-2 224
Isaiah 34:1-3 223
Isaiah 40:8 94
Isaiah 43:8 26
Isaiah 45:21 20
Isaiah 48:16 36
Isaiah 5:16 19
Isaiah 53:12 30
Isaiah 53:9-12 66
Isaiah 59:21 72
Isaiah 6:1-7 125
Isaiah 6:3 126
Isaiah 6:8 36
Isaiah 60:21 229
Isaiah 61:1 54
Isaiah 61:1-2 36
Isaiah 63:10 74
Isaiah 63:10-11 72
Isaiah 66:1-2 192
Isaiah 7:14 66
Isaiah 8:1, 11, 12 94
Isaiah 9:6 17
Isaiah 9:6-7 230

J

James 1:13 .... 15, 38, 199
James 1:3 199
James 2:14-26 171
James 2:17-18 174
James 2:26 107
James 3:13-17 85
James 3:13-18 .... 22, 114
James 4:1-7 206
James 4:5 216
James 5:14 169
James 5:17 216
James 5:20 112
Jeremiah 1:7 94
Jeremiah 13:12 94
Jeremiah 17:9 KJV 17
Jeremiah 30:1-2 94
Jeremiah 30:7 223
Jeremiah 31:15 66
Jeremiah 31:31-34 .... 77, 143
Jeremiah 31:33 .... 217, 229
Jeremiah 31:33-34 .... 65, 229
Jeremiah 31:34 85
Jeremiah 33:16 27
Jeremiah 36:1, 2, 4, 11, 27-32 94
Jeremiah 7:27 94
Job 1:8 206
Joel 1:15 223
Joel 2:2 223
Joel 2:28-32 78
Joel 3:1-2 224
Joel 3:17 229
John 1:1 52
John 1:1, 14 52
John 1:1-3, 14 .... 37, 95, 141
John 1:45-46 48
John 10:11, 14 51
John 10:30 52
John 10:7, 9 51
John 11:25 51
John 11:35 .... 21, 52
John 12:27 .... 13, 52
John 12:49-50 81

Reference	Pages
John 14:1-3	84, 152
John 14:15-26	81
John 14:16	71, 139
John 14:16-17	30, 74, 82, 131
John 14:17	87
John 14:2-3	52, 153
John 14:25-26	30
John 14:26	10, 71, 74, 83
John 14:3	82
John 14:6	51, 229
John 14:9	52
John 15:1-5	51
John 16:13-14	30
John 16:13-15	81
John 16:7-11	86
John 17:1-4	54
John 17:17	22, 89, 167
John 19:34	66
John 19:36	66
John 2:22	96
John 20:28	52
John 20:30-31	52, 97
John 3:1-18	182
John 3:16 HCSB	20
John 3:3	147, 164, 180
John 3:6-8	15, 69
John 4:24	13, 69, 72
John 4:6,7	52
John 5:39-41	100
John 6:35, 48	51
John 6:37-40	172
John 8:12	51
John 8:28	66
John 8:34-36	131
John 8:44	204, 208
John 8:58	52
John 9:35-38	37
John 9:39-41	112
John 9:5	51
Jonah 2:9	113
Joshua 1:8	130
Jude 6	132, 224
Jude 9	122, 127
Judges 6:24	27

L

Reference	Pages
Leviticus 11:44	19
Leviticus 17:7	129
Leviticus 20:8	27
Leviticus 24:16	28
Leviticus 26:11	13
Luke 1:26-28	122
Luke 1:26-33	186
Luke 1:28-33	56
Luke 1:30-33	40, 153
Luke 1:31-33	192, 226, 228
Luke 1:46	110
Luke 15:10	126
Luke 16:17	94
Luke 16:19-31	195
Luke 17:30	213
Luke 18:42	138
Luke 2:27-32	44
Luke 2:4	48
Luke 21:24	222
Luke 22:19	168
Luke 22:24	64
Luke 22:69	51
Luke 23:34	66
Luke 24:27	100, 141
Luke 24:44-49	64
Luke 24:45	113
Luke 24:45-47	51
Luke 3:23-38	46
Luke 4:1-13	73, 79
Luke 4:16	48
Luke 4:41	129
Luke 5:8	37
Luke 6:22	127
Luke 7:30	220
Luke 7:30-35	138

SCRIPTURE INDEX | 247

Luke 7:31-35 44
Luke 7:50 138
Luke 7:6-10 37
Luke 8:30-33 129
Luke13:16 130

M

Malachi 3:6 .... 15, 18, 38
Mark 1:1 50
Mark 1:14-15 142
Mark 1:15 .... 149, 221
Mark 10:18 201
Mark 10:44 50
Mark 10:52 138
Mark 12:24-25 100
Mark 12:26 94
Mark 12:28-30 64
Mark 13:31 189
Mark 15:39 50
Mark 16:14 64
Mark 16:16 220
Mark 16:6-7 66
Mark 3:11 50
Mark 6:52 63
Mark 7:37 63
Mark 8:14-21 63
Mark 8:29 50
Matthew 1:1-17 43
Matthew 1:18-20 73
Matthew 1:23 66
Matthew 10:28 194
Matthew 11:2 64
Matthew 12:22-27 129
Matthew 12:25-30 130
Matthew 12:26 123
Matthew 12:28 191
Matthew 12:33-37 202
Matthew 12:39-40 197
Matthew 14:33 37
Matthew 15:18-19 135

Matthew 15:28 138
Matthew 16:18 160
Matthew 17:15-18 130
Matthew 18:10 119
Matthew 18:15-18 161
Matthew 19:28 146
Matthew 2:11 37
Matthew 2:18 66
Matthew 2:2 57
Matthew 2:23 66
Matthew 21:28-32 142
Matthew 21:33-42 99
Matthew 23:39 221
Matthew 24:14-30 222
Matthew 24:15 222
Matthew 24:21 222
Matthew 24:29-30 222
Matthew 24:31 119
Matthew 24:35 95
Matthew 24:36 119
Matthew 25:31 127
Matthew 25:37 229
Matthew 25:37-38 224
Matthew 26:38 13
Matthew 26:53 121
Matthew 27:34 66
Matthew 27:46 66
Matthew 27:57-60 66
Matthew 28:18-20 167
Matthew 28:7 51
Matthew 28:9, 17 37
Matthew 3:11 73
Matthew 3:16-17 18
Matthew 3:2 .... 189, 190
Matthew 4:11 ....119, 127
Matthew 4:17 142
Matthew 4:1-7 99
Matthew 5:16 .... 167, 172
Matthew 5:21-22 193
Matthew 5:22, 29, 30 193
Matthew 6:9-10 190

Matthew 7:17-20 174
Matthew 7:21-23 181
Matthew 7:24 141
Matthew 7:24-27 101
Matthew 8:2-4 37
Matthew 9:29 138

N

Numbers 11:17 72
Numbers 12:5-8 93
Numbers 14:24 71
Numbers 17:2-3 93
Numbers 23:19 89
Numbers 27:1-11 45
Numbers 32:14 18
Numbers 36:1-12 45

P

Philippians 1:1-2 179
Philippians 2:5-11 37
Philippians 4:13 130
Proverbs 12:22 91
Proverbs 15:11 .... 123, 128
Proverbs 16:32 71
Proverbs 2:6 86
Proverbs 27:20 128
Proverbs 30:27 128
Proverbs 4:7 86
Proverbs 8:13 .... 111, 128, 206
Psalm 10:16 56
Psalm 100:5 201
Psalm 103:20 126
Psalm 104:24 23
Psalm 106:37 129
Psalm 106:44-46 18
Psalm 11:5 13
Psalm 110:1-3 229
Psalm 110:4 .... 18, 55
Psalm 110:5 54

Psalm 119:160 .... 89, 167
Psalm 119:68 20
Psalm 119:89 94
Psalm 138:3 130
Psalm 139:7-10 14
Psalm 145:17 19
Psalm 145:9 201
Psalm 147:5 17
Psalm 16:10 66
Psalm 2:1-12 39
Psalm 2:6 56
Psalm 22:1 66
Psalm 22:18 66
Psalm 24:10 56
Psalm 25:8 20
Psalm 33:4-6 99
Psalm 34:20 66
Psalm 45:6 11
Psalm 51:11 72
Psalm 53:1-3 .... 113, 135
Psalm 65:4 20
Psalm 69:21 66
Psalm 72:7 229
Psalm 78:69 16
Psalm 8:1-9 23
Psalm 85:10 229
Psalm 88:11 128
Psalm 91:11 .... 119, 126

R

Revelation 1:1 73
Revelation 1:8 .... 17, 121
Revelation 11:15 .... 128, 153
Revelation 11:2 222
Revelation 11:5 230
Revelation 12:6 222
Revelation 14:19-20 213
Revelation 14:7 223
Revelation 15:4 .... 20, 223
Revelation 16:1 213

Revelation 16:5	20
Revelation 16:5, 7	223
Revelation 17:14	54
Revelation 19:15-16	213
Revelation 19:19-20	224
Revelation 19:2	20, 223
Revelation 19:20	198
Revelation 20:10	133
Revelation 20:10-15	198
Revelation 20:11	231
Revelation 20:11-15	225
Revelation 20:12-15	231
Revelation 20:1-3	133, 196, 214
Revelation 20:1-3, 10	225
Revelation 20:1-3, 7-10	230
Revelation 20:13-15	198
Revelation 20:14	112, 136
Revelation 20:14-15	193
Revelation 20:1-6	218
Revelation 20:20	194
Revelation 20:4-5	225
Revelation 20:4-6	225, 229
Revelation 20:7-9	227
Revelation 21:1	228
Revelation 21:1-6	192, 198, 231
Revelation 21:3	67
Revelation 21:6	121
Revelation 22:13	121
Revelation 3:10	200, 223
Revelation 4:4	147
Revelation 4:6-8	123
Revelation 4:8	126
Revelation 5:8-12	147
Revelation 6:15-17	213
Revelation 6:16-17	223
Revelation 7:9-14	221
Revelation 9:11	123, 128
Revelations 1:1-3	96
Romans 1:1-4	30
Romans 1:16-20	140
Romans 1:18-21	99
Romans 1:18-27	108
Romans 1:2	19
Romans 1:7	11
Romans 10:14	141
Romans 10:14-15	102
Romans 11:11-32	76
Romans 11:15-24	216
Romans 12:3-8	81
Romans 16:1-15	166
Romans 16:26	17
Romans 2:11	82
Romans 2:4	144
Romans 3:10-12	32
Romans 3:10-18	20, 206, 208
Romans 3:23	208
Romans 3:25	22
Romans 3:9-18	114
Romans 4:14	174
Romans 5:12	32, 206
Romans 5:12-15	65
Romans 5:12-19	41
Romans 5:16-21	149
Romans 5:9-11	148
Romans 6:15-18	156, 174
Romans 6:23	112
Romans 7:19-23	216
Romans 7:19-25	152
Romans 8:14-17	149
Romans 8:15-17	78
Romans 8:15-28	79
Romans 8:16-17	83
Romans 8:35-39	21
Romans 8:38-39	130

T

Titus 1:1-3	90
Titus 1:2	15, 38, 91, 227
Titus 1:5-9	177
Titus 1:9	9
Titus 2:11-14	30

Titus 3:4-7 148
Titus 3:4-8 22
Titus 3:5 146

Z

Zechariah 12:10 66

Zechariah 13:8-14:5 222
Zechariah 13:8-9 224
Zechariah 14:20 229
Zechariah 7:8-12 94
Zechariah 8:3 229
Zephaniah 1:14-15 223
Zephaniah 1:14-18 222
Zephaniah 1:15-18 223

SUBJECT INDEX

Amillennialism, 216
Biblical Hermeneutics, 215
Chapter 2 Discussion Notes, 63
Christ's Divine Nature, 36
Christ's Divine Nature Attributes, 38
Christ's Human Nature, 38
Church Defined

    Chruch Defined, 159
    Church Defined as the Body, 161
    Church Established, 160
    The Body Defined, 162
    Universal Church, 164

Church Ordinances, 167
Church Polity

    Church Creeds, 182
    Local Church Membership, 180
    Offices of the Church, 176
    Types of Local Church
        Government, 174

Creation of Gender, 106
Creation of Humanity, 105
Davidic Kingdom, 225
Divine Simplicity, 24
Effects of Sin on Humanity, 112
Fall of Humanity, 110
God's Moral Attributes

    Goodness, 20
    Holiness, 19
    Love, 20
    Mercy, 22
    Moral Attributes Defined, 18

    Righteous, 19
    Wisdom, 22

God's Natural Attributes

    Eternal, 15
    Immutable, 18
    Natural Attributes Defined, 13
    Omnipotence, 15
    Omnipresent, 14
    Omniscience, 17

Good and Evil, 199
Heaven, 189
Hell, 193
Holy Spirit in the New Testament, 73
Holy Spirit in the Old Testament, 72
Holy Spirit's Deity, 74
Human Nature as a Dichotomy, 108
Human Nature as a Trichotomy, 109
Image and Likeness of God, 105
Importance of the Scriptures, 99
Issue of Free Will, 136
Kingdom of God, 191
Kingdom of Heaven, 190
Lake of Fire, 198
Languages of the Scriptures, 97
Millennium, 226
Names for God

    Adonai, 28
    El Shaddai, 28
    Elohim, 27
    Jehovah, 26
    Jehovah-Elohim, 27
    Jehovah-Jireh, 27

Jehovah-M'Kaddesh, 27
Jehovah-Nissi, 27
Jehovah-Shalom, 27
Jehovah-Tsidqenuw, 27
Yahweh, 26
YHWH, 26

Names Used of Christ, 57
Nature behind fall of Humanity, 111
Nature of Angels

   Fallen Angels, 127
   Judgment of Angels, 132
   Tasks Performed by Angels, 126
   Their Creation, 120
   Their Numbers, 121
   Types of Angels, 122

Nature of Christ, 35
Nature of God, 11
Nature of Good and Evil

   Evil, 203
   Good, 200

Nature of the Holy Spirit, 72
Need for Salvation, 135
New Heaven and New Earth, 192
New Testament Local Church, 165
Other Names for the Devil, 127
Other Names for the Holy Spirit, 87
Person of the Holy Spirit, 69
Postmillennialism, 217
Premillennialism, 218
Purpose of the Church, 166
Reality of Angels, 119
Resurrections, 225
Scriptures Represent Revelation from God, 96
Second Advent, 224

Second Advent Associated Judgments, 224
Sheol, 194
Soul and Spirit, 12
Terms Used in Eschatology, 211
The Effects of Salvation

   Adoption, 149
   Inheritance, 152
   Justification, 147
   Regeneration, 146
   Sanctification, 150

The Life of Christ

   Christ's Birth, 42
   Christ's Ministry, 48
   History behind Christ's Birth, 46
   The Childhood of Christ, 48

The Person of Christ

   Christ as King, 56
   Christ as Lord (Messiah), 54
   Christ as Priest, 55
   Christ as Prophet, 54
   The Messianic Message, 52

The Question of Demon Possession, 130
The Salvation Process, 140
The Work of the Holy Spirit

   To Baptize Believers, 76
   To Bear Witness, 75
   To Bring Assurance, 82
   To Bring Wisdom and Understanding, 85
   To Convict the World of Sin, 86
   To Empower the Believer, 78

To Guide the Believer, 79
To Provide Spiritual Gifting, 81
To Seal the Believer, 83
To Teach the Believer, 84

Tribulation Period, 221
Trinity, 11
Understanding the Kingdom of God, 221
Uniqueness of the Scriptures

    Claim Christ is the Word of God, 95
    Claim to be Eternal, 94
    Claim to be Inspired, 91
    Claim to be True, 89

www.ingramcontent.com/pod-product-compliance
Lightning Source LLC
Chambersburg PA
CBHW071228080526
44587CB00013BA/1540